The Eighth Promise

A Memoir

By William Poy Lee

Original Publisher North America Edition. Rodale Press

Previously Represented by
Marly Rusoff (retired)

Table of Contents

III. INITIATIONS (1964-mid-1972)

VI. CHAOS UNDER HEAVEN (mid-1972-1978)

V. RESURRECTION (1979-1983)

EPILOGUE

Prologue: Return to an Ancestral Village

Suey Wan is the name of my ancestral village, a small, unchanged place in the Pearl River Delta in China's semi-tropical southeast corner. Well, actually it's my ancestral village on my mother's side. My father's own village is quite nearby, but I don't ascribed to it ancestral village status. By far not. Nor as I look back on over fifty years of living, I source my essence, for better and not worse, back to mother's village. I have come to see, and accept, that it was my mother's earthbound spirituality, of the Toisan-Chinese people, that kept me safe, sound, and sane, all these tumultuous decades.

But the journey back was twisting, long, and almost never made. I finally trekked my way over rivers, rough roads, hills and fields to there. Oh, how invaluable it has turned out.

Like so many Americans, I wittingly pushed my way forward in our restless, mobile, attention-zapping, and energy depleting culture. All too many decisions were financial driven whether the "right" choice of college, mate, work, friends, where to live, and what to wear. It wasn't always so, but certainly during my mid-thirties to mid-forties I was racing this marathon in overdrive. Perhaps not so surprising, after several decades of hitting the American marks of university and professional milestones, I was pounding out that last lap towards the finish line of financial freedom, a final burst of a frenzied strategically focused workaholism that would pull it all together, a time I personally dubbed as the " the brain sweat" decade.

And then I paused.

Full-stop in 1995.

Actually, I came to a complete stop, a paralyzing, crackling, debris filled breakout, as I departed business, home, and a fading love. I stopped for over a year as I considered whether there was more to my journey. I knew there was more of course, and I knew I had lived with more dimensions of being and values, more personal, immeasurable, and deeply enriching throughout my earlier life. How had I had lost touch with those deeper places, spending an entire decade burying them over with all too shiny, expensive, and attention getting, material marks of success and in excess? Carefully, I took back my time, spending days walking beaches and state park trails, haunting bookstores, bicycling along San Francisco Bay to under the Golden Gate Bridge, and basically rethinking life. I made new friends, people like me, who by choice or circumstance, were not only questioning, but ahead of me, redesigning meaning back into their lives.

And that's when I completely opened up to my ancient past, in another land and culture, China, a place then still considered a struggling third world economy. This was not a Luddite romanticization of some pastoral, agricultural Shangri-la of self-sufficiency. If anything, it turned out to be a rediscovery of old ways, values, and yes, tried and true wisdom, of immense value to my modern American life. Having now integrated those lessons, this way of being into my still metropolitan lifestyle, a once daily, pulse-pounding, thigh burning leg race to the finish line has morphed into a rhythmic glide - in the Zone as it were - where I not only can smell the roses, but have time to plant a few, and observe their stages of coming to blossom...and still complete the Tour d'Amérique race in the winner's circle.

I suggest this kind of journey to all Americans, it may well reward one with a level of wholeness and happiness so elusive for too many.

 That year, I slowly realized that I came from a wonderful beginning, from even before I was born in San Francisco, from a people in an old, old unmapped village located in the southeast corner of China. I rediscovered that I am born of ancestors who were farmers, and lived not as individuals, or the mobile nuclear family unit, not even just as an extended family, but as a Clan of many extended families in one village, of hundreds of people. They had lived and loved in one locale and harvested the same fields, for a millennium or more. I had forgotten that place, and the tried-and-true wisdom of that Clan culture, and had, ever so slowly and carefully, reached back to it for resuscitation, revival, and not for only a new, but a critically transformed fresh start.

Suey Wan is an innocuous farmer's village nestled among remote hills in the backwater heart of the fertile Pearl River Delta of Guangdong province. My people's six counties are collectively known as Toisan (or "Taishan" as it's pronounced in Mandarin, the official dialect of China). Toisan's origins are more legendary than historically established, but unquestionably, the first Chinese settlers arrived here around 1,000 AD, fleeing the chaos of the declining decades of the once expansive, wealthy, culturally rich, and cosmopolitan T'ang Dynasty, hoping to find peace in this then far-off corner of the Chinese empire.

And for a millennium, my forbears lived relatively unperturbed, rarely traveling farther than twenty miles away from their village. These farmers developed their own cuisine, honed their own farming methods, learned to resolve community problems without government interference, and eventually evolved their own version of the Cantonese dialect, the rustic, rough-sounding and salty tongue of Toisanese.

In 1983, I was the first of my family to visit Suey Wan since the 1949 victory of the Communist forces of Chairman Mao Tse-tung over the American-backed Nationalist armies of Generalissimo Chiang Kai-sek. The new government's quick imposition of a "bamboo curtain" around China terminated emigration abroad and access to returning migrants alike. That was why, it took some thirty-four years after my mother fled to America, before I, a Chinese-American was the first of my family to return. I did not expect much from this little village, which did not even have electricity or running water in the early 1980s, as I was soon to discover.

Even so, the Suey Wan visit was more an afterthought than the purpose of the trip, pinned on to the end of an official five-week grand tour of China's width and breadth: of hiking crumbling portions of the Great Wall, climbing verdant holy Buddhist Mt. Emei to overnight in still practicing Buddhist monastery, and measuring myself against Xian's life-size terracotta warriors, to name just a few of the splendors. Why should I bother visiting just another peasant village, one of millions dotting China? What did Suey Wan have to offer me beyond the obligation to pay my respects to unknown relatives, a vague promise I made to my mother before I left San Francisco that summer?

If I believed in signs, I may never have made it and would have missed the most meaningful, and richest part of my trip.

The first contrary sign was Mother herself, as she was against my going. Her family had fled newly installed Communist China when newly arrived Cadres drove her older brother, a western educated man just like me, to commit suicide by leaping off the family roof. She feared the same fate for me. But from my perch as an international banker and lawyer with Bank of America, I assured her that those times had changed.

As those final few days drew near, I became concerned that for the first time in five weeks, I would be completely on my own. Mr. Wong, the senior China Travel Services (CTS) official who had smoothed all our travels throughout China would not be there to solve the any connection problems. Still he provided me with letters of introduction to my hotel (he had personally booked the reservation) and to the local CTS manager, to ensure I got to Suey Wan. But disturbingly, Mr. Wong's first letter of introduction proved ineffective, for after a great show of opening and slamming drawers, looking for my "lost" reservation, the night manager booked me into a poorly lit, humid dormitory for male travelers, barely several rows of wooden beds, each covered with a mosquito net. I considered heading straight to Hong Kong at the crack of dawn, to rejoin my traveling companions, more kin now than accidental colleagues, and dig into a T-bone steak laden with grilled onions, a side of Heinz ketchup, and well-done *pomme frites* in a Sheraton Hotel.

Then, during my late night stroll along the Pearl River, with Hong Kong pop-songs booming from radios secreted in the inky dark -- a weird parody of Top 40 tunes, eroding any chance of nocturnal tranquility -- a young Cantonese couple emerged out of nowhere and roundly cursed me out for nearly bumping into them. We hadn't even been that close to collision and a polite "Excuse us," would have warned me away. All this brought back to mind the true horror to come, that my travel companions emphatically warned of -- opportunistic Toisanese villagers fleecing returning American-born Chinese, like me, searching for their roots: relatives demanding gifts of TV sets, refrigerators, expensive watches, and stylish clothing; of vastly "extended" families running up large banquet bills, night after night, to celebrate the return of one of Toisan's own; and finally, playing off the guilt of having done well, living free and easy in America, while the home-folks had suffered during Communist China's reconstruction into a modern nation, indelicately demanding hundreds, if not thousands of dollars, on the eve of their departure,

No, on the eve of this leg of the trip, the omens kept warning me away. But I stuck it out in true Toisan character whenever confronted with adversity. In the early morning, Mr. Wong's second letter of introduction proved effective. The young and amiable local CTS manager, eyes wide open, recognized Mr. Wong as the national second-in-command of China Travel Services, immediately secured me a chauffeured private car at a good rate, and departing in an hour for Suey Wan. He then returned to the hotel with me, investigated last night's mishap with the day manager, and then made sure that I would have my private, air conditioned room with bath upon my return in three days (I did!).

And so, finally, I was on my way through: wrenching out way through a veritable obstacle course of endless construction sites and traffic jams of a miserably smoggy and dusty industrial metropolis. Eventually, we reached the clean countryside, cruising along a two lane tarmac road, past green landscapes filled with men and women farmers, faces brown from the sun, some working their fields while others bicycled to market, precariously balancing baskets of vegetables, trussed pigs, or caged chickens across their handlebars and rear tires; and of course, the occasional child ubiquitously and delicately astride the back of a muscular, horned water-buffalo.

All very charming, but in previous weeks, I had come to consider these picturesque farm-scapes as time-consuming but necessary passages to the world-class cultural treasures of China, i.e., the China worth seeing. Only today, I wasn't heading towards any place arising to the level of a heritage site. While not exactly heading into the heart of darkness, I was certainly struggling upstream towards an unmapped, tangential backwater of the nondescript, and wondering about my sanity the whole way.

In truth, it took many more hours and much patience to get to Toisan, even if there were no "there" there. Without air conditioning in the car, the heat and humidity increased as the morning turned into noon. My patient driver and an impatient me stood in the sun for long stretches while waiting for the slow, flat-bed ferries to transport us across each of three rivers blocking my path to Suey Wan. The only sign of modernity was a beat-up, light-blue Mitsubishi tractor, more the size of a well-off child's battery-run toy than a full-size John Deere. My driver informed me that Mitsubishi could run on practically any fuel, even the peanut oil my mother cooked with. At some point, he driver decided it was time for lunch, selecting an unexpectedly nicely appointed, air-conditioned restaurant (a mini-banquet for two which I paid for of course) given our location in China's countryside. But fine cuisine is a first and foremost necessity for Cantonese, and of course a three star establishment could be found, even on the way to Toisan.

Late in the afternoon, we reached my first destination, the small town of Hoisin, the only town in this region of rice paddies, vegetable fields, low hills, and farming villages.

Auntie Kow Woon lived here. With my mother's handwritten address in hand, my driver easily found her quite modern, apartment style, two-story home with a balcony.

Auntie Kow Woon came out and immediately broke out into a never ending smile. She touched my arms and shoulders, pinched me, again and again as if to convince herself that I was really in front of her. In no time at all, she began chatting merrily, then introduced me to an old childhood friend of my mother, Hung Yick, the town postman. To my surprise, Hung Yick was loud, boisterous, and opinionated, far different from the mostly quiet and reserved Chinese I knew in America. Within minutes, he and Auntie Kow Woon were laughing out loud, moving and gesturing as if they owned the streets. Well, they did own the streets, in a way that Chinese-Americans of my father's generation and generations before did not; grimly and quietly knowing that other Americans – white Americans - owned the streets of San Francisco. In the American of my father's youth, Chinese-Americans moved swiftly, then, eyes averted downward, quickly walked around white Americans, and stealthily like shadows to avoid the glare, ire and inevitably, the violence of these everyday enforcers of America's then racial caste system.

But here I was deep in the homeland of my own people, marveling at my relatives free and easy body language, as natural as that of any free people, so unlike the reserved, contracted bodies of many Chinese-Americans, and now that I could compare, a constriction obviously inflicted by our harsh historical experience.

And everyone, but just everyone, spoke Toisanese, as if it were the universal language of the world, the only language. Here, it felt that by contrast, only those with a limited education were stuck with Big City Cantonese, and as for those Mandarin speakers, well, they must be foreigners, official dialect of China or not.

Auntie Kow Woon and Hung Yick remarked on the purity of my tones, beyond the surprise of an American-born Chinese able to speak any Chinese at all, for many did not, but that I spoke like a native who had never left. Because of Mother, I said, and that to this day, that's the language we converse in.

Auntie Kow Woon and Hung Yick booked my driver and me into a local inn. Small, but clean and quiet. Compared to the dormitory, my room was a welcomed, cool comfort. In fact, compared to Guangzhou, the town of Suey Wan resembled the old-time, pastoral Chinese villages in the Hong Kong movies of my youth: white-washed low-slung homes trimmed with reds and blues; long, tiled, garden walls between portals; uncrowded streets whose town folk frequently stopped to chat as they made their way through their day; naturalistically trimmed trees and blossoming flower pots splashed colors on earthen streets; and oh, such a pacific quiet, free of speeding and honking traffic, radios blaring Hong Kong pop music, and unsolicited, rude Cantonese put-downs.

In this idyllic antiquity, I would not have been surprised to pass two young lovers bedecked in flowing silk gowns and elaborate royal head-gear singing a high-pitch duet to the lyrical strumming of the two stringed violin-like erhu in the background, or to duck our heads as a score of martial arts fighters cartwheeling from roof-tops over our heads, fists slashing and legs whirling in honorable duels-to-the-death.

Over dinner at the inn's restaurant -- simple, traditional dishes just like Mother's cooking, I explained to Auntie Kow Woon and Hung that I wanted to visit my mother's village Suey Wan and her childhood home, abandoned when everyone left for Hong Kong, but maintained since by Hung Yick. I wanted to visit father's own village, the house he was raised in, a home now occupied by his childhood schoolteacher. I didn't know the name of father's village, but of course, Auntie Kow Woon knew it and the exact house. Hung Yick had his postal rounds and couldn't join us, but arranged a time to give Auntie Kow Woon the keys to my mother's childhood home.

Then, unexpectedly, Auntie Kow Woon picked up the check, over my protests. I noted that they had ordered a few dishes only, not a lavish banquet. Amazingly, no large crowds of unknown extended family members had spontaneously appeared to "celebrate" my return. Nor had anyone hinted they could use a new refrigerator or television.

So far, so good as despite my traveling companions' well-meaning warnings, perhaps my relatives were different.

Early the next morning, after a night's rest so deep it made up for my restless night in Guangzhou, my driver drove Auntie and me to Suey Wan. I felt like an overseas Chinese tourist intruding into the daily movement of this ancient village for I had not been able to announce my homecoming since telephone lines did not reach here. So I was happy when we had to park our car at a narrow pedestrian footbridge for a much more low-key hike in. My dapper driver declined our invitation to accompany us, ostensibly too "country" for a Big City Cantonese like him. Even Auntie Kow Woon said, "I never come here anymore, only for you," and then suddenly pressed a handkerchief against her nose as we rounded a bend into the uncompromising fragrance of a large outhouse.

"I am definitely in the furthest realms of backcountry China now," I thought to myself, for the outhouse struck me as symbolic of a different sensibility. Not only was it the largest I'd seen in China, but shamelessly placed at the official footpath entrance, as if to suggest that a toilet was the happiest welcome a village could offer a rustic traveler after such a long journey. Huge and freshly painted red characters screamed the location of the women's entrance towards one end and the men's towards the other end. No shame about natural bodily processes here, I thought.

We then passed a simple temple, perhaps a pastoral traveler's second-most-desired facility, a place to give thanks for a safe journey. Was this the temple of my parents' wedding, I wondered to myself? As we continued along the earthen footpath, the sun burned hot on my face, but here it was pleasant, not sticky, and I enjoyed the walk across clear fields of rice paddies crisscrossed by red-hued mud retaining walls. The green semi-tropical plants and the rich brown earth were suffused in iridescence, as in a French pointillist painting. The pristine air refreshed me. On three sides, forested hills cradled the distant, dusky-gray stone buildings of the village.

As we came closer, I saw a long row of houses, their doors faced south in order to catch the sun. A young girl walked to one house, carrying a bundle of reed grass, then placed her bundle by the hearth fire visible on the other side of the open door and started cooking the midday meal, alternately pushing the reed grass into the flames and tending the pots. She was dressed in wide black trousers with a traditional flowered blouse buttoned off her right shoulder,

At the end of this row of homes was a simple, unmarked open area, that served as an informal village square. Adults squatted there in silence as children chased chickens, and ducks pecked the ground for food. Auntie Kow Woon announced me to them, by my Chinese name Poy Jom, the son of Chun Poy Jen, invoking my mother's maiden name.

No one had known I was coming. No one there had seen my mother in thirty-four years.

An elderly man looked up into my face, gazing briefly, but directly, into my eyes. "Yes," he announced. "You look exactly like your mother. Welcome home."

This man had not seen my mother in three-and-a-half decades, yet he spoke as if he had seen her only yesterday. His words stripped away my outsider conceit. No longer the tourist, I began to pay attention, the kind of attention that shakes itself free of the broader but shallower passage through a typical day, that narrows and focuses like a laser beam, honing in on and then affixing itself to a clue that had just loudly announced itself, a vital, significant clue to a lifelong mystery, one that may even had hitherto been unconsciously puzzling until this moment.

After greeting me, this elder returned to his silence as the children continued their play, the ducks and chickens their running around. The other adults smiled, uttered short phrases of welcome, and then also returned to their quiet and mysterious communion.

No one asked me how my mother and father, or my mother's sisters and brother, were doing. No one asked about opportunities in America or whether I was rich. No one asked what I did for a living or whether I had come seeking a wife. The conversational politeness of Northern Chinese was absent, as was the chatter of Auntie Kow Woon and Hung Yick, for this day, she too sank into this reverie of silence. Yet the villagers' silence was not rudeness, nor were they disinterested in me, for their smiles were genuine and their welcomes sincere. They reminded me of monks, cruising silent in deepest meditation behind temple walls. But instead of being removed from the world, these Toisanese villagers were sitting smack-dab in the midst of their real lives.

So there we all were, with the ducks and chickens, caring not whether we were in China, America, or Burkina Faso. Everyone and everything appeared so changeless, so present. Sitting in the warm sun. Connected in silent companionship.

Life could be that simple.

At that moment, something happened inside me. Or maybe it was already happening, and because I was not distracted by conversation, it was only at that moment that I began to notice. My skin, feet, my toes, all began tingling with some extraordinary energy. I started to effervesce, as if I were showering in bubbling champagne. Then I felt the energy go deeper like a running stream that started in my guts and surged through my chest, up my neck, and finally shot out the top of my head. What came out was joy, the deep, hearty joy of coming home, of knowing fully whom I was and where I was from. This was the joy of belonging, the joy of a simple village, of these quiet farmers, who knew who I was despite over three decades of separation. Here my spirit could bubble up from the soulful, artesian wells of my kin, on our land.

None of China's abundant grandeur affected me as profoundly as coming home to the village that had been my family's ancestral home for over one thousand years. Living America's hustling, bustling, mobile lifestyle, I had not understood the power of place, or how place could mold a people's character. In Suey Wan, I sensed that when a people live for generations in one place, dependent upon the very soil to sustain them, they internalize a resonance unique to them, and most powerful only in each other's presence. Standing upon my ancestral land was like standing next to the tuning fork of my soul. There, and only there, could my innate vibrations sound.

So many questions bubbled forth: What makes the resonance of a place? What makes the Toisan so Toisan? Hawai'ians speak of the *mana* of the land, the spirit of the land that nurtures those who live on it. Australian aborigines trek the mysterious song lines of their land in rites of initiation. Had the demands and bounty of this land forged a uniquely Toisanese character?

I have spent over two decades since that day in 1983 pondering these questions. Until that moment in the village square I had felt as if I had been dropped out of the sky, birthed one perplexing day in America, focused exclusively on an American future, unconnected to the ancient past of my parents.

That day I knew that, even before my birth, I had a complete past and came from a complete people. That day, for the first time, I sensed the power alive in the soil of my ancestral village, that underneath the soil was a gargantuan mother root bulb from which I was inseparable, as one of the thousands of shoots darting out from her deeply rooted fecundity, streaming Toisan *chi* essence into me -- wherever I called home. As I stood in the small square of Suey Wan village, I knew that, despite my exotic American markings, my DNA was here, the best of Toisan.

I knew then that this land, with her Toisan energy, had fueled me during my years of initiation in the 1960s and 1970s. This was the mysterious strength that sustained me when America's civil rights struggle and anti-Vietnam War resistance stomped into San Francisco's Chinatown, followed by the horror of my younger brother Richard's wrongful conviction for murder in 1972. This was the source of power that helped my brother and me to retain our Toisan character, the moral compass that kept us both on track, so that during our bleakest hours we eschewed the violence of retribution as an instrument of justice.

Just as suddenly as I felt my Toisan connection, I knew that my mother was the connecting link. Despite our resistance, she had succeeded in keeping us rooted in the Toisanese ways. She had kept her promise, the Eighth Promise that she had made to her own mother and the Clan Sisterhood thirty-four years earlier, in this very village. Like Toisan mothers before her, she promised to teach her children compassion by instilling in us the ways of Toisan.

That day, I finally understood that when my mother admonished me to "stay Chinese," she wasn't telling me to learn the facts of Chinese history or the lineage of the outrageous emperors whose Great Walls could be seen from the moon. My peasant farmer mother wasn't that well versed in Chinese history and culture. Nor was she suggesting that I decorate my home with tasteful Chinese antiques and landscape paintings. Except for her free Chinatown bank calendars, my mother's own home was devoid of art. Nor was Mother asking me to subscribe to an ethnic or nationalistic sense of superiority, for she never taught us to consider ourselves superior, or to look down on any other race.

In truth, my mother didn't know much about any of those things; she was a simple daughter of the earth. For her, to "stay Chinese" meant to retain, nurture, and pass on the virtues of intuitive cooperation and recognition of the humanity of others that are embodied in the ways of the Toisanese people. She meant for me to internalize the strength, flexibility, and pragmatism of a people who lived joined at the hip to nature. She wanted me to recognize that I am a child of Toisan.

Had Mother's Toisanese ways any chance of surviving in America? Did her first two sons, Richard and me, stay Toisanese or did we strand ourselves in a psycho-geographic limbo neither fully Toisanese nor fully American? As children, we were caught in a tug-of-war between two worlds, between my mother who sought to sustain Toisonese culture and my father who sought to assimilate to America. Unaware and unappreciative, we struggled to meet both sets of expectations.

This is the story of how my mother transmitted Toisanese ways to me even as I occupied myself with becoming completely American, of how those Toisanese ways helped me to navigate the great national divides over civil rights and the Vietnam War and the personal tragedy that tore through our family and even the frame-up of my brother Richard for murder in the first degree.

This is the story of my mother as my greatest wisdom teacher, who ensured that I received the best of both heritages. This is the story of how my mother's eighth promise kept the ways of Toisan strong within us through life's ten thousand joys and ten thousand sorrows.

SECTION I: SOURCE (1930–1950)

Chapter 1
One Story, Two Voices

But it was nearly two decades after that 1983 visit before I recognized my mother as the connecting link to Toisan. Responding then to an inner call to write, I started with short stories, then organized reflective essays, and finally struggle to craft this memoir. Eventually, I asked mother whether I could interview her, audio tape our conversations. Mother was initially hesitant, genuinely self-deprecating even.

"What does a simple woman like me have to say?" she asked.

"Probably a lot, but why don't we try it and find out," I responded and she agreed to at least a couple of sessions. The first one took place in my writing studio in my Berkeley home one weekend, when she and father slept over one weekend. It went well, and eventually we recorded thirty plus hours of her remembrances of her Toisanese upbringing, a way of life relatively unchanged for a millennium, and how and why she sought to preserve this sensibility in America. That's when I began to discern the quiet, but key role she had played in my upbringing, for as children, my brother Richard, younger by two years, and I had resisted her. She had succeeded after all in keeping us rooted in the Toisanese ways.

Over the course of these interviews, I came to understand that this connection to the land and ways of Toisan were the source of power that helped my brother Richard and me to retain our strength of character, the moral compass that kept us both on track, so that during our bleakest hours, through the social upheavals of the 1960s and 1970s, and our roles in a desperate power struggle in our community of Chinatown San Francisco where over 30 people were shot dead in the streets, my brother's wrongful conviction for one of those slayings, and then my attempts to get him a new trial, how we both ultimately eschewed the violence of retribution as an instrument of change and justice.

Realizing this, I finally understood that when my mother had admonished me to "stay Chinese," she wasn't telling me to learn the facts of Chinese history or the lineage of the outrageous emperors whose Great Walls could be seen from the moon. In any case, my peasant farmer mother wasn't that well versed in Chinese history and culture. Except for her free Chinatown bank calendars, my mother's own home was entirely devoid of art. Nor was Mother asking me to subscribe to an ethnic or nationalistic sense of superiority, for she never taught us to consider ourselves superior or to look down on any other race.

In truth, my mother didn't know much about any of those things; she was a simple daughter of the earth. For her, to "stay Chinese" meant to retain, nurture, and pass on the virtues of intuitive cooperation and recognition of the humanity of others that are embodied in the ways of the

Toisanese people. She meant for me to internalize the strength, flexibility, and pragmatism of a people who lived within the cycles, embracing both the abundance and the fickleness of nature. She wanted me to recognize myself as a child of Toisan.

I know now that mother's story leads into my story, and in fact, preordained many of my life choices. So, I share this memoir with her. That is why every other chapter is hers, in her own voice, from my audio recordings of interviews with her in Toisan dialect. Mother's chapters are italicized, to clearly mark her voice -- of how she lived her life, loved her two men, and raised her three sons -- even as, with Toisanese as her lifelong exclusive tongue, I am entrusted, as son and author, to capture that voice and project her personality onto these pages.

My own chapters remain in plain text. Also, my narrations of many of the key conversations and scenes of her upbringing in Toisan and early life in America, although based on our taped conversations, they are complemented and confirmed by other interviews, with her two younger sisters and a brother who now live America, and those village Clan Sisters among whom I was raised in San Francisco. Much later, I interviewed her Clan Sisters in Toisan, first in 1983 and then again in 2001.

Chapter 2 Toisan A Toisan Village

I was born on May 26, 1928. I was named Poy Jen. My name means "one who deflects negative events and generates positive outcomes." It means that when misfortune dislodges our family, I am the one who returns us to the center, and keeps us centered.

I am a direct descendant of the first families who settled in our village one thousand years ago. Suey Wan is the name of our village, and it is a thriving village to this day. We still have a house there. It has sat empty for fifty years, awaiting our family's return. We are a Chun Clan village, and so my maiden name is Chun. Your father was born and raised in a nearby Lee Clan village, before he left for America at the age of thirteen. Years later, he came back to marry me.

We were farmers, and we came from somewhere else in Northern China about one thousand years ago. We are people of the T'ang Dynasty, that's why we still call ourselves T'ang Ren *or, as we say it in Toisanese,* H'ong Ngeen—*people of the T'ang. Our soil was* how sek—*rich and wet, for Toisan is in the Pearl River Delta. Water so shiny you have to squint to see it. Our village faced a large paddy where we grew rice and other crops for market. All of us helped with farming, even the kids. Together, we prepared the fields, fixed the mud walls, planted, fertilized, and harvested. Every family raised their own vegetables in their private garden patch. Cabbage, scallions, bok choy, mustard greens, lettuce—so many vegetables. Fruit trees grew in yards throughout the village, for the weather was hot and moist for most of the year. Oh, so many kinds of fruit trees—red apples, bananas, plums, peaches, and many, many more.*

Our hills were full of trees that we used for building houses, wheelbarrows, plows, and furniture. Our water came from a village well. Deliciously cold, clean, and sweet water. When I was old enough, the first thing I did every morning was to fill two pails and carry them home. This kind of life makes you strong. Even today, I am strong. Until a few years ago, I still could carry a twenty-five-pound bag of rice several blocks, from the store to our home.

Chickens and ducks ran freely through the village. "Gop, gop, gop," pecking away at this and that. We ate them or sold them. Many families raised pigs for market. We didn't raise pigs— "uggghh"— too stinky and messy.

Instead, we raised fish in the village fishpond, for eating and for market. As kids, we played in the fishpond. We weren't supposed to because none of us could swim. But we liked catching tiny fishes. With my younger sisters, Tien and Yoong, and our girlfriends, like Kow Woon, we would sit on our heels, and, with tiny nets, catch baby fish. "Hslout, hslout, hslout," was the sound of the fishes squirming in our hands and flapping on the ground. "Ha, ha, ha," we laughed so much. We always got a little wet, but the sun dried us off before we got in trouble with mother. Then, we put the fish into a bowl, and played with them for days.

Every few months, village men dropped nets in the water to catch fish for market. We chased after the fishes that flipped free, flopping all over the ground. We'd grab one or two for dinner. The men scolded us, "Eating money instead of putting it in your pocket!" as we ran off, half-closing our eyes as the thrashing fish splashed water all over our faces. But no one really minded a few fish being taken. Especially not for special occasions like Chinese New Year or a wedding.

Life was not easy in the village like it is in America. Farmers worked constantly. Sweating and breathing hard. Worried all the time about enough rain and sun, daily checking for insects and rats that ate our crops. Our clothes were patched over and used until they fell completely apart. But still, we had lots more time to relax, to chat with one another, and to play. Once everything was done, it was done. You can't make the crops grow any faster by acting busy.

Life was simpler in the village in that way and safer—that is, until the Japanese Army attacked us.... The nearby Wong Clan fought back, killed some soldiers. We heard what happened, a dawn attack. Everyone was slaughtered – women, children, old people, too – whoever was in the village. They burned every building, wrecked every chicken coop, duck yard, and the fields. Two Wongs survived by jumping into the outhouses, ducking their heads under. We heard they kidnapped women from other villages, young girls, from villages and took them to Suey Nam, where their garrison was, and made them work, other things the elders wouldn't talk about in front of children. If a girl fought back, they tied her up like a pig on a pole and took her with the anyway.

At first we couldn't believe that the world had any people that cruel. We scratched our heads, lifted our eyes wide, rocked on our feet, placed on hands on our hips, and scrutinized the person trying to convince us, but just couldn't imagine any people under the heavens behaving so crazy. It's just people mean talking because we're at war, we said. Until the survivors of the Wong massacre, people we knew, hid with us. Our village is at the end of the valley and so we were the last one they attacked. But I can still remember the sound of their airplanes that first day. "Woo, woo, woo." And later the rhythm of their boots when they raided our village. Such big boots. "Bawk, bawk, bawk."

Chapter 3

The Butterflies of Death

It was 1938, and I wish my Mother could tell you herself about that tragic first day, and then of the near-fatal events of the second day, which I recount at the end of this chapter. But my Mother does not believe in revealing the sorrows in her life. She says it kills the spirit to recite bad times. Brings them back. She says I should focus on the positive, look ahead, think good thoughts no matter what happens, and the future will be happy. I've pressed Mother, but except for a few grunts of acknowledgment that "Yes, something like that happened." She goes no further and I've used my best trial lawyer's techniques to corner her, including relentless "yes–no" cross-examinations. But Mother waves her hand like a judge, simply vanquishing this irrelevant line of inquiry.

So, I must fill in the gaps for her and tell the stories of the sorrows in her life. I do so in order to understand her and the nature of her gifts to me. To learn the story, I have interviewed my father, who is more Americanized and thus more forthcoming. I have also spoken with several Clan Sisters who live in San Francisco, and with relatives in the village who knew Mother as a child. Her two sisters and brother, San Franciscans too, are like her —they haven't been very helpful. Besides, they don't understand me, and, because of that, they don't think particularly well of me. To them, I am the lawyer who irresponsibly decided to become a struggling writer. I am the successful businessman who thinks that while making money is only okay, it is not the primary purpose of life.

I should explain that my mother is not afraid of hearing bad news or facing hard times. Nor is she afraid of tackling the sorrows of life on their own terms. Quite the contrary. She speaks her mind, clearly, loudly, and emotionally when she is unhappy. She wraps her arms around unhappiness in a bear hug. Then slowly, steadily, and with great care, she turns misfortune around, one problem at a time, one day at a time. Perhaps it was her first near-death experience as a girl that taught her that tragedy could be averted, or, if unavoidable, turned around.

That morning in 1938 was the first time a Japanese Zero fighter plane attacked Mother's village. No one had actually seen an airplane before, and so no Toisanese warning shout was issued. How could backcountry farmers know that airplanes killed? Kow Woon was orphaned when that first plane flew over the old village—a clutch of cottages of no strategic importance. It was the *woo-woo-woo* sound of the plane that caught the children's attention. Curious children, they rushed out of their classrooms, jumping up and down and scanning the skies. Parents soon joined them outside their homes, shading their eyes with their hands as they too looked into the sky, in the direction of the *woo-woo-woo* sound.

The Zero discharged its machine-guns, raking the ground toward the school children. The bullets were red and orange, arcing down through the air, bouncing along the play fields. The children thought the red and orange bullets were butterflies. They ran closer to catch them. "Butterflies, butterflies," they gleefully shouted. Suddenly their laughter twisted into screams of agony. Children fell everywhere, shrieking. Blood spread and gathered in pools. Then the bombs fell into the crowds of confused adults and onto the row houses.

Thereafter, whenever the sound of *woo-woo-woo* was heard, the villagers would cry "Run and hide. The butterflies of death, the butterflies of death are coming."

Kow Woon's family was killed that day. In the way of the village clan system, there were no orphans. Grandmother Chun adopted Kow Woon as her own child, simply declaring that she was now Kow Woon's mother. Compassion meant that no child was ever homeless, and if Grandmother Chun was known for anything, it was for her compassion.

Years later, on a singularly stormy day in 1942, at the height of the Japanese invasion of China, the specter of death came again. Expanding their occupation of China, the Japanese war machine persisted in their indiscriminate slaughter of the unarmed peasants of China. It was part of a brutal, inhumane strategy of genocide designed, to break the will of the people and enslave them of the nation they had invaded. All too well known were the tales of captured young teenage girls and young women, their subsequent rape, torture, and murder of captured young teenage girls and young women. Or worse, to be programmatically raped as sex slaves by entire units of men, euphemistically designated as "comfort women," until they died.

After the first few raids of the mid-1930s, the villagers devised a verbal alert system and everyone would flee into the hills and hide until danger passed for the villagers. They learned that for soldiers on foot, it was just too much hiking for a day's ration of rice and vegetables, or even for the thrill of capturing young girls. So Japanese soldiers would not foray there. They'd raid the village, but no further.

This day, however, some villagers could not make it to the safety of the hills in time including my grandmother, my mother, her two younger sisters, Yoong and Tien, and their adopted sister Kow Woon. Perhaps the loud hard rains had muffled earlier warnings, for not even the shouted, loud, harsh sounds of Toisanese syllables could pierce athe deluge's clatter deluge. Only too late did they hear the cries "Japanese soldiers!" Japanese soldiers! Run! Hide!" Grandmother Chun quickly hustled the girls outside, Poy-Jen, her sisters Yoong and Tien, and their adopted sister Kow Woon, dashed outside, but then realized they could not cross the rapidly rising water level of paddies and into the safety of the hills. Mute with horror as the water level kept rising before their very eyes, they realized that death was here.

Grandmother knew of an abandoned house situated on the outskirts of the village. The obviously fallen structure was far enough from the main footpath that maybe the soldiers would skip it. They'd see that the roof had fallen through, that the windows were broken and the wind and rain blew through freely. They'd conclude that any food would be spoiled. If they came close anyway, they'd see that the inside was too cobwebbed and dirty for a hiding place. Yes, perhaps the Japanese soldiers would ignore it. That was Grandmother's only hope.

She scooted the girls toward the house. Once inside, she found a hiding place, a large pile of reeds used for cooking fires stored in a shadowy corner. She pulled aside the tied bundles of long reed grass, shooed her four girls onto the floor. She piled back the reeds back on into a womb like cave big enough for all of them. She carefully tucked in their little feet and hands and finally crawled in. Only then did she hide herself, hovering over them, spreading her arms over them, two on each side, like a mother hen.

Through the sound of the pouring rain, they could hear the soldiers' advance. Their boots beating an advance towards them. *Bawk, bawk, bawk.* Yelling loudly in Japanese, they kicked down the partially rotted front door. They yanked open doors to bedrooms, closets, and cupboards. They shouted what sounded like angry curses.

They huddled, frozen together, and swallowed their terror.

A soldier trampled in their direction, closer and closer to the stack of reeds. Soon, it would be all over but the screaming—and the bullets in the head. Maybe they would at least be spared bayonet practice. But just then someone outside shouted and miraculously, the soldier stopped, muttered, and then turned around and then the entire unit stomped outside. Their voices died down, then the "bawk, bawk" rhythm faded into the cadence of the falling rain. Silence. Longer silence.

"Be quiet. Don't move. It could be a trick." Grandmother whispered carefully, keeping her arms over the four girls. They remained still for a long, long time. But the Japanese soldiers had indeed left and they were safe.

Grandmother's quick thinking had saved them all; they would live another season. "Ten thousand joys and ten thousand sorrows—this is the promise of life," she undoubtedly muttered to herself as she thanked Kuan Yin, the Bodhisattva of Compassion who aids all beings who are suffering.

Chapter 4
The Clan Sisterhood

The most important thing a Toisanese girl learns is this: that all the females of our village are hung dee moy, *Clan Sisters. Age doesn't matter, little girl, wife, or elder, all village females are Clan Sisters. It doesn't matter if you were born in another village, like a Lee or Wong surnamed village, and married a Chun man. A wife automatically becomes a Chun Clan Sister once she moves into her husband's house. The new Sisterhood treats her the same as one born into the village. It also doesn't matter if you marry and move to another village: you remain a Chun Clan Sister.*

The Clan Sisterhood is like your best friend for life. We're a family that will always welcome you no matter what. We're a huge women's club, so you always have friends to drink tea with, share gossip with, and who will baby-sit for you. A Clan Sister will always help you no matter where you are, no matter what you do. We will raise each other's children as our own and teach them the good things, which is to know right from wrong, study hard, respect everyone, save money, and help take care of the family. The Clan Sisterhood has been a big part of my life. Perhaps you've noticed that my Clan Sisters have always been involved in your life?

That's why when someone I have never met is introduced to me as hung dee moy, *Clan Sister, I immediately give her the same respect, assistance, and affection I would to a* hung dee moy *I was raised with. I would help a new sister in any way I can.*

In Toisanese, hung dee moy *means all sisters together, or singular, a sister of our village clan, like "she is* hung dee moy." *Hung dee moy* can be title, like auntie or niece or grandmother. That's why, when you sometimes ask me who was that lady we just met, I say "She is* hung dee moy." *Not "auntie" or "elder" or "friend." The younger sisters call the adults "yee-yee" or auntie. The Aunties called the younger ones "moy-moy," or little sister.*

To understand the workings of the Clan Sisterhood, you have to understand a few things about our village, like our customs, our daily life, and how we were organized.

There was a lot to do every day because we were on our own—there was no government to provide social assistance, regulations or emergency services. But we got things done—all of it, in a village with no social services, no regulations. We had no repair shops to call to fix broken things, like in America. But broken tools got fixed, roofs replaced, and levees repaired. We even built our own grammar school.

There were no college-educated experts telling us how to farm or build canals and levees, like in America. Yet, we fed ourselves and made money selling vegetables, rice, chickens, pigs, beef, and even fish to the towns. And hundreds of years ago, we built a canal that connected us to Guangzhou. We built levee walls for each village all along the way. Over the centuries, the widest boats traveled to Guangzhou, Hong Kong, and back. That's why Toisan people are all over the world—the canal took us to the sea. The canal is there today, still being used. When you drive from Hoisin to the village, you can still see it along the road.

To get it all done, men and women had separate jobs. That's how we were divided, by our jobs. This has been so for many centuries, and so the Clan Sisterhood started to meet and talk, to do things better and better each year based on that. The men had a Clan Brotherhood, but you'll have to talk to your father about that. Hmm, no he left the village to early. Better to talk to my younger brother, your Uncle Wah. I can only talk about the Clan Sisterhood.

I am telling you all this so you can see that even though we were farmers in a village that's not even on a map, we were smart people and good to each other. You think we could have lasted one thousand one hundred years if we weren't smart people? Famine, flood, sickness, bandits, and the Japanese war? You think we could go through all those hard times together if we didn't treat each other well, no matter how bitter life was?

The Clan Sisterhood had special knowledge that men did not. Elder Clan Sisters cooked herbal medicinal soups to heal illnesses. Mothers cooked season-change herbal soups to adjust their children's chi *levels, so they wouldn't catch cold when the chilly north wind swept far south into our village. Aunties spent hours preparing the chi energy soups for a birth mother during her postpartum rejuvenation.*

Each generation of younger Clan Sisters learned the older generations' knowledge and then added on. So you see, the Clan Sisterhood was like a college for women. We taught one another what we had to know, passing on women's expertise and wisdom, generation after generation.

Women had to know how to plant different types of crops, how much to water each plant and when. Men were not the only ones farming! "Szooon, szooon, szooon"—plant by plant, we checked the stalks in the mud and water. Women knew how to harvest the crop, how to separate the grain from the husks. Women tended the vegetable gardens, protected them against insects and rats, and picked the vegetables at the best time to eat. Green, sweet, and crunchy! "Lok-lok"—that's the noise vegetables should make when you eat them. Women preserved food, like salted fish, fatback pork, sun-dried oily duck, sausages, dried vegetables, and dried fruits. Women even raised chickens, pigs, and fish for market.

At the age of six, I was raising the chickens for our family and I was good at it. Every morning I fed them rice husks and vegetable leaves. "Gawk, gawk, gawk, gawk," they said as they ran down from the chick coop. That's the best food to feed them so that they grow sweet to the taste. These were real chickens, not like the American kind with chemical injections to make them look tasty. Even my hens tasted good after they stopped laying eggs. My chickens ran around all day and at night jumped back into the coop by themselves. I counted them to be sure and if any didn't make it home, I went out in the dark, held my thumb and index over my lips and called to them "ject, ject, ject." Wherever they were sleeping, like leaning against a corner or lying, under a bush, they'd recognize my voice and wobble out to me, very sleepy-headed. Easy to carry, about a foot tall when full-grown. Always found them for nobody stole anyone else's chicken.

And women ran the household for the entire family. Cooked everyone's favorite foods all the time and all the special dishes of Chinese New Year and the Harvest Moon Festival. Women raised the children. Toisanese believe that mothers must raise their own children, that's what mothers have to do if you want happy children. Yes, no matter how busy we were in the fields, we saw them several times each day, even if we had to walk fast back and forth, back-and-forth. Kept them healthy and taught them manners. Tutored them in Chinese, history, math, and the three principles of democracy. I mean, it seems sometimes that women did everything.

I was working when I was five years old. Started early every morning. Got two pails of water from the well. Cut reeds for the cooking fire. Checked plants in the paddies to make sure there were no snails. Sometimes it was so cold, my hands would be numb from sticking them into the paddies, and my breath would blow out like smoke. "Phoo, phoo, phoo." I blew into my hands to keep them warm. "Bum, bum, bum." I jumped up and down to warm up.

I tended the vegetables in our garden plot and carried them home to cook. As I got older, I learned when a chicken was best for eating and when it was too old. I learned how to defeather and cut up a chicken, and how toto cook it so the skin was chewy, the meat juicy, and the inside of the bones still red.

The Clan Sisterhood—that's teaching by working together, not through books. Oh, girls went to school too, for about six years. But that was to learn how to read and write Chinese, add and subtract, and learn a little Chinese history. We studied Sun Yat-sen, because he was Cantonese like us. We celebrated his democratic revolution of 1911, which ended the imperial system. Every year on October 10th, or "10-10-Day." We memorized his Three Principles of Democracy, ideas he got from America. But only some really smart men kept going to school. Like my oldest brother who became a schoolteacher.

Over the centuries, the Clan Sisterhood had a special way of making decisions, the "speaking round-and-round." This "speaking round-and-round" is not like gossiping or socializing. That's more like "ji-ji-ja-ja...ji-ji-ja-ja..."—everyone talking at the same time. But when a "speaking" began, everyone quieted down. Each person could speak, and no one would interrupt until she was finished. The "speaking round-and-round" was part of everything we did. Before we planted the new crop, we gathered in a "speaking round-and-round." Before we built a new house, we met in a "speaking round-and-round." Before we helped a mother give birth, we assessed any health dangers and assigned duties in a "speaking round-and-round."

Actually, in Toisanese, we call it "Gong loi, gong huie," or "speech coming and speech going." But I think you understand it better as "speaking round-and-round" because it's not like arguing back and forth, like lawyers. You know what I mean, you're a lawyer. We stand in a circle and take turns listening until we understand the situation.

The Clan Sisterhood solved many village disputes using this way. There were no courts to settle matters and no sheriffs to enforce the right thing to do. Everyone who wanted to could get involved. This had to be done without taking sides, even if one party was a stinky, rotten rind. The solution had to be fair for each party to accept the solution. You see, we couldn't have someone so unhappy they wouldn't work with someone else. There was always some task that needed everyone's help— flood repair, seeding, harvest time, or fixing a roof. In this way, the "speaking round-and-round" kept us united and cooperating as one village.

So this was how I was raised and taught, surrounded by women of all ages, from many villages. Witnessing and learning from their deliberations. Knowing what to do by helping out with my own hands. Self-reliance, acting for the common good over one's own needs. Finding common ground and lasting solutions when there were problems.

From them, I not only learned to cook meals, but the recipes for the medicinal chi soups, and how to gather herbs and heat them up for poultices, to cure sprained ankles and wrists, bruised muscles.

Finally, one of the most important jobs of the Clan Sisterhood was to ensure the future of the village by finding a husband for each little sister—and, hopefully, a kind man, too. Every sister wanted a say, but you wouldn't bring everyone to the" first meeting" between the prospective bride and groom and their families. Only the elder Aunties went, the ones who were good at sizing up a man. The younger sisters could meet him later, if he was acceptable to the elder Aunties.
Like with your father, the first time we met, before we became engaged.

Chapter 4
Go-between Man

In 1948, a go-between arranged a marriage between my mother and a young Toisanese-American man named Fook Toon Lee. Traditionally, China had never subscribed to the romantic ideal of marriage. Marriage was a group decision, decided upon by the family of the prospective bride and groom, and in the case of Toisanese villagers, with the communal consent of their respective village Clan Sisterhoods. Within their cloistered farmers' lives, Toisanese families were typically oblivious of the identities of young men and women coming of age in even nearby villages. Many hired professional marriage-brokers to scout out the best marriage prospects. Others entrusted discerning villagers, often life-long friends of the family, who worked in professions or trades that exposed them to the children of many villages. These individuals were not full-time marriage brokers, but more like skilled go-betweens with successful track records of matches. So Fook Toon's mother, still in Toisan, hired his childhood grammar school teacher, someone who knew him well, and a member of the Lee Clan village, as the go-between, to match him with a suitable bride.

My father Fook Toon, was Toisan, born on November 14, 1922, in the nearby Lee Clan mere miles from Suey Wan. At the age of thirteen, he joined his father in America, a US citizen who lived in Chinatown, San Francisco. In 1948, when the go-between reported he had identified three bridal prospects – Poy Jen being one of them, Fook Toon was twenty-six and Poy Jen was twenty-one. Fook Toon and Poy Jen had never met each other. Dating was not customary, so neither one had ever had a romantic relationship.

The marriage go-between was a respected schoolteacher, Fook Toon's grammar school teacher. The go-between's biographical sketch of Fook Toon's life gave Poy Jen's mother assurance that he could be a good match for her first and favorite daughter. He told her that he had taught him as a child.

"Fook Toon was a good student, bright and eager to learn. He loved writing poetry and even at that young age, had achieved a level in classical poetry equal to scholars from wealthy families." He told her.

The go-between recited Fook Toon's intentions: he wanted to marry and raise a family, but in America, not China. Having immigrated to America as a boy, and now a successful worker, his bride must be willing to start a new life in America. The go-between didn't know all the details, of course, but if Fook Toon must wasn't well off, how else could he afford to travel back and forth across the Pacific, instead of finding a bride by exchanging photos and letters?

What a go-between really knows versus what he chooses to portray, is often a more idealized version of the starker truth. So, in this way, even arranged marriages don't seem so different from the romantic process, i.e., each party puts their best foot forward during the mating dance, and similarly, often sees what one needs to see, the harsher traits diminished in significance to be worked out later.

In truth, Fook Toon's father, an American citizen who lived in America, had summarily ordered Fook Toon to join him in San Francisco in 1935, not sentimentally requesting his presence because he missed him or out of fatherly love, wanting him to receive an American education.

In fact, his father wanted him for his earning potential: to put him to work full-time.

But at the age of thirteen, Fook Toon knew none of this and of course did not question this summons. He was not only an obedient son, but also alert enough to notice that there just wasn't enough inheritable farm land for him and his younger brother in the village for each to support a family. So, he gladly left Toisan for America, or *Geem San*, the Gold Mountain, the whispered promise of boundless wealth that lingered long after the California Gold Rush of 1849, when Chinese first arrived in California. America was a new and strange land and with a language which Fook Toon did not speak: but he trusted his father, whom he had not seen in years, had paved the way for him. So, culturally and linguistically ill-prepared, this dutiful son unhesitatingly left by sea on a huge ocean he had never seen before, for, a voyage of many weeks, below-decks in steerage class on a rusting ship that stopped only once, in Honolulu, for fresh provisions.

After passing through its golden gate entrance into San Francisco Bay, all other Asian immigrants, for example Japanese immigrants, sailed directly to the piers and disembarked immediately onto the streets of San Francisco. Not so for Chinese. Fook Toon was quarantined on Angel Island, a West Coast Ellis Island maintained exclusively for Chinese immigrants.

The reason was that the birth papers of many Chinese males claiming to be sons of US citizens, a priority preference for immigration and citizenship, were presumptively suspect, probably fraudulently obtained. The Immigration and Naturalization Service devised very detailed tests to separate genuine claims from false ones. Depending upon your performance during the oral examination, detention could sometimes last less than a week. But more typically, it was several months, and occasionally sometimes eighteen months or longer.

Why this draconian test? For decades, the era's anti-Chinese exclusion legislation severely limited the number of Chinese migrants, and the few who were admitted had to be related by birth to American citizens. So, when San Francisco's great earthquake and fire of 1906 destroyed City Hall and all its birth records, the Chinatown community seized the opportunity, claiming mythical sons and "re-registering" their apocryphal births at the new City Hall. These newly minted fathers then sold these false birth certificates for huge profits throughout the Pearl River Delta. Their numerous counterfeit sons came to be known as *hoo jee doi*, or "paper sons."

Responding, the immigration services devised authenticity tests. In order to do, they obtained maps of the main Toisan villages of origin of Chinese immigrants, the names of neighboring families, several generations of relationships by name, and other detailed information that only a genuine offspring could know. A male who did not know the layout of the village of origin of his father was deemed a paper son and immediately deported. A boy who did not know relatives by name for several generations was immediately deported. Thus, the test had unintended and cruel consequences: often legitimate children failed, for the questions were frequently based on information that was old or poorly reconstructed, wrongly mistranslated, or misunderstood by the interrogator, to the horror of a genuine offspring.

To have come so far, to have paid so much money for the passage, and to never have the shining streets of the Gold Mountain, and only to be sent back to China: the shame of failure. Many threw themselves overboard during the long passage home.

Fook Toon knew from letters from returned Toisanese who had been sent back to the village back to the village of that the heartbreaking consequences of giving even one wrong answer could be devastating. On that first day on the island, as if he needed reminding, he could read their bitterly worded calligraphy, carved on the barracks walls, that recited of detentions for months on end, testing and testing until each test became a torture session, consequences ominously echoed on calligraphy carved into the wall of the detention barracks.

Fook Toon even encountered the broken spirits of awaiting their deportation back.

So, Fook Toon had spent weeks studying the layout of his village's streets, memorizing everyone's complete formal name and diagramming charts of everyone's relatives for three generations. He walked every lane of his village, memorized who lived next door to whom, when a particular building had been torn down, and that one built. He drilled himself on all the most mundane but exacting details of his village's life and history, because this was the difference between admission and deportation. The sinister reputation of the tests was so great that Father had prepared crib sheets to study during the voyage, sequestered in an inside coat pocket, finding quiet corners for his secretive daily review. When he was less than three days out from San Francisco, he tore them up, tossed them into the wind so they could not be used in any way by the suspicious authorities against him, as evidence to accuse him of only memorizing the village layout, but that he had never lived there in fact.

The go-between impressed upon Poy Jen's mother Fook Toon's forethought, confidence, and youthful derring-do. He said that father had refused to fail. His interrogation day at Angel Island dawned: Fook Toon passed completely. A few days later, he ferried over to San Francisco, reuniting with his father.

While the go-between impressed upon Poy Jen's mother Fook Toon's persistence and planning, yet the chillier truth was that within days of his arrival, instead of a loving family welcome, his father immediately delivered him to a job as a live-in domestic, in that era what was called a house-boy, and a Chinese house boy was all the rage back then, a "must" for any proper home. Fook toon was delivered to the home of a physician in wealthy Marin County, and within the racial caste system of the time, a completely wealthy white enclave just north of San Francisco. Fook Toon was left on his own, at thirteen years of age, literally fresh off the farm, clueless about American society, and speechless and illiterate in English.

During that the first year, his father came knocking on his door once a month, on payday, and took all his cash. Eventually, he knew to hide a few dollars before the hour of that knock on the door.

The go-between continued, saying that Fook Toon diligently attended American school, and learned to speak and write the American language. What he didn't know was that even though Fook Toon had graduated with very good grades from the local middle school—with test scores oftentimes higher than those of his American-born classmates, as one history teacher opined several times in an attempt to shame his native-born fellow students into do better.

Yet, given the racial climate of the times, Fook Toon knew that prospects for a Chinese-American immigrant in Marin were severely curtailed if not downright non-existent. Too, he grew tired of the endless cleaning up to maintain a certain household immaculateness. It was often not until 10 P.M., when all his chores were finally done, that Fook Toon could study, and then was often berated for using up the light bulb, running up the electric bill, and his late dinner limited to a simple tomato sandwich despite bountiful left-overs often tossed a few days later (by him of course).

And the family's frequent Saturday night soirees kept him on duty for entire weekends: all day Saturday in preparation, all evening serving food and drinks, with a preliminary clean-up into the wee hours, and a complete clean-up all day Sunday, as if there had never been a party.

So Fook Toon departed Marin, giving up his chance at the superior high school education offered by Marin, one of the finest public school districts in the Bay Area, and whose graduates typically matriculated into America's best universities. When he informed his employer of this decision, the physician sardonically responded, "I knew you would quit" Fook Toon construed this as revealing a not-so-hidden agenda, that the doctor had intentionally worked him hard so as to discourage him from staying on in Marin, to close the doors that might have opened to him had he finished high school in this enclave of wealth and privilege.

Whatever the reasons, Fook Toon headed for Southern California, too far away for his father to take his cash. First he traveled to Los Angeles to search for better work than a houseboy, then wandered inland, where along with Mexican, Pilipino, and Japanese migrant workers, he worked the bountiful Central Valley. When that harvest season was over, he headed back to Los Angeles before finally settling back into San Francisco's Chinatown. Exploited by his own people, the Chinese-owned restaurateurs: double shifts, six and sometimes seven days a week, low wages where the owners kept the tips, he eventually refused to work for them. He soon realized that the Chinatown powers-that-be were completely complicit with this exploitation, as well as the city's political establishment, and in fact enforced it by busting unionization efforts in the most union town west of the Mississippi. This system repulsed him, for he was raised in the communal sensibility of mutual fairness and cooperation. He understood now why his own father had so coldly exploited him, that

that was just the way things were in Chinatown, and his father had lived there too long. Still, Fook Toon refused to work any more Chinatown jobs.

But the diligent student Fook Toon, the childhood classical poet, the one who had passed his Angel Island test on the first interrogation, had indeed learned to read and write American English in his Marin County middle school well enough and with a certain glibness that he could join the restaurant worker's union. Equally important, he had not been overwhelmed culturally and isolated despite his hostile household load, but had learned invaluable social skills, especially on how to get along with mainstream Americans. So, Fook Toon found worked for white-owned restaurants serving white customers, and the owners loved his uncomplaining diligence, clockwork attendance, and good-humored optimism. The union guaranteed him steady wages with paid vacations and a health plan, and with its grievance procedure, the union protected him from arbitrary firings, unpaid wages, and race-based mistreatment. But the union also kept Chinese-American men in second-tier jobs—as busboys, dishwashers, and backroom supply men. Typically, union busboys eventually moved on to become waiters, but Chinese union men could not become waiters who received tips, tips so lucrative that waiters often earned more money than their customers did. But a union man was as he got in America, Fook Toon was safely employed, and in his old age, he would still have a health plan and receive a monthly pension along social security.

Still, it was a devil's bargain as he would remain stuck in a lower-income bracket, unlikely ever to advance into the middle class.

The go-between simply assured my grandmother that Fook Toon would always have a steady job with a regular paycheck -- this was accurate as far as it went.

My Grandmother Chun then asked whether Fook Toon sent remittances home to his mother. The go-between assured her he did, regularly. Besides, only those with cash and a future could return to Toisan to find a bride to take back to America. The go-between continued idealizing Fook Toon's attributes.

Grandmother Chun knew there were tens of thousands of unmarried Toisan men in America, and very few eligible Toisan women. She fully understood the value of her first daughter as a bride for any Chinese-American man. America had historically kept out Chinese women, granting visas only to Chinese men in order to exploit their cheap labor, then expecting them to return to China when old and physically spent. She knew of that there were anti-miscegenation laws and customs against a Chinese-American man marrying American women of other races.

Yes, she could afford to be selective, for there were a lot of lonely Toisan men in America. But not too selective, for Toisanese men coming home for a bride also became a way out of China for Toisan women, and many families now wanted their daughters to leave. Chinese society had been disintegrating for decades, a breakdown accelerated by the decade-long Japanese invasion, and now, in the fourth year of the civil war following the Japanese defeat, China was surly in its final stage of collapse. Who knew who would win, the Communists or the Republican Nationalists, but especially, who knew how the new China would turn out? Would this ancient sleeping dragon of a civilization continue to thrash about in death throes for several decades more, or would it, like the other favored Chinese mythical creature with whom the dragon is often symbolically portrayed, the Phoenix, arise from its ashes, reborn whole, singing life's song, and soaring into the new day.

No one knew. The future was at best, uncertain.

Grandmother had proven herself a pragmatic, resilient woman. After all, it was her quick thinking that had saved her children and Kow Woon on that noisy, stormy day, when they were stranded when the Japanese soldiers raided. I finally met her in the mid-late 1960s, when she arrived in America. Then I had a chance to witness her undemanding kindness as she watched over everyone's comfort. She never corrected, only suggested. I can imagine her practical yet loving rumination for her daughters as she raised them.

So I surmised that my grandmother must have surely thought more of her daughter's future happiness than her own. "We survived the Japanese war, but I lost my husband, killed during a Japanese air raid in Burma. A bomb hit the laundry that he had started there to earn money to send home to us. Yet, even with the Japanese war over, our village has not been safe for years," she must have thought.

"And now the Communists are winning the civil war and we are Nationalists." I knew that with her family active members of the republican Nationalist party, and her eldest son a Nationalist official, she understood we're on the losing side of the civil war.

So in 1948, my pragmatic and flexible grandmother decided the wisest course was to marry off her favorite daughter, her first-born daughter, Poy-Jen, not to a local suitor, but to a Toisanese-American, as a way out to America where she would be safe. Poy Jen would then be a bridge for her family, finding Toisanese-American husbands for sisters so they could leave here—Yoong, her my second daughter to be followed by Tien, her my third daughter, and even Kow Woon, her adopted daughter. Squire them away to the safety of America. After all, they could always come back later when China modernized, when the village was safe again. I imagine my grandmother hoping, "Perhaps I can join them later when they are safe in America." But because she so reflexively put her own needs behind those of others, she had dared not to hope it out loud, for in her traditional way of being, life and opportunity should always pass to the younger generation.

"No matter, for I am old."

There was never a chance that Poy Jen could end up an old maid: she was too pretty, too nice, too skilled and too much like my revered grandmother. So she had time and many marriage options. But after hearing the go-between speak on behalf of Fook Toon, I believed that this was her thinking, of why Grandmother Chun so readily agreed to a so-called "first meeting." Desperation drove her now, that of fundamental survival.

This first meeting was not really a first encounter between Fook Toon and Poy Jen, but a meeting between the Chun Clan Sisterhood and the Lee Clan Sisterhood. The first meeting was not even a formal meeting, but was intentionally set-up to look like an accidental encounter. That way, if despite the hopeful prospects, one party or both decided against it, no one would appear to be rejected, and future prospects would left unsullied. At an agreed-upon date, time, and intersection in the town of Hoisin, both Clan Sisterhoods, along with Poy Jen and Fook Toon, arrived at a busy street and stood on their own corners, diagonally across from each other. They pretended not to notice each other, like they were just casually hanging out on the street corner chatting, although their evaluative stares were quite obvious.

Mother remembers the Chun Clan Sisterhood slyly first evaluating examining Fook Toon, the only young male among the Lee Clan Sisterhood. With sly glances up and down his body, they whispered that Fook Toon was still a young man, probably mid-twenties, and that he certainly seemed healthy. He was around 5'4", which was a good height for a Toisan male. He was slender with sinewy muscles. Delighted he wasn't one of those wrinkled, spindly, old-time bachelors in the fifties and sixties who had finally earned enough to come home for a bride, Fook Toon was stacking up as a suave looker.

Then the Chun Clan Sisterhood decisively moved into the most important stage of their "speaking round-and-round." They assessed, Fook Toon's character.

"Certainly, he must work hard," said a Clan Sister.

"Not one to sit around all day eating and gossiping," chimed in another.

"These are good traits for a husband and father," said my Grandmother Chun.

"He's not dressed like a dandy, but wears practical, clean clothing," noted all the Aunties.

Thus, they concluded he didn't waste the money he earned, that Poy Jen would send money home to her family in China.

"These are good points," concluded all the Clan Sisters.

Seeing the smiles of satisfaction on the Chun Clan Sisters' faces and hearing the raising volume and uplift tone of merriment of their a "speaking round-and-round," their glances no longer guarded but staring smack-dab at Fook Toon, the marriage go-between decided to decisively move the encounter to the next stage. He would bring the two groups together. He casually walked over to the Chun Clan Sisterhood and evenly assured them that Fook Toon always sent money home to his mother. Then, he let drop that Fook Toon had substantial savings, not only enough to bring his new wife to

America, but to start a home with new furniture, pots and pans, and a wardrobe of American fashions.

"Well, a thrifty man who saves is a good match," said several Clan Sisters.

"Fook Toon's success in America is a point in his favor," concluded all the Clan Sisters.

At this point, the marriage go-between summoned the Lee Clan Sisterhood over and introduced the two groups, beginning with the elders. He saved Fook Toon's introduction for last, a good son returning from America to visit his mother. He encouraged Fook Toon to say a few words in American.

"Hello...how are you today...nice to be home," Fook Toon rattled off in his best American.

"Well, he certainly knows how to speak the American language, and he didn't before he went to America. Smart—that's a good point in his favor," whispered an elder Clan Sister as several buzzed in their agreement.

Fook Toon then switched to Toisanese and carefully offered the most polite Toisanese greeting: "How are you Mrs. Chun. Have you had a chance to eat today?" In the world of the village, asking whether one had eaten was the American version of "How are you doing? Are things going well? How is your health?"

As they carried on a polite conversation, Poy Jen, hiding behind her Clan Sisters, took several careful but full looks at Fook Toon.

"But his Chinese is behind the times and his accent is rough," hissed a Clan Sister. "He's not Chinese enough—too Western," she concluded harshly.

An elder auntie balanced this defect. "He left many years ago, as a child. It's not fair to fault him for speaking poor Chinese if it's in his favor that he speaks American. It's not fair to say he's not Chinese enough if America is where Poy Jen will live," she countered. "It's good that he's American. The more American the better." She drove her point home.

After some reflection, all the Clan Sisters agreed it would be unfair to hold his inadequate Chinese against him or the fact that he didn't seem Chinese enough anymore.

Although Fook Toon seemed shy, he struck everyone as a nice enough man. "He will probably treat my daughter decently," said Grandmother Chun. "I think he should provide well and Poy Jen will be happy. He sends money to his mother." My Grandmother Chun's summation was the stamp of approval of the match, and so the Clan Sisterhood knew they were near the end of this "speaking."

All in all, the match was shaping up better than expected. After a last turn of "speaking," the Clan Sisterhood unanimously approved of Fook Toon Lee, the overseas Chinese from America, as an acceptable husband for their beloved younger sister, Poy Jen.

But my canny Grandmother Chun knew that the Sisterhood had left unspoken was Fook Toon's main attraction ,that he was offering Poy Jen a safe passage out of a disintegrating Chinese society. Fook Toon and other Toisan-American men were lifeboats for entire families as this old China slowly sank and new China had yet to emerge. Ultimately, this would have overridden any of Fook Toon's or another man's shortcomings. Others mothers had agreed to marriages to much older, even to elderly men, who had turned out to be mean and abusive men, men of questionable character habits just to get their daughters out of war-torn China. Sometimes this was done on the basis of a few letters and outdated photographs of someone now much older. Once married, their letters home chronicled their growing misery. So, my grandmother was deeply grateful. "At least Fook Toon is young, pleasant enough, and a good worker. He honors his mother and he will honor me," she sighed out loud, happy at the outcome.

"There in America," Grandmother Chun thought, "Poy Jen would acquire citizenship. She could legally bring over her two brothers, two sisters, and perhaps even me. She could scout out a husband for Kow Woon and other Clan Sisters so they too could leave to America."

The " accidental" meeting now shifted to its final stage. All present declared that the engagement should go forward. Only then did the go-between introduce Mrs. Chun and Mrs. Lee. After exchanging pleasantries and their mutual hopes for the future, the two mothers finally introduced Poy Jen and Fook Toon to each other.

As he later told me turned out, my father took to Poy Jen right away, the best of the three prospects scouted by the marriage go-between. He had met the other two "accidentally," but those encounters had not advanced to an actual introduction. Not even close. In his mind's eye, Poy Jen was the prettiest and the kindest of the three young women. Fook Toon posed only one question to her: "Are you willing to make your home in America?"

Fook Toon knew that his best prospects for himself and of his children were as Americans. Despite his hardships in the States, he had no desire to return to China. He had to know that his bride could leave China completely behind, for the rest of her life.

Poy Jen replied clearly and unequivocally, "Yes."

The marriage go-between beamed. He had served his prized former student and younger Clan brother well. He had earned his fee. He then closed the deal by arranging a time for the two mothers to work out the details, especially the selection of the astrologically ideal wedding date using the ancient moon calendar.

Both Clan Sisterhoods smiled and merged together as everyone unabashedly chatted away—"Ji-ji ja-ja, ji-ji ja-ja."

Poy Jen and Fook Toon took turns smiling and blushing, as they exchanged nervous glances. That was the first time they had stared directly into each other's eyes.

Chapter 5
A Village Wedding and Lucky Day

My marriage celebration lasted five days and five nights. "Ohhhh—gow-hen, how gow-hen"—happy time, happy-happy. People came from nearby villages and slept over to help with the preparations. Our village simply opened its doors and the guests made themselves at home.

My mother hand-sewed a red silk dress with matching pants decorated with dragons and phoenixes for my bridal dress. No, I didn't wear the traditional heavy red headdress with the tassels in front hiding my face until I was presented to the groom. That was out of fashion then. Nor was I carried in a sedan chair with a blaring band of musicians to your father's village. After all, I was going to America and that's why the wedding took place in my village. Your father was dressed in a blue satin scholar's gown imprinted with medallions of dragons. A crisp, shining red sash hung across one shoulder down to his waist. He wore a scholar's cap with a red band. Tucked into the red band was a sprig of clover, freshly plucked out of the ground that morning. This sprig symbolized the start of our fresh future together.

Weddings were a special time for everyone in the village, because that's the only time we got new clothes. You see, though the year, all of us wore old clothes, patched over clothes we passed down until they fell completely apart. But for a wedding celebration, everybody bought bolts of cloth to make new clothes. We spent days designing, cutting, fitting, and sewing. We loved weddings as that's when everyone got brand-new clothes!

Everyone kept os busy during over those five days of the wedding celebrations that even visitors helped: organizing the feasts, baby-sitting, keeping the children out of our way, and with chopping and cooking and just everything. Lots to do. Lots and lots. "Ji-ji, ja-ja. Ji- ji, ja-ja" everyone running around and chirping away like baby chickens.

On the first day, everyone took out their best bowls, plates, chopsticks, and serving spoons. No one family had enough bowls for a big banquet, you see. Just enough for their own families; We pooled everything together, washed and cleaned them. We then decided who would contribute which vegetables or chickens or ducks.

Those who didn't have much helped out with the cleaning up. They dusted and wiped down our house, even. They even washed the floors. They cleaned the temple where the wedding banquet was to take place. They cleaned other houses in the village where relatives would sleep over—like a giant slumber party.

On the second day, everyone prepared for the feast. We picked the best vegetables from each family's garden. Organized the plates, bowls, pots, and pans. Who would cook, who would serve, who would clean up, and so on. We made sure that enough meat had been ordered from Hoisin, and that it would be delivered on time. Hoisin is the nearest town and that's where you could buy barbecued pig, roast duck, and cuts of beef.

On the third day, the food preparation really got busy. Everyone washed the vegetables, then chopped and sliced them. The sisters minced the meats for the wedding dumplings and oh, so much to do. We decided which chickens and ducks to kill for the next day. You see, young birds tasted sweeter and are not fatty, like old birds. You can't just serve any old chicken or duck at a wedding!

There was plenty of food everywhere. Some of the poorer people pilfered food for later. But everyone knew and no one cared. It was a celebration and there was plenty of food, even if some was "borrowed."

On the fourth day was the private banquet for the families of the bride and the groom. My own Clan Sisterhood cooked, served, and cleaned up afterwards.

At last, the fifth day, the wedding day, arrived. More guests came from other villages, bringing more cooked chickens, fresh roasted duck, barbecued pork, cuts of beef, homemade dumplings, and so many special treats. There were endless plates of fresh fruits, dried fruits, watermelon seeds, and oh, so many, many gifts. Everyone gave us red packages with money.

The banquet itself was held in the temple, which was the only building large enough to fit everyone. Traditionally, men were seated and served first by all the women. Then, after they finished eating, we cleaned up and then we women had our very own banquet. No, the men didn't serve us: we served ourselves. All dressed up in our wedding clothes, your Father and I went from table to table, toasting with strong liquor.

We ate the same kind of food prepared as for Chinese New Year as after all, that's positive food, full of hope, good thoughts, and looking forward to a great year. Eight precious ingredients in vegetarian jai, *because its long rice noodles symbolized a long-life for us, chock-full of luscious black mushrooms, crunchy water chestnuts, chewy flat bean curd noodles, earthly black cloud fungus, salty seaweed hair, thin-sliced lotus root, and very green cabbage…all well cooked and dripping with a stewy soy and sesame oil sauce. Lots of very fresh, very green vegetables. Must have lots of green, for green is the color of life.*

Musicians played the whole time, trumpets and gongs and drums. Very loud the whole time, playing over our own loud gossiping, laughter, and toasts of good fortune. There were all these trumpeters, "Doot, doot. Doot, doot." All day long and into the night.

Then, there was a special tea ceremony for the parents, your Father's parents and my mother. The ceremony was to thank them for all the time, work, and love they have put in to raising and protecting us. The ceremony was to say we were adults now and can make our own way and raise our own family. But we would remember them in gratitude. We would take care of them whenever they needed help. Especially when they got older, we would take them into our homes as valued members of the family.

Well, after those five days, your father left. Tradition required that during the time, I spent the entire month with my family before I could leave with my new husband to his home in America. Your father went to stay with his family as we would reunite at the end of new-bride month to start our journey to America.

I did my daily chores, of course. Drew water from the well. Gathered reeds for the cooking fire. But, mainly, I performed new bride rituals. I burned incense and red paper with blessings before the family altar. I thought only good thoughts for the future. Like Chinese New Year, banish bad thoughts. Think positively, every day about every little thing. Your husband. Healthy babies. Boys! Prosperity. A good home. Happy, happy, everything happy, happy. Prepare your attitude for a happy future and the years will turn out well.

This period was also a final time to spend with my sisters and especially my mother. This was a last opportunity for her to teach me whatever else I would need to know as a woman. As the first daughter, she was even closer to me than to my younger sisters, and this turned out to be a very special time for us.

Even as a child, I had always known my mother was special. My village revered her like a saint. When my mother was out of earshot, older people often said to me, "Your mother is just the best person. She is so good. Grow up to be like her." She never said a harsh word or passed rumors behind people's backs. She only said only good things. She helped anyone who needed help, without hesitation or to get anything back. They pointed out how she was raising Kow Woon, as good as her own daughter, after she was orphaned by the Japanese plane attack. She always took the initiative to help everyone in the village solve difficulties, always encouraging everyone to talk things through, work things out — "speaking round-and-round." And whenever she spoke-up in a "speaking," I noticed the entire circle quietly paused for a longer time than usual, as everyone mulled over her words before adding their ideas, and oftentimes, their agreement.

"Ai gah, how pang yu. Hung toon yeet maan nian lah, chah-um-dall (everyone, please let's not forget we are all kin, one village, one clan, for close to a thousand years now)," she constantly reminded everyone. Her reputation was as the finest person of the village, reminding us that we have more in common than in dispute—and that if we could remember that, nothing was really worth fighting over for long. We could work anything out.

That was the main thing she reminded me several times that last month: to always try to work out difficulties out for the better, for everyone. Not just for yourself or just for your own family. But for everyone's good. In this way, I was raised to be very much like her. Even today, people in the village and in America say that of all her daughters, I am the one most like her.

Finally, I had only a few last days remaining. Everyone prepared special good-bye dumplings. We gathered the ingredients, chopped them fine, mixed the dough and put it all together. It was great fun and we joked and gossiped as we made these dumplings. But for me, I felt sadness. Those were the closing days of my life in my village. Soon, I would no longer see my sisters, my Clan Sisters, and especially my mother. I was going to a new land, very far away and did not know when we would be reunited. But, of course, I remembered to stay positive, stay focused on a happy future.

Somehow, I knew that we would become one family together again.

The last day of my final month with my mother was called Lucky Day, and soon enough, Lucky Day dawned. During that whole month, I wasn't allowed to wash my hair. But on Lucky Day, my mother trimmed and washed it. She had to do everything herself. Not even my sisters could help. Not even an elder Clan Sisters could help.

First, she set some water to boil. Then, as we sat in our living room, the sun streaming through the windows, mother took my long hair into her hands and slowly cut it with scissors, a few inches at a time, then higher and higher. A few days before, she had purchased a special soap used for this day, a kind of shampoo. She then washed my hair, lathered it up with this special soap, and washed it out again. Mother slowly toweled my hair and head dry. Finally, she carefully combed out my hair. She took a long time, much longer than usual. I was glad she did.

At the end of this last day, I paid my final respects to my mother.

The next day, I left for Guangzhou with my new husband, your father.

Chapter 7 The Eight Promises

It was during Mother's new bride time, that precious month of womanly isolation, the chrysalis within which my grandmother transmitted to her the final measure of feminine knowledge so that Poy Jen could reemerge as a woman, a wife, and a soon-to-be-mother that she made her eight promises to Grandmother Chun, to her family, to the Clan Sisterhood, and to her village.

Whatever unshared wisdom my grandmother Chun, whether personal, practical, emotional, or concerning community dynamics, could or would impart to her first daughter, this was the special time, in the Toisan way, to speak all that now. Whatever unspoken, known, or unknown difficulties came up for her during her marriage, and how she coped with it, she revealed those lessons now.

Then too, they reviewed the practical knowledge, ensuring that Poy Jen knew all the village recipes of favorite Toisanese dishes and especially of the medicinal chi soups for each change of season in order to strengthen the family's health, which soups to drink during her own pregnancy and postpartum recovery, and of course the ones that build the internal energy field of her newborns. And perchance she may actually have a garden plot in her American life, what seeds might sprout best under those new conditions, of how to amend the soil with which nutrients, and what each plant should look like, from shoot to just before harvesting.

Who knew when they might reunite again, whether in a few years or not for decades, or perhaps even, never to meet again. Who knew what awaited Poy Jen and her children to come. Because of this greater urgency to their conversation, my grandmother impressed upon Mother more clearly certain obligations that in another time, need not had even been broached.

And so mother described to me the eight promises that evolved during new bride month, eight promises she swore to her mother to fulfill. My grandmother, a compassionate person by all other accounts, a quality I experienced myself during her brief years later in America, of course did not sit my mother down, wag her index finger at her, and laid down the law in some stern, edict like fashion. When mother described each one of the promises to me, she smiled, remembering her happiness at being entrusted with each one. She remembered them with a faraway look in her eyes, that suggested that despite her youth, her lack of exposure to the larger world, that my grandmother had asked of her only that which she could fulfill. Weighty promises to be sure, but with the same steadiness of daily application in all that Poy Jen had learned from the Clan Sisterhood's way of passing on new skills, firmed up by the bonds of love of the Clan, and feeling her mother's complete lifelong confidence in her as a child, then as a teenager, and now as a young woman. I could hear in my own mother's tone of voice, see in her eyes, the way her back strengthened even more upright, the quality of the sacredness of these familial vows, her awareness at the time that she had been trained, prepared, and was more than ready, perhaps eager even, at the this young age, not only to assume, but to live up to these promises.

Although, mother did not recite them to me in order, nor do I think, did she and my grandmother ever bothered to count them up, these are the eighth promises a she described them to me, the ones which emerged and then blossomed forth during the her new bride month, that special cocoon of farewell intimacy between Toisan mother and Toisan daughter:

The first promise was to raise her children to be Chinese, so they could return to their ancestral village when the difficult times had passed.

The second promise was to find suitable Chinese-American husbands for her two sisters, Kow Woon, and other Clan Sisters, so that they might immigrate to America as soon as possible.

The third promise was to become an American citizen and sponsor the immigration of her mother and two brothers to America.

The fourth promise was to keep alive in her children the dream of a democratic Nationalist China - the dream of Sun Yat-sen, the George Washington of China, who was a Cantonese like them. Later, when her oldest brother was driven to suicide by a Communist investigation in Suey Wan, the fourth promise was expanded to include keeping alive his memory as a teacher and as a Nationalist official for the village.

The fifth promise was to keep her children connected to the village. Mother agreed to write letters describing their progress. She agreed to send back photos so they could be recognized when they returned. The photos would be mounted in her childhood home so her children's life force could join with the ancestral fires.

The sixth promise was to seek out the Clan Sisterhood in America and keep the Sisterhood traditions alive.

The seventh promise was to cook the traditional mind-body balance and *chi* energy soups for her family to protect their inner *chi* and their outer energy body.

The Eighth Promise was to live her life in complete compassion, starting with her own family and Clan, but especially her own birth children; then expanding out to all people regardless of who they were, where they came from, or whatever their livelihoods; and finally, to instill this same compassion in her children by teaching them the ways of Toisan.

In truth, the other seven promises, in their specificity, were permutations of the overarching Eighth Promise. The other seven promises, though equally heartfelt and dutiful, were simpler and could all be completed in a matter of years.

But it was the Eighth Promise, to live with compassion towards all, that I think of as the ever-living promise, for all of one's days. And this was the promise, perhaps arising to the level of a moral or spiritual path of living, strikes me as the distillation of all the wisdom of my kin, from a millennium of life in the Toisanese way, in one small locale, self-reliant, with the same families in each house generation after generation, as everyone faced daily life, equally at the mercy of nature as well as the drama of humanity. I think that during those last days before her departure, mother realized that it would be this Toisanese compassion, specifically honed by our clan experience, that would get her daughter through her days to come in an unknown land, all her days, including whatever it would take to fulfill the other seven promises, through all the days of life.

In coming to embrace this last promise, Mother was clearly guided by the quiet example of my own grandmother's life. Even on the eve of this momentous separation, Grandmother Chun had carefully put Mother at ease about the promise to pull the rest of her family into the safety of America.

"Don't worry about me. Just get your sisters to America, one way or another." She said kindly and added that she'd do fine in Toisan, or in Hong Kong, if they managed to get there, that anyway, she was simply too old to start over in a new country.

Poy Jen knew this last words weren't true, but that in her compassion, her mother didn't want her young daughter, a simple, farm girl, to feel overburdened. Poy Jen implicitly recognized that Grandmother Chun was expressing the Toisanese way of caring for the emotional and mental balance of the other. Never overburden another with your needs and fears. Stay strong. Endure. Most of all, trust that your children, having been raised right, will be the best people they can be, even if you are not present. They will remember you and they will help you even when you do not ask it.

From the day she was born, Mother had experienced the Eighth Promise as it was lived by her own mother and by her village Aunties. She learned from them that a mother always gives to her children, first and foremost, the fullest, deepest, greatest, never-ending measure of nurture, time, sustenance, and at times, rescue. This promise was not discharged even after one's children grew into adults, which by Confucian familial ethics, adult children should caretake their elder parents, never the other way around. Regardless of the hopelessness that may enmesh her, the Eighth Promise required a Toisan mother to reflexively charge into the center of any of life's dangerous spider web traps, fight off the relentless horror of the moment, and wrest free her child, and return home to safety.

I could feel from Mother's descriptive tone that her embrace of the Eighth Promise was a deeper commitment than of the other promises, as burdensome as they all were to an eighteen year old. From the viewpoint of spiritual sensibility, this struck me in retrospect as the deeper intuitive rite of an unspoken Clan Sisterhood initiation. By birth and now marriage, she had already qualified for membership in the Chun Clan Sisterhood, and later, their honeymoon lovemaking would elevate her from maidenhood to womanhood. Yet, as New Bride month drew closer to its end, she was no longer a girl, but had already become a full woman in the eyes of her Clan Sisterhood; she was no longer a little sister, but had transformed into a full-fledged Auntie of the Clan Sisterhood; for in the moment of the making of that deeper commitment meant of the Eighth Promise, by some alchemy of our time-tested ways, Mother now had what it took

For Mother, the eighth promise would turn out to be her truest. The other seven promises were ones she had made aloud, to answer the needs of her family and Clan. The Eighth Promise was a silent promise, one that Mother made to herself, was more powerful because it was unspoken. I think such soul promises, as this one, are the ones we are most loath to break, most determined to keep, and in a mysterious way, they do not chain us or deplete us, but rejuvenate us in each turn of their keeping. Soul promises are spiritual in nature, like the adult confirmation of a swaddling baptism or of being born again (and again!) in Jesus Christ, or the taking on of lifelong vows to live in accordance the seamless Eight Point Matrix Path of the Buddha, or the making the haj to Mecca and Medina, or praying before the Wailing Wall. Like a magic spell, the Eighth Promise not only demanded energy, dedication, and sacrifice but in each fulfillment, renewed the body, mind, and spirit. The Eighth Promise was paradoxical in this way: it could never be completed, but would always be fulfilled time-and-again, as life presented each of its ten thousand joys and ten thousand sorrows.

A compassion so intrinsic could not be contained to just one's own children, but as Poy Jen knew from the clan's daily, communalist sensibility, naturally extends itself beyond family to Clan, to other villagers, and even total strangers: evolving into a kind of telltale Toisanese personality trait.

I have often wondered how this kind of compassion could have embedded itself so completely into our Toisanese character. Was its genesis in a coping strategy? Did it arise from the lessons of living in one locale, practically indistinguishable from the land that fed them and the four seasons that blessed the peasant farmers with timely and bountiful rain and sun or, alternately, destroyed their fields with too much sun or too much rain? That in order to make it, year after year, generation after generation, one must always let go of grievances, resentments, and disappointments; and so they imbued kindness, acceptance, and forgiveness at all times, under all circumstances. It certainly wasn't because Toisan families were devout Buddhists, Taoists, or Christians guided by formal teachings; for except for an ancestral hearth, they barely gave a nod to religion in their daily lives.

I only began to learn the answers to these questions as I sifted through the fragments of my life, and the life of my mother. Just as my mother learned the ways of Toisan from her Clan Sisters, I had to go back and study my own past. My story traces the story of the Toisanese-Americans, of the how the Eighth Promise was brought to America.

That final day of new bride month, the day Mother made her Eighth Promise, Lucky Day, was to be her last day in the village. Her family decided they would soon follow, within a year or two, but only as far as Hong Kong. There, they would wait for Mother, first to find grooms for her two sisters, and then to become an American citizenship to legally sponsor her mother and brothers' immigration into America.

Poy Jen's adopted sister, Kow Woon, decided to stay, staking her future in the village on a new China under the Communists. Many others also decided to stay, and so the village would not become a ghost town, but would remain vital, with living roots for the emigrants who may later choose to return. Arrangements were made for Hung Yick, a decorated officer in the People's Liberation Army, to feed the family's ancestral fires. He agreed to open the house once a year, during the lunar New Year celebration. Then, he would burn incense and offer food and wine in our names in front of the family altar, in ritual renewal of our unbroken connection to those who came before us. Thus anointed, he was entrusted with the only set of keys to the home.

On the eve of her departure, mother spent her final hours scrutinizing her home and the village, as if to burn it into her memory. The house was a stand-alone building, built of the same uneven, dark stones as all the other homes. Yet, it was the only two-story house in the village, paid for by remittances from an uncle in Seattle. Facing the broad paddies, the house received bright, warm sunlight all day long. The entrance was a red, wooden double-door, unusually ornate for this village, letting air and light into the reception hall. Windows all around allowed in even more light, along with cooling breezes and a lovely view of the glistening wet fields and forested hills. The interior walls were painted a wash-yellow. Hand-painted vines of many-colored flowers graced the trim of windows and doorways. Ceilings delighted upturned faces with painted platters of green, honey-yellow and rust-red floral arrangements. Poy Jen's childhood home had been a happy one in design as well as spirit. She was leaving all this behind now.

That night, as Poy Jen completed her final packing, Grandmother asked her to take several Nationalist Army uniforms. "Raise your boys to return the Nationalists to power in China. Your eldest brother is a Nationalist official. And remember, Sun Yat-sen, the George Washington of China, was a Cantonese," she admonished. The Wah Kue, the Diaspora of over forty-million overseas Chinese, had funded the Nationalist Party's overthrow of the last Emperor in 1911, the revolution which introduced democratic principles into China.

"You are and your family will be Wah Kue—the overseas Chinese, China's bridge between other nations, but Chinese always. You can do the same, you can support the Nationalists from America, to retake China once again," she concluded.

"Ah, Mah, how can I ever forget that I am Chinese, and Cantonese, like Sun Yat-sen, and that I am of the Toisan people." Poy Jen assured her mother. "And that you are my mother. I will keep my word to you in all things." Even the unspoken vow of the Eighth Promise, she said to herself.

She then left to sleep in her childhood bed since childhood, possibly for the last time.

Chapter 8
Crossing Three Rivers

Your father's younger brother accompanied us to Guangzhou to register our marriage and start the immigration process.

Was I scared? The only people I was ever scared about were the Japanese Army, and they had surrendered. No, I was more excited than anything else. After all, I was going with a good man to a good country, America, our friend in the war with Japan, and now in the anti-Communist civil war. Besides, Toisanese sons and daughters had left for foreign countries for hundreds of years—to America, South America, Europe, Southeast Asia, Australia, and even Africa. Some came back and some stayed, but they always remained in touch with the village. This is part of the Toisan way, to go out into the world, learn the ways of the new land, make friends with people of other cultures, and earn money, all without forgetting the ways of Toisan. I was just another Toisan bride joining a Toisan man overseas somewhere far away. Our roots remain in Toisan, but our own lives were to blossom in a new land.

No, I didn't know anything about white people or modern cities. But I was young, excited by the adventure. Still, I was gladder to be going to San Francisco with its own Toisanese speaking Chinatown than to a city with few Chinese.

To get to Guangzhou, we boarded these long boats where we sat single file and didn't dare move. The boatman warned us that we could tip over if anyone moved. You could lie down flat or sit up, but whatever you decided, you were stuck and you couldn't change position for the entire trip. Men with long paddles grunted and groaned and through sheer muscle rowed us toward Guangzhou. It was really uncomfortable, and hours before we could step off the boat. We changed boats three times, over three rivers. Finally, we caught a motorboat that took us the rest of the way.

I was very happy to go to Guangzhou. As kids, we dreamed of Guangzhou. You see this was our big city, and getting married to your father got me there. Otherwise, there would have been no chance. I would have lived all my life in my husband's village. Died in the village.

Ahhh, Guangzhou. Those were happy days. It was the first time I spent alone with your father. No daily chores like carrying buckets of water or cutting cooking grass. It was all new and fun—pretty clothes, dinners, and sightseeing. We stayed in a hotel with a mattress bed—and sheets that they changed every day! They brought fresh tea and hot water to our room every morning and whenever we wanted more!

We didn't have a private bathroom. We shared a shower and a squat toilet at the end of the hallway. But a hot-water bathroom and a flush-toilet for a country girl who had known only outhouses, run around barefoot all day, and bathed in the river, what an idea anyway! This was already "first class!" As far as I was concerned, all Guangzhou was "first class!"

The next few weeks, your father and I filled out so many papers—marriage license, immigration, and medical—just a lot of papers. Doctors and nurses examined me to make sure I was healthy and wouldn't bring any diseases to America. You see, in our village, we were barefoot most of the time, picking up hookworms and who knows what other germs through our feet. I was lucky and had no diseases. Still, they tested me three times before giving me an okay. They x-rayed me too. Others that had diseases were given medicine until they were well. Then tested again. They weren't trying to stop anyone from going to America. They wanted to make sure you were 100 percent "okay-okay."

The first time I saw a Westerner, a white person, was in that clinic where I was tested so many times. The doctors and nurses were all Chinese. I guess the Westerners worked for the American government. Maybe immigration officers. They were taller than Cantonese, with huge, long noses and kind smiles with large, perfect teeth. Sure enough, Americans must be nice people indeed to help make sure we were healthy enough to go to America.

This went on for several months, testing and waiting, more testing and more waiting. After I passed all the medical tests and all the immigration papers were completed, we waited for the visa. Then one day, we were told that it would take "some more time" and they didn't know how long. "Maybe months." Always maybe, never "for sure, for sure."

Your father thought it best to return to America to his job. He had spent quite a lot of money for the wedding, the immigration papers, and waiting in Guangzhou. He wanted to earn some more money instead of waiting around day after day, not knowing when the visa would be issued. But before he left, his younger brother agreed to escort me directly from Toisan to Hong Kong once I got my visa. He would make sure I safely boarded the ship to America.

I returned home to wait. It was like a present to spend more time with my family. The visa was eventually issued, of course, and I left Toisan once again. The long, narrow uncomfortable boat and the hours unable to move—again, I thought! But this time, to my surprise, the boat went only a short distance before we boarded a motorized ferryboat direct to Hong Kong, no stopping in Guangzhou. "Boot, boot, boot..."—you could hear the motors all the way! But what a difference! We could walk around and breathe the air. There was a restaurant, food stands, bathrooms, and comfortable chairs.

In Hong Kong, I boarded a President Ocean Liner to America. I was in steerage class, with other Toisan women joining new husbands in America. I slept in a bed in a large dormitory. Others who paid more shared four or even as few as two to a room. Crew members changed our bed sheets every day. That was a luxury!

And they sold us large, fresh, sweet oranges for a dollar an orange. Oranges were a real treat. "Orrr-lan-geee! Orrr-lan-geee!" Since we didn't speak English, they would raise a finger to show the price—one US dollar—and hold up a big, bright orange in the other hand. Good thing one of the ladies had changed some Chinese money into US dollars. They wouldn't take Chinese money. She bought us all oranges. So sweeet!

We all got seasick the first few days. I was okay after two days. By the time we got to Honolulu, everyone was used to the ocean. Most of our time was very relaxed, walking around or sitting on the deck chairs gossiping, wondering about America, and watching the ocean.

The boat stopped in Honolulu for several days for fresh food and new passengers, but we couldn't get off. Hula girls danced and Hawai'ian men dove into the water for coins. We saw the green hills and then the night lights of the city. The air was warm and pleasant.

Soon enough, we reached San Francisco. I cleared immigration and customs.

Your father was waiting for me on the other side. "How was the voyage? You didn't get too seasick, did you?" he asked. He looked very happy to see me.

"Seasick only the first few days. Voyage was easy, very relaxing." I, too, was very happy to see him, to be in America.

"Welcome to America. This is your new home," he said.

On January 16, 1951, a little over a year later in the Chinese lunar Year of the Tiger, you were born in Chinese Hospital, San Francisco Chinatown—my first son.

SECTION II
AMERICA (1951–1963)

Chapter 9
Red Egg Day

The Clan Sisterhood organized women's business, like giving birth. Men did not get involved. No hospitals and no doctors—it was all up to us. The Clan Sisterhood took care of the mother when she was pregnant. When she was ready, we midwifed the baby into the world. Then we took complete care of her during the first thirty days following birth. We really had to work together then as a Sisterhood, and so we used the "speaking round-and-round" to organize everyone.

At least one auntie was a midwife, but no one had formal training. We learned everything by watching, listening, and doing. We would recognize that Auntie so-and-so was really good during birth. Or we noticed little sister Ling-ling really liked helping out with birthing, so we would make sure she always assisted the midwife. Yes, even as young girls, we helped out at births. Not in the room, but cooking, boiling water, cleaning. Like that.

This is how we took care of a pregnant mother all the way. The Clan Sisterhood cooked the special chi *soups for the health of the mother and the unborn child during pregnancy. Every day, little sisters picked the best vegetables, scooped out the best grains of rice, and slaughtered the tastiest young chickens for the mother. Aunties boiled a big clay pot of herbal soup the whole day, down to a small bowl of broth. Slowly, we fed the mother, saying good things about the baby, always staying positive in intention, feeling, and words.*

As the birth time neared, the Aunties talked more and more about who would do what during the birth. All day long, we checked up on the mother. Her facial color, her appetite, what she had been eating, and the size of her stomach. We felt for the kicking of the baby, which way the head was facing, and so on. We made sure her husband left her alone and treated her well if he was a mean man. We helped with her chores.

After the birth, the mother and baby stayed in their own room for thirty days. During this time, Aunties prepared special soups to rebuild her chi energy and her outer energy body. Toisan people know that pregnancy and birth depletes internal chi energy and makes holes in the outer energy body. So a new mother had to avoid wind blowing, or chu feng. *If the wind blew through the holes, she lacked chi to fight back. She would get sick in winter. Later in life, she would get arthritis, rheumatism, or bronchitis. Toisan people know that it takes one moon cycle with special care to rejuvenate a new mother's chi.*

How do I know this? I learned as a little sister, by watching, listening, and doing.

Only a few people could visit during this month. Just close family members and elder Aunties. Everyone else stayed away. The isolation was so important that new mothers stayed in bed, even in the middle of harvest. The baby remained inside too.

These are the soups we cooked for this special time. The first-week soup cleans out the system of any leftover blood and membranes that did not come out during birth. We cooked this soup with hok mook ngee *(black wood ear fungus),* keem jeen *(related to lonicera flower),* nganh nah *(ginger root) and* gai *(chicken). The black wood ear fungus grows on the bottom of tree trunks. It's shaped like a human ear, is black in color, sometimes dark brown. She drank this soup in the beginning, two or three times only. You see, this soup has a very strong yin quality, enough to bring down her chi fire if we are not careful. So, it's only served once or twice in the first week.*

The second-week soup ensures that the mother's milk is plentiful, nutritious, and sweet so the baby will drink lots of it. This soup's main ingredients include smooth bean curd, ginger, and a little bit of pork for taste. About half-a-bowl three times that second week.

We served one main soup throughout the month, cooked with our five basic herbs. Always lots of ginger-root for fire to rebuild the chi *inside the mother. Cook ginger in everything. Also,* bok kee *(astralagus) sliced to look like a doctor's tongue depressor;* hong on *(codonopsis), which looks like a dusty brown twig;* gee doc *(red lycium berries), which are tiny, soft, and wrinkled like raisins; and of course* hung dow *(red jujubes), marble-sized wrinkled berries with a pit inside. These five herbs had to be in each pot of this main soup. They add a sweet taste, build fire, and provide every nutrient a mother needs to rejuvenate. Like a soupy multiple-vitamin.*

And at every meal, we cooked a fresh pot of herbal chicken soup with liquor stock and boiled it for one hour, down to a small bowl. Then, we fed her steamed chicken, the white meat only, no skin, with ginger over rice. Or salted preserved fish with ginger over rice. Salted preserved pork is okay too.

A new mother is so weak after birth that there were foods she could not eat because they would affect her in a bad way, possibly for life. No vegetables, because during this time, vegetables easily cause diarrhea. Why leak away the nutrients we spent so much time cooking! No fresh fish, because the scales weaken the chi *body, causing the mother to get sick in the chest every winter. No beef, because it causes incontinence in old age. No duck because too many toxins in the meat. Oh, no fruit too because it flushes out all the special foods and will cause the same problem as beef when you're older .*

These soups have another purpose: they produce good milk for the baby. Milk is all the baby should have for the entire month. If for some reason, the mother was not making enough milk, we boiled up rice broth for the baby. After cooling it, we slowly fed the rice soup using a tiny, tiny spoon. Sometimes, we used a finger to spread the rice broth onto the baby's lips. The baby would lick the liquid. This is not like jook, *the thick rice soup, but much thinner.*

By the end of the month, both the mother and the baby were strong enough to come out. This is the red-egg-party time. We hard-boil chicken eggs and dye them red color. Eggs symbolize new life because chicks come out of the eggs. The egg also symbolizes strength, because an eggshell is very strong. And of course, red, the color of blood symbolizes vitality. The red-egg party reconnects the mother to the village and introduces the baby to the Clan Sisterhood. This time, it's the birth mother turn to cook up a huge pot of special herbal soup. This is her thank-you soup to her sisterhood, to give them back some of the nourishment they have given her—maintaining the balance of giving and receiving is important—and to show she is back on her feet. This soup must have pig feet, chicken, and liquor cooked for hours in sweet and sour soup. Served so steaming hot you have to blow on it—"phoo, phoo, phoo"—before you can sip even one spoonful. Oh, and men came to red-egg parties, to have some soup and say hello. And even the little sisters could eat a little soup, despite the liquor.

The red-egg party was also a special kind of "speaking round-and-round." Men usually all left after the first serving of soup and so did not take part. This "speaking" started as each sister cradled the baby. She would look into the baby's eyes, formally introduce herself by name, and state her family relationship. As if the baby understood every word. She then diagnosed out loud the baby's strength, skin color, size, and so on. Then she passed the baby to the next sister. Oh, we were serious, like real doctors. The mother listened very carefully because this was how she learned from our collective experience, especially when the eldest Aunties spoke.

Sisters advised on what foods this baby should eat or which soups to drink for increasing health. If the baby had a cough that came from the chest, a sister might say, "My first-born daughter had this kind of cough. Be sure to give her lots of the medicinal tea made from this and that plant. It cured her of the cough by the age of seven."

Sisters remarked on personality characteristics, like "This one is really smart." An auntie may say: "See how his eyes watch and follow every movement. He should go to school, perhaps a maybe university in Guangzhou."

Another sister might notice, "This girl is kind of deliberate in her movements. She clutches my thumb very tight. My sister is like that. She's really strong and will be a good farmer ."

Or "This boy has a kind face. His smile is big and his eyes are soft. He will be a good son to his parents. Send money home all the time."

In this way, each sister knew the baby's strengths and needs and could help care for the baby if for some reason the mother could not. Like Kow Woon, when the Japanese airplane killed her family. My mother already knew her like one of her own when we adopted her. You see, in this way, in our village, there's always someone to care for a child, for an afternoon, a moon cycle, or for life.

Little sisters learned a lot about each baby from the red-egg-party speakings, training us in motherhood even as little girls.

Which is good because we babysat when the Aunties went to market or worked the fields.

Then everyone gives a lay see *or* hung bow, *a red envelope, very pretty with gold characters and money inside for the baby. Money symbolizes the support of the village for every child. A slang term for money is "water." By giving money, the big trees were giving of their own precious "water" to the baby shoots until they were rooted enough to get their own water. Red, the color of blood and life force, means vitality. Gold symbolizes the providence of family, friends, water, sun, good harvest, peaceful times, and wealth. This is the same sentiment when grown-ups give red envelopes to kids during Chinese New Year—the older trees giving of their own water to our young saplings.*

But you were born in the United States, in a hospital, not in China, even if it was a Chinatown hospital named Chinese Hospital.

Your paternal grandfather immediately gave you a power name, Poy Jom. Poy means someone who stands strong, is thoughtful, and can figure things out. Jom has the water symbol in it, signifying someone who is placid on the surface, but whose waters run deep, possessing a deep reservoir of wisdom and resources. Your family name, Lee, is comprised of two Chinese characters: "tree" is on top, and "young or new life" is on the bottom. This is like the tree of life. Toisanese are like that for we have many branches throughout the world, but we grow from one tree.

Your grandfather also gave you an English power name, William, after the English monarch, King William the Conqueror. He knew from his own harsh life as a Chinese-American that you need a power name to succeed here. All your given names, Chinese and American, are power names. And because your American middle name is also Poy, your Chinese and American names are linked.

Your birth here was very different from it would have been in the village. I tried to keep the traditions, as I promised my mother. But it was much harder to do so since most of my Sisters were back in China. There was no midwife, but at least Doctor Chun Hong Gum-feng was a woman, Toisanese, too! Very nice lady. And she assisted the birth of every baby in Chinatown for many, many decades! Yes, I did stay home for 30 days. But there wasn't a Clan Sisterhood to help me during the 30 days isolation. If we had stayed in China, I would have moved to your father's village and become a member of the Lee Sisterhood, and they would have made my soups for me. But there weren't enough Lee Aunties or Chun Aunties here for a Lee Clan or Chun Clan Sisterhood. The new-style Chinatown Sisterhood was of sisters from every village—Wong, Fong, Lee, Chun, Lew, Lum, Tom, and so on. Well, they were mainly the wives in the apartment building. We all seemed to understand the same things anyway, and they knew what to do. So I guess all the Toisan sisterhoods are similar.

Another difference was that I had to cook all my own soups and foods. Oh, the neighbors would help me out by buying whatever I needed every day. They took turns shopping for me so I wouldn't go out and risk chu-feng.

At your red-egg party, everyone remarked how big you were, nine pounds at birth. We called you Ai (big) Bee-bee *and* Lao (adult) Bee-bee. "Ai" *because of your size.* "Lao" *because your features were formed like an adult. The sisters considered you wise and intelligent beyond your years. Everyone said you were strong, would grow up healthy. Maybe because the sisters were not really my sisters in the village, they didn't speak as much or in such detail as back home. This was America, and our motley Clan Sisterhood did the best we could.*

Two years later, we had Richard's red-egg party. Richard was sweet-tempered, obedient, and healthy, many said. Richard was handsome, others said. And mainly, how lucky I was to have two sons. Then, something terrible happened. No one was watching you, William, and you knocked over the pot of hot soup. Thankfully, it only scalded the right side of your ribs and not your face. That's how you got your scar. I know you don't remember anything. I try not to think of it either.

Heahhh—this never would have happened in the village. I don't know why, but a put-together Clan Sisterhood wasn't as alert, didn't watch out for each other as well. Maybe we felt a little fuzzy because of the bigness and strangeness of San Francisco. Maybe we felt less powerful, not so important, because Chinatown was much more complicated than home. We could only try our best and it was mostly good enough.

Thirteen years later, your youngest brother John was born, and that was the last red-egg party I gave. Everything was happy, happy at that one. Who thought I would give birth at thirty-five—and to a third son!

Still, the early years were wonderful years. Only a few sad things happened, like the hot soup and your scar. Every week, I wrote letters home, sometimes sending photos and sometimes money, just as I had promised my mother. The letters they sent back said they had sent the photos back to the village and how helpful the money was. You see, they were now living in Hong Kong, all five of them squeezed into a small hovel in a very run-down part of town. Every dollar I sent made a difference. But it wasn't easy sending back money. Your father made me write down every cent I spent: 7 cents for salt, 50 cents for a bundle of chopsticks, 25 cents for beef, and so on. He turned out to be a cheapskate, making me account for every cent, prohibiting me from sending money home. But I did it anyway. I would lie, say I forgot to write everything down. This is the only thing we ever argued about—money.

To make my own money, I worked part-time as a waitress near Union Square, and later on Washington Street near Grant Avenue. Chinese restaurants, of course. Later, I sewed clothes in a Chinatown sewing factory. You and Richard slept next to me or played on the floor, lost in piles of cut-up fabric. Your father picked up the two of you on his way home from work so I could attend

Americanization classes in the evening. I loved learning the American language and all about America. I really enjoyed America.

Working, attending Americanization classes, raising babies - you just don't know how much work babies require of a mother - shopping, cleaning, cooking, washing clothes, writing letters home, missing my family, and arguing about money. That was how it was when you were babies. I was no lon choon, *a lazy bug sunning on a branch. But when Richard was about three years old, I couldn't do it anymore. I started crying for no reason. Some days, I couldn't do anything. I quit work. I dropped out of Americanization classes. For a few months, I dropped Richard off to a baby-sitter in the afternoons to a Clan Sister from the village. He cried every time. I felt bad because a Toisan mother should always take care of her children herself. It's best for the child. No one ever cares for a child the way a mother will. That's the Toisanese way.*

But your father insisted on the baby-sitter even though she cost money. He wanted me to get well. He felt bad, I could tell. Like he had let me down, or failed to protect me. But I got better and soon could take care of Richard, too. I never went back to Americanization school. I only worked a little once in a while. Who had time anyway—with two boys? And then you entered kindergarten.

Chapter 10
Mrs. Ransom's 48 Steaks

I remember well that first day of kindergarten, for that was the day I crossed over. That was the day of my formal introduction to the American language and the American way of life. My first attempt at complete American sentences was on that first daỹ—a recitation of the Pledge of Allegiance.

"Okay, children, we will now pledge allegiance to the flag of the United States of America. Please stand up everyone," said Mrs. Ransom, the gentle, soft-spoken kindergarten teacher for Washington Irving Grammar School. Thirty or so Chinese-American kids remained firmly seated, silently staring at the teacher. Not a one of us understood a word of American.

"Hmm, well let me help you," she said as she moved from person to person, gently taking each one by the hand, helping us to our feet.

"Now, all of you stand up." She held her arms wide, palms up and pumped them up higher toward the ceiling. We understood. This was the signal for us to rise.

"Now place your right hand over your heart," said Mrs. Ransom.

No one moved.

"Here, like this," as she placed her right hand over heart. "Like this." She gently took a right hand here and a right hand there, placing them over the heart.

Most of us placed our right hands over our hearts. I placed my left hand, going the other way. "Billy, let me help you." Mrs. Ransom had pinned a name tag onto my new school clothes. Prior to today, I had always been called by my Chinese name, *Jom*. Father had said "William" was what everyone would call me in school. To be called "Billy" instead was news to me. Mrs. Ransom had assigned me this nickname as if it were the most natural thing in the world.

"Okay, everyone. Please repeat after me: - I pledge allegiance…"

Silence.

"Okay, everyone look at me. Look at my lips." As she pointed a finger to her lips.

Mrs. Ransom bent at the waist so we could see her lips better. Her lips were the brightest lipstick red.

Mrs. Ransom was the first Caucasian I had ever been able to examine up close and for countless hours. This is why, even to this day, her image remains so clear in my mind. She was quite tall, at least a foot taller than my mother. And she was slender. Her ash-blond hair fell evenly to her shoulders, curling up at the ends. She wore a tan, short-sleeved V-neck sweater that disappeared into the waist of a tight brown plaid skirt, which in turn blossomed out to mid ankle, just above her black high heels.

She repeated the first line several times. Then she made a circular motion to include all of us, making eye contact with each and everyone one of us. She slowly opened her lips to start again.

Suddenly, all at once, we hollered out, in unison "I pleck al-leak-gance..." "To the flag..." continued Mrs. Ransom. Again the inclusive circular finger. "Toot dah flack…"

"Of the United States of America." Mrs. Ransom kept going.

"Ahf dah uni-ked steaks of Amal-lee-ka." We bravely blurted it all out until we reached the last word of the Pledge.

Mrs. Ransom then reviewed the design of the American flag, that the red and white stripes represented the thirteen original "steaks," and something about each star representing one of the forty-eight "steaks" making up this huge country called the United "Steaks" of America, to which we had just pledged allegiance.

She went onto to say that there is a father of the entire country, known as the "Pres- za-dent."

"Can you say Pre-za-dent?" she coaxed, pointing to her lips and then making the inclusive fingering circle.

"Pleh-see-dun-tah..." several of us bravely attempted.

"The President's name is Ei-sen-how-er," she said. "Can you say Ei-sen-how-er?" At this point, we sucked in our breaths, unable to say a sound. She seemed perplexed that we stopped after doing so well with the pledge on this, our first day.

The reason was that Chinese-American family names are single-syllable: Lee, Chan, Wong, Ng, Fong, Kwok, and Kwan. The longest Chinese family names were limited to two syllables—Leong, Louie, or Owyang—and those names were rare.

So, here was Mrs. Ransom telling us there's a guy who is the father of our country whose family name alone is four syllables long. Then he sports a title that is three whole syllables long and we don't even know his first and middle names yet, which we knew he had to have! And just how long were each of those names? Why he had enough syllables for several families! We were boggled mute.

Finally, Mrs. Ransom said, "But everyone calls him Ike."

Thirty kids, our first day of kindergarten, suddenly released our collective breaths. Loudly. "Ike, Ike, Ike…," we gladly chanted back, over and over, so relieved that we didn't have to use a four-syllable name with a three-syllable title to refer to just one person. Even if this very important man was the father of our big country of forty-eight steaks.

I first found out I was going to kindergarten in late January of 1956, forming a mid-year class of twenty-five or so. Mother explained that every kid had to go to school when they became five years of age. I asked whether Richard was going too. We were so close, sharing all our toys, racing, and wrestling with each other all the time that I couldn't imagine going to school without him. She explained that Richard wasn't old enough yet, but Henry Lee from the Chinese-American restaurant down the street and Donald Soo from next door would be attending school with me. Then we went shopping for new clothes and new shoes.

Although I was born in America, I had spoken Toisanese exclusively for the first five years of my life. Toisanese was our household tongue, the only one spoken by our neighbors as well as the merchants along Grant Avenue. I did not start speaking "American" until that first day at Washington Irving Grammar School. We called the language "American" because we knew what English sounded like: the British in Hong Kong spoke "English." Later, in the 1980s, when I spent a great deal of time in England, I discovered that the English agreed with us, that Americans did not speak "English," but a dialect they labeled as "American."

Mother registered me inside the school auditorium. I came to know this auditorium well. We played there when it rained, and it rained a lot in the winter months. Mrs. Lau, a Filipino-looking Chinese-American teacher translated for the mothers, most of whom didn't speak American. She spoke Big City Cantonese and didn't seem too friendly or very respectful of the Toisanese mothers. She directed us to the kindergarten room, across from the auditorium. Mother gave Mrs. Ransom my forms, said good-bye and would pick me up later. Some of the kids were crying as their mothers left. I was scared too, but didn't cry.

After completing kindergarten with Mrs. Ransom, we moved up one floor to first grade. Our next teacher was the very warmhearted Mrs. Stephens, who introduced us to Dick and Jane and their dogs Rex and Skippy, reading, 'riting, and 'rithmetic. We finished second grade with Mr. Walsh, a dapper, slender gentleman who regaled us with his clever jokes and stories of his garden snakes and his warty gourd, which was on display at the science table. Richard started kindergarten about then, with Mrs. Ransom. Hearing what I had been through, he was a little more prepared, a little less shocked at kindergarten goings-on. Later, my classmates and I moved up to the third floor for fourth, fifth and sixth grades. Education was like climbing a ladder: the higher the grade level, the more stairs to climb.

All too soon, American became my dominant language. I still spoke Toisanese with Mother though. Mother listened as Father tutored Richard and me in the evenings. Even with her promise to teach us written Chinese, Mother knew we had to master American first. For my part, it seemed natural that we were switching from Toisanese to American. Everyone in class had spoken only Chinese when we entered kindergarten, but as the teachers smoothly guided us over the linguistic divide into straight-ahead American, it felt like that was how life worked, that this was the natural order of the universe.

Mother constantly contemplated the most opportune age to enroll me in Chinese language school. Wait too long and she risked my becoming irredeemably "Americanized."

In the 1950s, Chinatown had about five Chinese language schools. Chinese school started at 4 p.m., an hour-and-a-half after grammar school let out. Most Chinatown kids attended one. As I progressed in American school, Mother undoubtedly noticed that her two sons were speaking less and less Toisanese. Worse, from her point of view, we were incredibly enamored of all things American. As it turned out, Richard and I were equally resolved not to enroll in Chinese school. Our battle with Mother ranged over three summer vacations. Since I was the older, Mother's efforts focused mostly on me.

That first summer, I informed Mother that I simply could not fathom the necessity for it. After all, I was conversant enough to talk to her, shop on Grant Avenue, and order take-out from Chinese restaurants. Besides, everyone else on the block spoke American. I listed them on my fingers: Sam of Sam's Cleaners and his friend Molly, Charlie of Charlie's Bail Bonds, Wallace the Carpenter, Mr. and Mrs. Jackson of Jackson's Bookstore, and the beat cop Danny the Wop. Even kind-hearted Benny of Benny's Smoke Shop and Tagalog was his first language.

I pulled out the stops -- Chinese School will take time away from my American homework and I won't win my scholarship to college. "This will be your fault if you make me go to Chinese school."

Richard listened with supportive bemusement, hands in pockets, standing with me. Two years younger, Chinese school was still remote for him. Still, he knew that my arguments were his. My desire for free playtime after school was his desire. He was as happy as I was when I prevailed that first summer.

And I prevailed the second summer using a new twist. I discovered that it was Cantonese, not Toisanese that was taught for the first two years; from the third year forward, it was Mandarin. So I marshaled new arguments. Well, everyone in Chinatown spoke Toisanese, so what was the point of learning Cantonese? Only Hong Kong movies at the Sun Sing Theater were in Cantonese and learning Cantonese to understand Hong Kong movies better couldn't be more important than doing well in American school.

And then by year three, I dramatically stressed, Chinese school taught exclusively in Mandarin. That was practically a foreign language as far as Chinatown was concerned. What was so important about learning Mandarin, a dialect no one used in Chinatown? I mean, we're in America, and we have no plans to go to China or anywhere near it anytime soon. Just what was the point of Chinese school when you thought about it all the way through?

But the tide turned by the third summer. Mother's happiness was important to Father, who still felt guilty about her emotional breakdown. And Father was not against us going to Chinese school. Even though he was firm that his sons would stay Americans, he thought that we should know our Chinese heritage and be fluent in Chinese. After all, in his youth, he had achieved some merit as a writer of classical Chinese poetry. This genre of classical poetry is extremely difficult to compose. Organized as a kind of a poem puzzle, with each word representing a number of concepts. Like an invisible scrabble! Depending upon their placement in the poem's structure, the meanings change— cross-cultural literary, cultural, and philosophical allusions with double- and triple-score brain tickling delights. He believed that speaking Chinese and knowing Chinese civilization would actually enhance my chances of winning that ever-important college scholarship.

Mothers being mothers, and with the Clan Sisterhood tradition and all, she must have called a speaking round-and-round. All I know is that one afternoon in the late summer of 1959, Mrs. Soo next door, Mrs. Yock from around the corner, Mrs. Lee of the restaurant down the block, Mrs. Lum from down the street, and my mother escorted each of their kids to the front of our apartment building. In a phalanx formation, they force-marched the whole lot of us, nine kids, to Nom Kue Chinese Language School, two blocks away on Sacramento Street between Kearny Street and Grant Avenue. Only after we were enrolled, seated in our classroom, and the teacher had called the class to order did this Amazon honor guard demobilize.

I have a confession to make. As a child, I was often ashamed of the Toisanese dialect. Of course, I spoke Toisanese at home without reservation. But in the company of non-Chinese neighbors, and against the perfectly enunciated American of television, Toisanese seemed unmusical, clunky, and too loud. In contrast, the American language flowed mellifluously, so easy on the ear. It was the language of modern times, of speed, military might, industrial capacity, and amazing technology, a language so unlike Toisanese, the language of farmers in some God-only-knows-where backward old village in China.

My shame always was deepest when our patient, beloved, otherwise kind public school teachers reprimanded us during our rare lapses into Toisanese. These rebukes inevitably happened at recess, the time when we gave ourselves completely over to the freedom and joy of play. Spontaneously, someone would slip into the briefest, happy flurry of Toisanese. As the recess teacher, scowling now, spun around in the direction of the offending sounds, she'd shake her large, loud, brass recess bell furiously, as she rushed into the offender's face. She'd shout over the clanging: "This is America. Speak only American. You will sit on the bench until recess is over."

Sometimes, a teacher caricatured Toisanese in the most awful way, twisting her neck and moving her head back and forth and sideways like a chicken, as if to say, "What self-respecting person would want to speak this gibberish?" The few times I was benched for speaking my first language, it didn't seemed to matter that I excelled in reading and writing American: the teacher somehow forgot that I had spoken American every minute of that day and every day since the beginning of the semester. These thunder-cracking harangues condemned Toisanese as a transgression equivalent to coming to school while burning with chicken pox and coughing in everyone's face. A gentle reminder would have sufficed, but was never forthcoming. In this milieu I began to doubt the worth of my first language, the place of my family's origins, and, finally, the place of my parents in American society.

It took me many years to feel right, once again, about speaking Toisanese and then many more years before I felt good about being a Toisan-Chinese. My awakening began tentatively when I entered Chinese language school. My acceptance of my background surged ahead in the late 1960s during the Civil Rights movement when many people of color reconnected with the roots of their suppressed heritage. In my childhood, however, not only was the America of the 1950s arrayed against the speaking of Toisanese, so too was the rest of Guangdong Province, the home of Toisanese. Guangdong's official dialect was Cantonese, and Cantonese speakers considered Toisanese inferior.

Even more invalidating was the fact that Mandarin was China's official language, and all Cantonese were forced to learn it. As far as linguistically differences, Cantonese and Mandarin were two radically different languages, as different as French is from Latin despite their links as romance languages. As for the relationship of Toisanese to the Cantonese language, Toisanese is a dialect of Cantonese. Just as the ears of Parisian French speakers feel assaulted by Quebecois French, so too Cantonese speakers consider Toisanese an embarrassing variant. Official China, with little use for Cantonese, knew nothing of Toisanese. As if salting a wound, China had historically considered the province of Guangdong a distant backwater in the lowest corner of the empire, a place to exile unpopular magistrates, rebels, and criminals. For Cantonese speakers, Toisan villages were their backwaters.

With Toisanese's reverse cachet as a hillbilly'ish, coarse, down-in-the-delta variation of Big City Cantonese, there are of course no Toisanese novels, poems, or operas. There is no legacy of Toisan royals with ornate Toisan summer palaces. The prolific Shaw Brothers Studio of Hong Kong did not make movies in Toisanese. Not even bit players speak Toisanese in Cantonese movies. Toisanese sounds signify sweaty, backcountry impoverished backcountry peasant farmers working oxen in mud all day, with syllables that are harsh to the normal ear and spoken at a decibel level equivalent to shouting. In truth, the normal volume of spoken Toisanese is a shout. When spoken angrily, the listener is sometimes finely sprayed with spittle. People coming from Toisan who wanted to pass for better in Guangzhou or Hong Kong dropped Toisanese and picked up Cantonese as if shedding soiled, ill-fitting, rough cotton work clothes for the blue silk garments of scholars and merchants.

And yet most of the first Chinese-American pioneers were Toisanese. Arriving in the 1850s to join the California Gold Rush, we stayed to build the first transcontinental railway from the West, as Irish immigrants built it from the East. Grimly, we stuck it out through the 1880s, a reign of terror of anti-Chinese legislation, anti-miscegenation laws, race riots, lynchings, and torching of

Chinatowns up and down the West Coast. The horror of life for California's Chinese residents was so unrelenting that it gave rise to a popular expression, "He didn't have a Chinaman's chance." Beginning in the 1900s, we eventually settled into an uneasy, institutionalized "Jim Crow" segregation within the surviving Chinatowns.

These Chinatowns prospered and became havens for later waves of Chinese immigrants: in the 1950s, refugees like Mother fleeing from Communist China; in the 1960s, refugees like Grandmother Chun who had been stranded in Hong Kong after the 1949 Communist assumption of power; in the 1970s, Mandarin-speaking Taiwanese and then ethnic Chinese-Vietnamese boat people; and finally in the 1980s and 1990s, Mandarin-speaking Mainland Chinese moving to America for freedom and opportunity. Through all those periods, the sons and daughters of the original Chinese-Americans, the Toisanese and Cantonese , the ones who built and maintained the Chinatowns, welcomed each wave of newcomers. These Toisan pioneers had not only built safe havens, but their children went on to become doctors, lawyers, decorated war veterans, US Senators, a state Governor, best-selling authors, movie stars, and Silicon Valley moguls. Their names are part of our culture: actors Anna May Wong, Bruce Lee, and Jason Scott-Lee, former Governor Gary Locke of Washington State, and best selling novelist Maxine Hong-Kingston, and

Over the years, I sensed that the linguistic characteristics of Toisanese might be reflective of the inextricable, interdependent bond between the Toisan land and its people. Like the language of the Basques of the Pyrenees, the U'wa Indians of Columbia, and the Hawai'ians and their islands, our tongue became inseparable from the *mana* or power of our homeland. Like these other people, the Toisanese people and their dialect are unofficial and under-recognized. Our character is unpretentious and practical. We became tough-skinned to life's difficulties. We focused with an incredible drive on family, land, home, education, and abundance.

Our dialect reflects life wrested from the mud, clay, and stone of wet delta land and the need to be heard over vast stretches of fields. Not surprising then that the sounds of Toisanese syllables come wrapped up like clogs of dirt embedded with stone and held together by the long, sinewy grasses used for cooking. Sentences explode out of the mouth like a mortar barrage, with consonants, vowels, all the tones meshed into a tight barbed clump of earthly linguistics. Toisanese can arc over rice fields, penetrate a flock of noisy geese, cut through a stand of bamboo trees, and curve around a hill. As the sentence lands, the remaining barbs of sound hook your eardrum so you know that, indeed, you are being addressed and the reasons why.

The dialect was designed for survival—year after year, day after day, sometimes minute by minute. A self-reliant village of farmers needs to know immediately of any emergency, and the Toisanese shout served as our warning system, one that could carry over the curvaceous metes and bounds of our countryside. A levee has just burst! A week's labor seeding a field will be lost unless all hands run to shore it up. This message would boom and echo across the fields.

During World War II, Toisanese warnings were of destruction and death. "Danger! Danger! Japanese soldiers are raiding the village for rice and vegetables, young girls to rape, and young men to kill. Alert—do not return to the village. Cross the river into the hiding place in the hills. Wait for us there. Make no noise. Don't come back tonight. Your life depends upon it."

In the land of Toisan, there were no excuses for failure. There could only be survival, and thus Toisanese evolved to guarantee survival. A nuance-free language whose meanings are harshly, crudely, and loudly clear, a language where layered linguistics of hidden meanings have no place, served its speakers well.

In contrast, Big City Cantonese is melodic like a stanza of music in its seven tones and spoken at a normal volume. The one-upmanship of city sophistication propels its colloquialisms. It's the language of overly clever merchants and the prickly double-entendres of the social elite. Big City Cantonese is conversed in urbane quarters, wearing clean, fashionable clothes, and with elegant manners. Its basis was politeness masking a withering wit, preferably while eloquently describing the subtle fragrances of this year's harvest of that rare tea handpicked by monkeys from misty high cliffs.

But even Big City Cantonese appreciated that the ear-splitting, spitty Toisanese attains its oratorical finest when downright rude and, disdainful to the bones of your family and especially your ancestors. It soars even higher when salty and sexually graphic. You know you've been told off when you'd been tongue-lashed in Toisanese.

Although Chinese school was the start of my eventual acceptance of my Toisanese heritage, it initially confirmed for me the shame and distastefulness of the Toisanese dialect. The Chinese school principal and the teachers trucked no Toisanese. My first grade teacher, Mrs. Wong from Hong Kong, enforced this linguistic reign of terror with a drumstick. Rap went the drumstick at the slightest offense. Speak Cantonese and leave Toisanese behind!

This created some problems with Mother because she tutored me with a Toisanese-accented attempt at Big City Cantonese. I often cringed, imagining Miss Wong's sharp correction of my recitals the next day. In frustration, I continued my attacks of the futility of Chinese school with a righteous vigor.

In time, however, my Cantonese improved. I did well in both my recitation and written exams. Soon enough, as with American school, my resistance melted away.

Oddly, the written language of Chinese, a pictorial symbolic system, remained constant and unified, with Mandarin, Cantonese and Toisanese all as one written language. I fell in love with Chinese brush stroke calligraphy; it not only captured my imagination and my artistic sense, but also validated my "Chinese-ness." Unlike American words that can be sounded out from the printed page, each Chinese word is a unique picture character unto itself, and has to be memorized as a separate creation. Different lines, boxes, dots, and commas constitute each word character, and each stroke has to be exactly where it belongs. To complicate matters, we drew characters with a classic bamboo brush dipped into black ink and, held in an upright position that required twisting several fingers awkwardly along the bottom of the brush.

At first, my brushwork resembled nothing more than a series of mini-Rorschach tests. Eventually, my brushwork improved. With brush poised over rice paper, I learned to run my first stroke clean, from a tiny dot down into a flower burst and, with a flourish, to lift the brush off the page, just so, without smudging or dripping ink. Suddenly, writing Chinese – and being Chinese - was fun.

But it was only when we studied Dr. Sun Yat-sen and his *Three Principles of Democracy* that China and America seem psychologically connected. Dr. Sun Yat-sen, considered the George Washington of China, formulated his principles from the writings of America's founding fathers, especially those of Thomas Jefferson. The good doctor had walked the streets of our very own Chinatown, tirelessly proselytizing for the funding of a democratic revolution, one which later overthrew the last Emperor Pu-yi, on October 10, 1911. Our own local newspaper, *Geem San See Bo* (*Chinese Times Daily*), which Mother and Father's favorite read daily, had been a voice for democracy and modernization in China for over half a century. Suddenly, Chinatown's humble streets—packed with three story buildings, vegetable and fish shops, souvenir stores, and functionally dressed men and women, took on a magnificent prominence. We had financed a revolution that ended thousands of years of a monarchy in a vast nation of millions, a revolution that, for better or for worse, propelled China into the twentieth century. China suddenly felt familiar, like a second cousin, and no longer a stranger.

My interest in Dr. Sun Yat-sen grew, my Chinese school selected me one year, during the "10-10 day" celebration of Republican China's Independence, to recite Sun Yat-sen's Three Principles of Democracy. I somehow managed to stand and deliver in flawless Cantonese - before the entire Chinese school. In time, the school taught us China's long history, nearly five thousand years of outrageous Emperors and Empresses who ordered up Great Walls, opulent palaces, and waged ruthless war that built and destroyed civilizations; about major Chinese inventions—astronomy, gunpowder, silk weaving; and of the large fleets of ships that navigated the stars and crisscrossed oceans centuries before Columbus accidentally landed in America.

Teachers read to us from the poetry of Li Po and Chuang-tzu. We learned of Buddhism and Taoism, Asian religions that had played great roles in Chinese civilization. These religions sounded and felt Chinese, with Chinese-looking people in their paintings and statues, so unlike the Chinatown churches with their Caucasian Jesus and ivory Mother Mary statues surrounded by the faces of European-faced angels.

We were taught about the sage Confucius and his philosophy of Confucianism, a hierarchical system of social cooperation and obedience between levels of society and within families. It was this system that united and built the ancient civilizations of China. A few selected rules, "Obey your parents…" and, of course and inevitably, "obey your teachers," were drilled into heads.

In time I understood more Chinese than I could speak, and eventually could switch easily over into Cantonese. If Mother's intent was to keep me Chinese by sending me to Nom Kue Chinese school, she succeeded. Yes, there was more homework, as I suspected, but for the three years I attended Chinese school, it did not take time away from my American studies. Yes, there was less playtime after American school, as feared, for we rushed home, gulped down our snacks and flew out the door in one move. With our ubiquitous Chinese School bags in hand, we flapped down the street all the way to Nom Kue, desperately trying to make the 4 p.m. bell, and looking for all the world like a flock of one-winged ducks.

As for Mandarin attitudes toward provincial bumpkins, well, if we had to, we'd master Mandarin, including the highest form, Beijing style, with its distinguishing and linguistically questionable "ar, ar, ar" word endings. But our historical Toisanese migrations outward were always overseas destinations. We take on Vietnamese, Malay, Filipino Tagalog, English, Spanish, and American— whatever the tongue of the dominant culture, Toisan immigrants will learn it and their children will master it.

Chinese school made being of Chinese ancestry feel better; and made being Toisanese feel lighter. American school teachers would continue to scoff at us through high school, but within the pragmatic, flexible, compassionate character of Toisan people, it never makes sense to dwell on the unfairness of life. Always the underdog linguistic tribe, we developed a thick skin to the cheap shots. Perhaps because of this, despite our insularity, we don't spend a lot of time demeaning other groups. Instead, our compassion often extends to others similarly marginalized.

For centuries, we have bravely gone forth to foreign climes, sunk new roots, spoken new languages, acculturated, and then blossomed for generations in our new home.

This too, is the Toisan way.

Chapter 11
Soupe du Jour

Toisan mothers must cook the special seasons-change chi-adjustment soups for their children. Especially so when they are young, but also well into their teen years. Our responsibilities go beyond washing, dressing, and feeding our children's physical bodies — we nurture the invisible chi bodies. These are not food soups, like the vegetable soup that Benny the Smoke Shop man treated you to from the Star Cafeteria or like CampbellCampbell's Chicken Noodle Soup, which you and Richard loved as children. No, these soups are like medicine, similar to the soups for rejuvenating postpartum mothers, yet very different. These soups are to adjust and strengthen chi energy for the climatic changes of the seasons so our children won't catch colds and flu. If eaten regularly during childhood, these soups will keep you strong and healthy throughout your lives.

During the hot days of summer time, I cooked oong-gwah hong *(winter melon soup). Winter melon soup brings down the* yang *heat in the body for it is* leang *or* yin. *The herbs are the same ones used in the rejuvenation soups for new mothers—*bok kee *(astralagus),* hong-ong *(codonopsis),* gee-doo *(lycium berries), and* hung dao *(red jujube). Lycium berries are good for your eyes for they keep your vision strong. Besides winter melon, I added peas, sliced pork, and eggs to make it sweet. Not sweet like sugar, but sweetly delicious from all the juices of the herbs and the meat mixing together over a hot fire. Even though they're medicinal soups, they taste delicious like American soups.*

Another summer soup was foo jook hong *(bean curd* hong*), also very yin and good for very hot days. I cooked it with the same herbs, but only for an hour, no more. Sometimes I added a piece of pork to sweeten the soup. You didn't like bean curd soup, but I made you eat it. Sometimes, you waited until the end of the meal when it was cold before you would finish it. But if you wanted to go out to play with Sonny or Donald, you had to finish your soup first.*

Most important was to adjust the chi as summer turned to winter. After you and Richard started school, you two caught everyone's germs, vomiting for days with really hot temperatures. I started to cook lots of soups around fall. These soups raised the fire in your chi so your body could fight off colds and flu. Ngow-mee hong *(ox-tail soup) cooked with these same herbs was especially good for this. We boiled the ox-tail for an hour and a half, until it was so soft, the meat slid off the bones. By then, the soup was so sweet. You really liked ox-tail soup. You'd dip entire pieces into soy sauce, slurp the meat off the bone, and then suck the marrow dry. You lifted up the bowl and gulped down the soup, your throat bouncing up and down. And then asked for another bowl. Well, that's the way you should eat ox-tail soup, suck up everything.*

I also cooked soups for your father and me. Adults need soups too because as we get older, our bodies change, lose vitality, and don't heal as quickly. Gee hong *(turtle soup) strengthens the body. Lots of nutrients, like a multiple vitamin. Same herbs as with ox-tail soup. You see, Toisanese always used the same herbs. Maybe it started because we were poor farmers, but really, there's no need to get so fancy with herbs, like Big City people do. They use this and that herb from Mount*

Emei, so and so tree bark from Szechwan and this and that tuber from Xinjiang - paying five hundred dollars an ounce and so on. Simple herbs with local vegetables and meats cost less and are just as powerful. The trick is to use your eyes and look for the glow of quality; use your fingers and feel the living chi stored in the ingredients. That's how to make good soups.

Turtle soup is best eaten just before winter. The turtle should weigh four to five pounds. The turtle should be alive with a healthy shell, shiny eyes, and active feet. The really important thing beforehand is to remove the intestines and organs that have toxins. And you have to remove it without spilling any of the toxins onto the flesh of the turtle. Otherwise, the soup tastes bitter. This is not hard to do once you know how.

For cooking turtle soup, we used the special lacquer pot that is used only for cooking herbal soups. It looks like a little bushel, reddish in color and covered with wires on the outside. Simmer turtle soup with the same herbs we always use, but add a lot of Chinese liquor to give it a very strong fire chi. Cook it for about four hours. Eat it just before bedtime, after dinner has been digested. That way, the balance of the medicinal ingredients is not upset. Dinner foods have another kind of balancing effect. So, you shouldn't mixed dinner foods with chi soups.

The first time I made turtle soup for my children, the turtle lived in the sink for a few days. You and Richard played with it every day, walking it in the hallway, placing it in the bathtub full with water. So you refused to drink the broth. You were sad that I had killed your new pet. But that was okay because turtle soup is really for adults. Kids have strong chi and turtle soup could add too much fire. But because you had been so sick the year before, your father and I decided you should have at least one bowl. "Turtle is a food, not a pet," I had to explain. You complained about the green color and the smell and so on. But we watched you drink it down until it was gone.

Sometimes I made ngow-now hong *(cow brain soup). Like turtle soup, cow brain soup strengthens the body, but it is especially good for removing the chill in the head area you get from* chu-feng, *or a "blowing-wind" that is so strong it tears holes in your energy body. Also, if you have a lot of headaches, cow brain soup cures that. Toisan people believe that* seck, *or dampness, can gather in your brain, and cow brain soup is good for clearing that. If you don't remove the dampness, you may not suffer right away. But when you're older, ohhh, you'll have lots of headaches and get sick all the time.*

Before cooking cow brain, you have to remove the red veins. This is not hard— soak it in salt water for a few minutes and they just come off in your fingers. Same herbs, some white Chinese liquor and add chung-koon *(wallachi tree bark) and* bok jee *(angelica root). Boil everything for about two hours. By then, the brain is white, smooth and soft like tofu. This is an adult soup, but because I wanted to strengthen you and Richard, I served you small portions, about a rice bowl's worth. It was funny. You were so skeptical. But the soup was oh so sweet, and after you dipped a piece in soy sauce, you couldn't stop eating until it was all gone!*

Jee-gek hong *(pig feet soup)* is definitely an adult soup because there's so much strong, white liquor in the soup, a child could get drunk. You insisted on trying it because you really enjoyed my soups. But one spoonful, your face grimaced and you said "Ugghhh," and coughed it back into the bowl.

There are lots more seasons-change and chi-adjusting soups—like yin wall hong *(bird's nest soup),* you chee hong *(dried scallop soup),* schloot ngee hong *(white fungus soup) and* hlee mee hong *(four-tastes soup). The four ingredients of four-tastes soup are* wai san *(Chinese yams),* len doo *(lotus seed),* bok hop *(lily bulbs), and* hah geen *(almond). The main soups I made for my children were winter melon, ox-tail, bean curd, turtle, and cow brain, and that turned out to be good enough. You were the weaker child—more colds and flu than Richard. And you had tuberculosis when you were eleven. But by your mid-teen years, you were very healthy. Strong body and a quick mind. Straight A's in everything, even gym. You played basketball for your junior high school. Not bad for a child with tuberculosis. Even now, you're still very healthy, alert, very strong, and everyone says you look ten–fifteen years younger than your age! Good Toisanese soups, that's why. Strong chi for life!*

Chapter 12
Ragtag Boy Scouts

During the 1950s, our family lived at 638 Kearny Street, in the heart of old San Francisco, across the street from historic Portsmouth Square. Surprisingly, this urban village, in a district called the International Section, replicated the characteristic of our Toisan village Suey Wan, with values of safety, respect, cooperation, and above all, protection of children. People from all over the world lived here in a surprisingly respectful harmony. Thus, our street was emotionally familiar to Mother that way, a clean, well-lighted, and compassionate place to raise kids. Trustworthy shop owners and caring neighbors watched over her kids, as if her own eyes and ears, just as her own village had watched out for her.

Portsmouth Square itself was a museum of the early history of San Francisco with monuments commemorating it's genesis as the plaza for the founding Spanish town of Yerba Buena, the site of the raising of first American flag after America won the Spanish-American war, the site of California's first public school house, and a favorite haunt of Robert Louis Stephenson.

In the 1950s, Chinatown itself surrounded the Square on three sides. Beginning in the 1850s, thousands of Chinese had made their way across the square to a Chinatown growing along Grant Avenue. They came to work the gold mines, ended up building the first transcontinental railroad from the West end, ten stayed to farm, fish, build businesses, and start Chinatowns up and down the West Coast. By the 1950s, when I played in the Square as a kid, Chinatown surrounded the Square on three sides. Our apartment itself was among the remnants of the lawless Barbary Coast, like the historic Bella Union Theater where the great opera singer Caruso once sang, and the row of Burlesque houses along Pacific Avenue were still in business. Across from the square was the old Hall of Justice—the city's police headquarters, jail, and courts. A block away from the square was the International Hotel and other bachelor hotels, home to scalawags from every nation and a community of Filipino-American veterans. Nearby was City Lights Books, the epicenter of Beat poetry.

It was here, on the Square, along the International District and in Chinatown that I enjoyed an idyllic, wondrous childhood in the heart of a big city. Our parents never admonished us to stay away from our neighbors based on their race, ethnicity, or language. They encouraged us to get to know them, to tell stories about them, and would drop by to thank particularly kind ones.

Like Benny Beltram, a Filipino-American who operated Benny's Smoke Shop, an 8'x10' hole in wall stuffed to the ceiling with pocket-size goodies for neighborhood bachelors, winos, the nearby constabulary, and kids alike. Exotically named cigars from all over the world: American cigarettes like Viceroy, Lucky Strikes, Winston, Kool's, and Kent's; rolling tobacco in glistening white sacks with drawstrings; round tins of Copenhagen chewing tobacco; Gallo's Thunderbird Port; and racing forms flew over the counter in rapid-fire exchanges from 7 a.m. to 6 p.m. six days a week. The front of the counter was an explosion of candies, gums, and cough drops—Mars, Almond Joy, Lifesavers,

Wrigley's, Smith Brothers—all tightly displayed against a terraced candy counter. In the front of the counter was a water-cooled Coca-Cola fridge with 7-Up, Squirt, Doctor Pepper, and, of course, Coke. On the wall across was a rack of Laura Scudder and Granny Goose potato chips. Outside was a rack of comic books—Archie's, Superman, Richie Rich, and Classic Comics, which introduced us to *Treasure Island, Two Years Before the Mast, A Tale of Two Cities, The Man in the Iron Mask,* and *The Count of Monte Cristo.*

Benny's Smoke Shop was an informal community center. Like the families in our building, he exemplified the village sensibility of treating other's' children as a communal trust. In summer time, we neighborhood kids met there to read comics, share sodas and chips. We earned extra money by running errands for Benny before deciding the group's mischief of the day. Hike up to Coit Tower to pick berries and catch bees? Triple feature and steaming hot dogs with mustard and fresh-chopped onions on Market Street? Walk through North Beach to Aquatic Park to catch baby crabs, wet our shoes, and get in trouble with our mothers? Benny knew our whereabouts and so, our

Mothers often checked in with Benny on our whereabouts or to leave messages for us. Filipino men came by to pick up letters from home, then dropped into a lilting, almost popping, Tagalog conversation, sharing as they shared gossip or argued Filipino politics. Benny shifted seamlessly from English to Tagalog and back as customers shouted out greetings or cigarette brands. Every morning, gamblers bought racing forms and shared tips about the horses before trekking off to catch the trains to Bay Meadows Racetrack only to return late in the afternoon to celebrate with a bottle of Thunderbird Port or to grouse about a false tip.

Over time, Benny quietly settled on Richard as his chief errand runner, and slowly trained him on how to order goods, pick them up at a nearby wholesaler, and to restock the shelves. Hence, Richard had more money than me, which felt strange at first because, as an older brother, I was supposed to do better. But since we shared everything, his generous treats soothed the stings to my ego. Besides, Benny made everyone feel wanted. He treated us to the daily soup from the Star Cafeteria a few doors down. Our favorites were vegetable and chicken noodle soups. We'd voraciously dipped the crunchy sweet-dough bun slathered with butter into the steaming broth. And every few days, he offered us soft drinks and chips.

Nor was Benny alone in this instinct. Molly, a blonde, buxomly, big-haired Irish-American woman spent her days with Sam at Sam's Cleaners & Alterations. Sam himself was a grizzled-faced, bespectacled Chinese-American who spoke American perfectly. They sat across from each other over Sam's sewing machine, facing the front door and catching the afternoon sun. Sam sometimes hunched over his sewing machine, hemming pants legs or pulling thread through a buttonhole with his teeth, while Molly painted her nails even redder or, touched up her face with lipstick, powder, and eyebrow pencils.

They sat like royalty, the King and Queen of Kearny Street, shouting greetings and joking with passer-byers. They shared bottles of Pabst Blue Ribbon beer and took turns blowing smoke rings through the other's smoke rings. Meanwhile, we petted Sam's collie, tied up in front by the fire hydrant, pretending she was the television hero dog Lassie. We played hide-and-seek under the racks of dry cleaning that filled up the back of the shop, pushing our bodies through them as if on a planet with a thick atmosphere. The hiss and steam created by Sam's workers pressing the adjacent ironing boards suggested an even more mysterious landscape, like that of Mars in the triple feature cinemas along Market Street. If one of us fell crying onto the concrete outside while playing, Molly would sit us in her lap and comfort us. But in the evenings, Molly left Sam's Cleaners for Smokey's Bar, where we could see her laughing, drinking, and smoking through the swinging door. Then, she acted like she didn't know us as she went back and forth with different men, arms around her waist, to her room at the Hotel Justice, a few doors away.

In an era when interracial couplings were taboo, Sam and Molly's unusual, undefined, and very public pairing was silent courage. They were not a traditional couple, but neo-outcasts, and perhaps living on the social margins rendered them tough enough to live as they pleased.

Sometimes Sam treated us to a hamburger from the Lee Family restaurant next door, especially if we had run back and forth several times bringing him and Molly cold Pabst Blue Ribbon beers. Mr. Lee seemed pleased at each and every order, as if we were calling upon his best abilities. We watched attentively from the counter as he personally patted each new burger by hand, dicing fresh onions and then melding them into the patty before placing it on the open grill. As the patty sizzled, Mr. Lee deftly sliced a fresh tomato, rinsed the bright, green lettuce leaves in the adjacent sink, and then lightly toasted the whites of the buns on the grill before slathering both sides with mayonnaise. He put it all together, sliced it into two perfect halves, and presented it to us on a white oblong plate with a side of crisp potato chips. All for twenty cents. Heaven was a bite into a Mr. Lee hamburger.

Jackson's Bookstore was on Clay Street, around the corner from Sam's Cleaners. The bookstore was a two-story cathedral stocked from floor to ceiling. A balcony stretched alongside the four walls, a slender second story of floor-to-ceiling shelves packed with hardcover literature, dangling precariously over the main floor. Everything was dark wood, cozy and quiet. Mr. and Mrs. Jackson played classical music all day long as they stacked and stocked books, explained titles to customers, and rang up sales on the brass keys of their noisy old cash register.

The Jacksons took time to point out certain books, especially history books, explaining their contents to us. We didn't always understand, but listened anyway, and got into the habit of perusing books. This early experience made books seem like friends, confidants who would tell you everything you ever needed to know; pals entertained you endlessly. Still, we habitually ended up among the pulp fiction with its horrific covers of ghouls rising from graves against a full moon, or of vampires carrying women into the midnight, or of women who looked surprisingly like Molly, cigarettes dangling from their reddened lips and holding a smoking pistol over a dead man lying at their feet. I wondered, "Had our Molly ever shot a man dead?" She certainly was tough enough and sometimes gave overly familiar customers at Sam's Cleaners a look so chilling it could kill.

In the evenings, the local beat patrolman, affectionately known as Danny the Wop, often paused in his brisk rounds of twisting and rattling the handles of closed shop doors to make sure we were okay as we played hopscotch and foursquare outside our apartment. Sometimes, he joined us in an ever so short game of toss or gave us change for potato chips and ice cream.

There was a small contingent of older African-American men who shared the bachelor hotels with Filipinos. They began their mornings with bottles of Thunderbird and cigarettes from Benny, and then whiled away the day sunning on the benches in Portsmouth Square. Or they gathered in front of their friend's shoeshine stand across the street from Jackson's Bookstore.

Ralph was tall and gaunt, forever gracing everyone with a smile. Killer Diller was mean, always growling at us, and sometimes pretending to chase us with a butter knife, behavior befitting his namesake. Yet once, when a very mean white man, a stranger to our neighborhood, shouted racially derogatory names at us—an occurrence so odd that we froze in confusion rather than consternation —and charged menacingly at me, Killer Diller came to the rescue. He shouted, "Leave that boy alone," and placed himself squarely between us. I had been paralyzed with fear, and had not Killer Diller intervened, I am sure I would have been injured. That was the only time he looked at me with open kindness, with unconcealed concern in his eyes, "You all right?"

"Yes! Thanks, Killer Diller!" as I ran off with my pals. I knew then that Killer Diller, for all his histrionics, could never hurt us. He was our Scary Man and we were his kids to scare, but always in play. On sunny Sundays, we often woke up to the robust praises of African-American spirituals. Perhaps young eyes see more sharply, but gazing out our windows, I could see Killer Diller in a fresh suit and a red carnation, along with Ralph, and the other bachelors seated on the park benches, suited up in glistening white shirts and ties in their glistening Sunday best. Large African-American women adorned in outrageous hats and shiny red, blue, and black dresses beat out rhythms on their clanging tambourines as they led the assembled in shouts and calls, prayers, praises, and song. Ralph and Killer Diller would raise one hand to the sky while the other rested on their hearts, shouting hallelujahs and praising Jesus. Sometimes, they leapt up to dance around, both hands shaking in the air, faces uplifted to the sunny, blue heavens.

Nurtured by this milieu of resilient, canny survivors, our neighborhood gang acquired an unusual optimism and resourcefulness. Is it any wonder then that we started our own Boy Scout troop?

Several weeks earlier, Donald Soo and I had visited the Boy Scouts of St. Mary's American Church. Donald lived with his five sisters in the house next door and was my best friend of the "outside-the-apartment-building club," as Sonny Cheong was my best friend of the "inside-the-apartment-building club," a four-story home for eight families.

But one night, Donald and I went to watch Sonny in his Boy Scout uniform go through his paces at St. Mary's Chinese Catholic School. As visitors, we sat on the top of foldout tables, as quiet as could be. Lined up perfectly, the Troop recited the Scout's oath, passed uniform inspection, and then drilled. Several merit badges were awarded, pinned and later, they worked on tying sailors' knots.

Donald and I wished to sign up for Boy Scouts but our families couldn't spare the money.

But one school night, as we sat around the apartment's central stairwell chatting, studying, and playing games, Sonny flipped through his Boy Scout manual with me. He taught me the Scout's salute, three middle fingers of the right hand straight up next to each other and the thumb curled over the baby finger. Then I practiced the Scout's oath, reviewed the sections about hiking tips, how to leave trail markers with twigs or stones, and building and extinguishing fires. We discussed what it meant that a Scout is always prepared. On another night, we practiced tying knots.

Soon enough, Richard learned the knots, too. Then Sonny's sisters, Maxine and Marie, joined us. We all memorized the Scout's Oath. Soon Donald and his sister Ruby joined us every night. Then, Henry and Harry from the restaurant dropped in.

One day, someone suggested, "Why don't we start our own Boy Scout troop?" A giant light bulb lit up over all of us. Yes, why not, indeed? What did we need? Well, we needed Boy Scout Manuals, Boy Scout kerchiefs, pocketknives, flags for each troop, and Boy Scout uniforms with caps. The rest of the merit badge activities we could take straight out of the Manual, practicing in the hallways of our apartment building.

For the flagstaffs, our mothers contributed old brooms and mops about to be thrown away. We sawed off the old bristles and mop tops with pocketknives. To make the flags, Mother gave us clean cotton diapers saved from our childhood. Cut diagonally, they made perfect triangles for the Troop Flags. A skilled illustrator, Sonny drew animals on the troop flags for Eagle, Bear, and Snake Troops. I headed up Eagle Troop and Richard headed up Bear Troop. Drop-ins and less devoted members lined up as Snake Troop. With the sidings from a crib, we built a lean-to command post against a banister. A large 7-Up soda box and a handcrafted stool served as a desk for Sonny. He was Scout Master. No question ever about it. He had the training, the uniform, and the only Boy Scout Manual.

But as the weeks passed, we dreamed of having our own manuals and uniforms. Richard and I approached Mr. Jackson of Jackson's Bookstore for some Boy Scout Manuals. You see, Mr. Jackson, we attempted to explain, we started a troop in our building. We did it because we couldn't afford to join a bonafide post, like at St. Mary's. Mr. Jackson rounded up several old manuals that were in fairly good shape. He would take only fifteen cents. A few days later, he gave us a couple more for free and presto! we each had our own manuals. Next acquisition, neckerchiefs. We saved our pennies, and eventually, Sonny ordered Boy Scout neckerchiefs through St. Mary's for each of us.

Every night, after homework, we assembled as Boy Scout Troop #638, Kearny Street Post, just outside my family's apartment door. We stood at attention in our assembly area, Richard and I in front of our respective troops as Sonny inspected and drilled us. We were so organized, serious, and sharp that the adults started to watch us, nightly--with big smiles on their faces. Like a panel of judges, they commented on our drills as we executed crisp right turns, about-faces, at-attention, and salutes to Sonny. But it became clear, that except for Sonny, we all the rest of us wore ragamuffin street clothes, the Boy Scout kerchiefs our only unifying feature.

Astounded that our interest did not wane, the adults must have discussed uniforms for us. Mrs. Cheong knew the cost, and that put a stop to the talk of buying uniforms. But my mother didn't stop thinking about it. After all, she lived by the Eighth Promise, to take care of her children regardless of the circumstances. Unbeknownst to us, she had stored the Chinese Nationalist Army uniforms her mother had given her so many years ago on a high shelf in our bedroom. One day, she and Father brought them out, handing them to us. The boxes exploded into a disarray of snatched garments. Our first reaction was that we couldn't fit into adult army uniforms, but to our surprise, the jackets, shirts, pants, and trench coats were children's sizes. Wow, I thought, the Nationalist Chinese Army must have been small people—like the munchkins in *The Wizard of Oz*.

And so we lined up in our uniforms, courtesy of Chiang Kai-sek's Chinese Nationalist Army, an army often of small underfed teenagers and hence, about our size.

When refugees flee, they take only what they need: food and drink, money and gold, addresses and phone numbers for cities they might go to, and perhaps a warm jacket and a change of clothes. What had possessed Mother to carry these bulky uniforms so many difficult miles, from Toisan to Guangzhou to Hong Kong to America and finally up three flights of stairs to our apartment?

Was it the dream that the Nationalists, with the help of their American friends, would one day retake the mainland that had kept her to hanging onto these antiquated uniforms? Was this part of the Fourth Promise to her mother, to keep the dream of Sun Yat-sen alive? Or was it in honorable memory of her older brother, a beloved teacher and Nationalist official who died for the Republican cause, a beloved teacher and Nationalist official, who was either driven off or thrown off the roof of our village home to his death during the early Communist occupation?

Guided by the imperatives of her Eighth Promise, she must have weighed the old Nationalist dream against her self-reliant children's concrete needs of today, and then cut the lingering sentimental ties to the closed reality of her former life, its dying dreams. Her life was now in America. Her children needed uniforms here, now, today, so they could be Boy Scouts of America.

And that's how the Boy Scout Troop, #638 Kearny Street Post came was formed. We exulted in our status as bonafide Boy Scouts. We recited the oath, tied knots, and left trail markers throughout our building. We drilled endlessly and tightly, executing sharp left turns, right turns, and about-faces in our narrow hallway and tight alcoves. We practiced being prepared, storing water bottles and packaged foods in case of an earthquake. With the uniforms, we were no longer poor kids.

Our neighborhood had given us the gift of resourcefulness. But it was Mother who had magically legitimized us. Now we were just as good as the official Boy Scout Troop of St. Mary's, each one decked out proper and grinning from ear to ear. Mother bestowed this gift not just on her own sons, but upon all the children of the troop.

Chapter 132
The Toisan Rules

There weren't many unmarried Chinese women in America. Not in the 1950s— many more Chinese men than women, I mean for Chinese who weren't born here, who didn't speak American well. You see, American-born Chinese women wouldn't marry immigrant men from China. They wanted to move out of Chinatown after college, not be stuck in a marriage with someone less Americanized. For them, Chinatown was for weekends, to visit their parents, buy Chinese food, view a Chinese movie, banquet with friends, and so on. They wanted American-born Chinese husbands, people like them. That was the way it was and so there were always lots of Toisanese bachelors.

I had promised to help my family get to America, but until I became a citizen I couldn't sponsor their application. Marriage to a Toisan *bachelor who was an American citizen, however, could get my two sisters here right away. So, I set out to find husbands for Yoong, and then for Tien, my youngest sister. This was during the late 1950s when the immigration laws were so tricky that sometimes an overseas wife would be denied a visa.*

I put the word out—to the Clan Sisters in San Francisco, the merchants on Grant Avenue, and all the family associations. We didn't marry for love, you know, or for good times. Go-betweens arranged marriages. I became the go-between for my sisters. What I looked for in a Toisan *husband was:*

Kun-lick—a determined worker, not easily discouraged. A saver, not a spender.

Jett—Truthful, reliable. Not a troublemaker.

How sheen foo—someone with a good strong body, of average height and build; someone who could put up with all kinds of difficulties, of all kind, day after day, without giving up.

Guai doi—A man who is not flamboyant and had no bad habits like gambling, drinking and womanizing

Leck doi—Intelligent enough to work and take care of the family, but no need for brilliance.

The Wong couple introduced Mr. Shleen-wah Wong to me. You remember the elder Wongs—who lived across from us at our Kearny Street apartment? They had met Mr. Lai who used to visit us. A very nice man with a car, who took us on Sunday outings. But he was too short, hunched over all the time. Also, he had a hearing problem and later there were rumors he had a wife in China anyway.

Anyway, elderly Mrs. Wong knew I was prospecting for my sister, and Schleen- wah was a Wong, so she arranged a first meeting between us. A "getting-to-know-him" meeting without talking about marriage. I cooked a special meal and, as it turned out, Shleen-wah Wong was very nice. In World War II, he served in the American Army, fighting the Japanese. He was captured and tortured. For months. Once he was buried up to his neck in dirt as a punishment. For a long time, he said. But he survived and received some compensation from America for his hardships. Maybe because he was Chinese-American and not a white person, the Japanese soldiers treated him worse. Still, Shleen-wah was strong and healthy. And he had all the qualities for a good Toisan husband. He was a chef. He was frugal and ambitious—saving money to eventually start his own business. He smoked a little, but that's all. In those days, everybody smoked cigarettes, even your father.

But there was one problem. Mr. Wong was older, much older than Yoong. About twenty years older, as a matter of fact. So we met a couple of more times so I could be sure, always over dinner at our home. Finally, I decided to show him a picture of Yoong. He thought she was very pretty. And I think because he had gotten to know me, he assumed that Yoong would be just as nice and as capable a wife.

That was why I cooked dinner for him, dressed nice and treated him nice. I knew that if he liked me, he could get to like Yoong. After all, Yoong was in Hong Kong and he was here. In those days, most people still traveled by boat—President Lines mostly. Airplane travel was new and expensive—only for rich people. You couldn't just fly over and have a long weekend date. Besides, Mr. Wong was not romantic at all, just very business-like. He still wanted children, time was running out, and basically, he wanted a reliable wife more than fun.

I agreed to tell Yoong about him. I wrote her a long letter with a photo of Mr. Wong. Yoong wrote back that she didn't mind his age. So I turned it over to them to decide the rest. After several letters, they agreed to a meeting. Mr. Wong went to Hong Kong and the next thing you know, they were married, and he returned to sponsor her immigration.

I was confident that the match would turn out fine because, well, Yoong is matter-of-fact about life. She doesn't need a lot of fun and she doesn't like to spend money. Very frugal, actually a kind of cheapskate. Yoong wanted security, to be taken care of. Mr. Wong could provide security. Also, Yoong looks older than her age, older looking than me even though I am the first sister. The way she is, she seems more like an old person anyway. Perhaps too for Yoong, it was a plus that Mr. Wong felt his time was running out.

Mr. Wong even asked your Father to partner with him in a business. He had the money, but didn't speak American well. Your Father spoke American well, but, mainly, he was very comfortable dealing with white men, since that's what he did all day in white-owned restaurants, chatting, debating politics, and joking back with white people every day. Well, Mr. Wong knew of a grocery store for sale near Hyde Street and California, you know, where the "dang-dang cheh," the cable cars, turned the corner? They even visited the store several times, but your Father decided to invest in another business. Mr. Wong bought an apartment building instead, near the same corner as the store.

Mr. Wong died sometime in the 1970s. Yoong still lives there, in the sunny penthouse, alone now since her two sons left for college and jobs. Yoong is secure, collecting the rents from four apartments. The building keeps going up in value—from the original $50,000 to several million dollars now.

She's still a cheapskate. Stays home most of the time, counting her money. Me, I'm not like that. If I have money, I take the train with your father to the Bay Meadows Racetrack and watch the horses. We gamble ten or fifteen dollars for fun. Win or lose, no problem. Or we ride the bus out to Serramonte Shopping Center in Daly City. If we have just enough money, we don't even hesitate— we eat the buffet at Sizzler's.

Or I'll fly to China and visit my Clan Sisters. Lots of good times there. If I come back broke, I stay close to home, gossiping with my Chinatown Clan Sisters. Lots of places in Chinatown for low-priced pastries and coffee or a decent 3-course lunch with a beverage. Take a walk to Fishermen's Wharf or downtown to look at the Macy's windows and hunt for sales. Why not, life is good.

But Yoong is not like that. She doesn't like to spend money even though she has so much now. That's why Yoong and Mr. Wong were a good match — they were both frugal —hang onto money, don't have fun.

My youngest sister, Tien, is very different from Yoong. She's prettier, very playful, with a fiery temper, and a very quick thinker. I knew she would be happier with a man who respected her opinions and treated her as an equal, rather than one who wanted to be in charge and put women down. So, Mr. Richard Lee was a good match for her. Same name as your brother—Richard Lee. Lots of Richard Lee's in America. He was pleasant and mild-mannered, in his early twenties, about the same age as Tien.

At first, I didn't think of him as a husband prospect. He was just a struggling college student who lived next door to us. No job, no money. Mr. Lee was so poor he had to share his small room with another student. He couldn't afford to eat in restaurants and he couldn't cook. I invited him to our dinners. Mr. Lee's favorite food was fish, pan-fried in black bean sauce and chopped onions. He salivated when he smelled the dish. He was always so hungry he'd wolf it down with two quick bowls of rice.

I guess I felt sorry for him, like for a younger brother. He was naïve too, a scholar with a gentle personality. That's why I always made his favorite dish. That kind of fish was very cheap—twenty-five cents for four small fishes, like the shiners you use to catch at Fishermen's Wharf. And four was more than enough to share. I even washed and ironed his clothes. You remember we had a washing machine at the time, the only one in the building? I was just helping him, not really thinking about his marrying my sister.

Many go-betweens had approached him, and he had refused them all. And that's what started me thinking. Maybe he would make a good husband for Tien. There must be some reason why all the go-betweens propositioned him. When I suggested that perhaps he and Tien might make a good marriage, he didn't say "No" as he had with the others. I think that was because of my kindness to him. Maybe he felt he owed me a favor. Maybe he had grown to like me, and so he was open to meeting a sister who, probably like Mr. Wong had thought, would be like me—and cook good food for him, too, especially black bean and onion sauce fish! Then, his eyes lit up at her photo—Tien was indeed very pretty. And later, after several letters, Tien agreed to meet him.

Richard didn't have much money or a steady job yet, so he didn't meet all the criteria for a good husband, especially kun-lick. *But he studied hard, read books all the time, and so I thought he would work hard when the time came. He spoke American quite well, although not as well as your father. Besides, as a college man, maybe he would do something else besides restaurant and laundry work. And everything else seemed okay. He voyaged to Hong Kong and there he married Tien.*

Well, as the years went by, Richard did work hard, as a busboy at the Commercial Club downtown. He ended up as a restaurant worker after all! But he saved his tips and his 13th-month Christmas bonus, year after year. They moved into the North Ping Yuen housing project, just like us. I had told them about it, when we moved in and it was still brand new, like a rich apartment building with a sunny view of the bay. Later, he and Tien bought a nice house in the Avenues, the Sunset District, with my brother. It's now worth lots of money, probably about a million and a half.

It turned out Mr. Lee and Tien are more like equals. Mr. Lee is actually a bit timid and indecisive, but Tien's fiery will and expressiveness balances him out. Sometimes they sound like two sides of the same person, thinking out loud with each other, and finishing each other's sentences. They really love each other.

So, this one too turned out to be a good match. And so I fulfilled the promise to my mother to find my sisters good husbands.

Your father helped me all along the way, even though we did fight about money. But that's little stuff. He didn't mind that I prepared expensive meals for Mr. Wong. Or the costs of Mr. Lee joining us for dinner night after night. Or my doing Mr. Lee's laundry in a washing machine that Father paid for. Father knew it was right for me to find husbands.

And it was your father who helped me to pass my citizenship test so I could bring my mother and brother to America. Father found and paid for the immigration lawyer who prepared me for the oral test. Every week or two, I walked to that financial district office to be tested on the last week's set of practice questions and to receive a new list. The lawyer assigned a Mrs. Wong, who spoke Cantonese only, and didn't seem very friendly at first, to work with me.

There was one problem: I didn't speak American and the oral test was in American. I didn't read American and the study materials were in American. Your father worked all day and couldn't teach me, so he assigned you to be my tutor. He explained that you earned Excellent and Very Good grades in every subject, good enough to tutor me, and it was summer vacation, so I had time. I think you were around ten years old then, maybe eleven.

You both ended up my tutors actually, because your Chinese wasn't that good. It was Father who explained the test questions to me in Toisanese. They were mostly about democracy, which I knew about from Sun Yat-sen's Three Principles of Democracy. Oh, there were questions about the three branches of US government, the election system, the most important presidents, the rights of citizenship, and so on. If the test was in Chinese, I could have passed it easy and saved a lot of money.

But as for the oral part of the test, your role was to help me to understand the questions and answers in American. Oh, we tried so hard. You read each question and, I tried to read it back. You read each answer and, I tried to read it back. Day after day—impossible to learn both the American language and memorize the citizenship test in one summer.

One morning, quite frustrated, I as I had started writing Chinese characters over each syllable, Chinese phonetic equivalents of the American sounds as a solution came to us. I don't know who thought of it or who had the idea first, but we realized that each question and answer had its unique sounding key words and no other. Then each answer had its own key words and no other. So, instead of trying to remember each sentence completely and then answer back in a perfect sentence perfectly, we realized that I only had to remember key words sounds. I furiously wrote in the closest-sounding Chinese characters over those key words and concentrated on memorizing them only.

If I heard the sounds "First Pres-za-dent," I answered "Wah-sing-ton." If I heard the sounds "Free the slaves," I answered "A-blah-hem Ling-kon." The one I had most trouble with was "Kur-rent Pres-za-dent." I tried to say "Dwite-dee-i-zun-how-wer," but his name was too long. But you told me that your teacher said we could call him "Ike-kee" and that became my answer.

Mrs. Wong didn't like this at all at first: she felt that we should answer everything in perfect American. I explained to her that we only had so much money and so little time, and I had to get my mother over. She's getting old, stuck in Hong Kong, and this was my promise to her. Even though Mrs. Wong was Cantonese and not Toisanese, and she was an American-born who looked down on immigrants like me, yet I think she felt what I was feeling, missing my mother and my brother. I think she remembered how hard being Chinese in America could be, that sometimes we have to help each other even if we are not in the same social circles. At first reluctantly, and then kindly, she cooperated. Instead of sending me home to perfect my language, she passed me and gave me the next set of questions.

Finally, the big practice day with the lawyer came. He was white, and I had to be able to answer all the questions in any order. I was glad you could stay in the room with me, as you had with every visit with Mrs. Wong. Well, both the lawyer and Mrs. Wong were smiling when we finished. He said I would do fine. I surprised Mrs. Wong when I shook her hand and said, "T'ank you velly much, Wong Tai-tai." She smiled back, "You're welcome."

Two weeks later, we dressed up nice and walked to the Immigration building. You found the right office and a man called out my name "Mrs. Poy Jen Lee." He was a nice man. I looked him directly in his eyes and kept smiling. At first he was a little surprised at my short answers, then, after he struggled with it, I guess he decided this was okay. After a long time, we finished. He was friendly as he showed me the door. I was sure I had passed, and a few weeks later, the lawyer sent a letter confirming this.

We went to swearing-in day together. I took my new patent leather purse with brass locks from Macy's in Union Square, a celebration gift to myself. We walked to the big courthouse, up the wide stairs with two-story columns, and into the dark wood and marble halls. You found the courtroom— hundreds of people there, all races and ages, new citizens with their family and friends.

The guard said to stand up for the judge, but then the judge asked us to sit down before we even got up all the way. He congratulated everyone on becoming a citizen, then asked us to stand up for real this time, and repeat with him the oath of citizenship:

> *I hereby declare, on oath, that I absolutely and entirely renounce... all allegiance and fidelity to any foreign prince, potentate, state, or sovereignty of whom or which I had heretofore been a subject or citizen; that I will support and defend the Constitution and laws of the United States of America against all enemies foreign and domestic; that I will bear true faith and allegiance to the same...that I take this oath freely and without mental reservation or purposes of evasion; So help me God.*

Then we recited the Pledge of Allegiance with him—loudly, with every kind of accent, echoing back and forth in that big room. I could hear you saying the pledge along with me.

To thank you, I took you to Manning's Restaurant, a fancy place with white tablecloths and bow-tied waiters on Market Street, near the cable-car turntable. "Order anything you want," I said. You did —all your favorites—chicken noodle soup, hot dog with French fries, cherry coke, and apple pie with vanilla ice cream.

A few years later, I sponsored my mother and brother into America. I was so happy to have my mother near me again—I had missed her so much all these years. Finally, we were reunited. Finally, I had someone I could really talk to someone about my children, and my marriage, especially about your father's meanness.

Chapter 14 Bogie's Man

During my 1983 visit to Toisan, I was stunned to encounter a near identical twin to my Father. Same small stature and sinewy body. Same thinning hair above the brow. He was a teacher at our village's grammar school. Unlike Father, his face was devoid of pain, frustration, and struggle. He seemed totally at peace in the world. Beatific, in a word. Upon our introduction he gazed deeply into my eyes, with total attention, as if nothing else mattered, he was feeling for our Clan connection. Only after he found it did we exchange the briefest of greetings before he nonchalantly turned back to his pupils, who were quietly hunched over, whirling brushes on rice paper. In spite of his startling resemblance to Father, the feel of the teacher's presence was, perplexingly, more reminiscent of Mother, as if Father had been emptied of his volatile personality, then refilled with Mother's steady kindness.

And yet he wasn't related to Father, at least, he hadn't responded in specific recognition as had my Chun Clan relatives in the makeshift village square, who recognized my mother in my face. It was more like the teacher felt for our vibe of kinship rather than any specific relationship. Kow-Woon also did not denote a blood status, and so the remarkable similarity may have sprung from the commonality of the Toisanese gene pool.

Later, I visited Father's ancestral home, a mini-townhouse of wood construction. The tenant, Father's teacher from childhood and later, my parents' marriage go-between, invited me in and then left. He didn't know I was coming either, and yet, his ease at my presence, and his complete hospitality, was as natural as if we had known each other all our lives.

Unlike Mother's spacious house, little sunlight penetrated the interior of Father's childhood home. I had to move ever so slowly to avoid bumping into the furniture. Farm tools, baskets, pots, and pans hung neatly on every wall. Every square inch was completely utilized. Mother's larger and sunnier home, although comforting, had felt like an abandoned sacred temple, temporarily dispossessed due to exigencies, its spirit fires burning low, patiently awaiting the return of the survivors of the dispersed Order to return and revitalize the space. This smaller, darker townhouse-style farmers house, though shadowed, felt cheery, felt lit up and energized by the thriving lives of the residents.

Only when I descended the steep stairs back down from the second floor, did the large sepia-tone photo of Father as a teenager confronted me, eyeball-to-eyeball. As in a graduation photo, his young face gazed upwards, optimistic and promising, someone so brand-new that his visage positively glowed despite the dim light of the stairwell. Father was once beatific, too, like his near twin, the village teacher. He wasn't always an unpredictable emotional pendulum.

I wondered, as I crouched in that stairway, about what price Father had paid to put rice on our, to make it in America, of what had it cost his psyche to work in a racially striated restaurant industry in a hostile society? Had Father stayed in China, would he be serene like, still possess the same serenity of his near twin? Would he have encouraged me to write or to paint as he had himself composed poetry instead of pushing me into a money-making profession? In my emotional memory as an adult, would his essence, then, have been felt 100% safe, nurturing, and comforting like Mother than erratic, wonderful alternating with meanness?

Perhaps that's the rub with difficult but not completely abusive fathers. I always wonder whether it could have been better, and why it wasn't. Whether Father could have been more of a mentor, and later as I aged and wizened, whether we could have been friends, even buddies. For despite his difficult personality, and his unpredictable rage, we inevitably reached back to one other. Many a time he would just call and suggest spending a weekend together. Or I would suggest an outing to some beach or nearby state park. On his turning 77, I invited him over for the day. On an old upright birdcage piano left by the previous homeowner, I plunked out and sang Happy Birthday to him. He seemed deeply touched and then whispered, "No one has ever sang Happy Birthday to me before. No one has ever played the piano for me before."

That was a good day, but his volatility invariably blew up the bridges between us, and many a time, I preferred to let them lay in ruins for an interminable period. It was usually Mother who brought us back together, by cajoling me to come home for dinner, or if I was particularly resistant, by springing him on me at some restaurant, despite her promise that she would come alone.

Mother always admonished me, "He's sorry. He knows he was wrong. You know how he is, *mo lo mo lah,* no sense, just say stuff. It's nothing now. It was said, it's out and over with. I lived with your dad for years. He's just like that. He doesn't mean it. Forget about it."

Father always confirmed her statement with his downcast eyes. He could never say sorry, but his apology was in his demeanor. Over those reunion dinners, Mother and I do most of the talking, as repentant (or biting his tongue) he said little if anything.

And then it was fine again until the next outburst. When I was younger, it was usually during these rages that I momentarily felt that syndrome most, if not all of us have indulged at one time or other, of having been switched at childbirth in the hospital nursery, that these weren't my real parents because my real father would have been kinder, understood me completely, and done better by me, emotionally, materially, and intellectually.

But of course, they were my real parents, and certainly Mother never lacked in my eyes. So over the years, I settled into loving him, accepting his wit, grace, and gifts when Good Father was present, but never, ever making excuses for Bad Father's behavior. And no, it never stopped being confusing. My childhood memories of Father are emotionally conflicted. Father was kind, gentle, and supportive, but intermittently abused his family verbally and physically.

Physicality—in my earliest childhood memories, it's his strength that stands out starkly. First to rise every morning, he'd drop to the floor for thirty push-ups followed by sixty sit-ups. Father labored in restaurants, a supply man and busboy who lifted vegetable boxes, sides of beef, two-gallon cans of tomato sauce, and trays stacked with dishes, eight hours a day and more. Only slightly over five feet and of a slender, compact build, his biceps were large, and hard, and round like a curled fist. His body was taut, with sinewy muscles and bulging, dark-blue veins.

Father was a fierce walker. In my earliest childhood, he walked to work even though the Meteor Restaurant was two miles away, and then back again. Rain, fog, or sunshine. On weekends, he propelled us, one on each side like mini-versions of him, to Market Street, San Francisco's boulevard of movie palaces, to catch a double or triple feature. Clutching our hands, he'd launch off as we half-ran to keep up. Eventually we got the hang of it, tossing our arms far forward with his and stepping large, like soldiers on a triple-time drill. Still, my thighs suffered wind-whip, and I'd scratched them while waiting in line for our tickets.

In play, he swung Richard and me around effortlessly and endlessly as we laughed and yelled, "Faster, faster." He'd hoist us high past his head to the ceiling so we could fly like Superman. At the playground, he'd push our swings way past the other kids'. When we headed home late and sleepy from a Cantonese movie, he'd cradle both of us against his shoulders and then up three flights of stairs to our beds.

But Father would explode without warning. Several times, Father became so angry that he beat Mother with his fists. We were so shocked the first time it happened, in the middle of dinner, that Richard and I stared incomprehensibly. We had no reference points for violence. We didn't know what was happening. Before we knew it, Mother had fallen on her back, futilely blocking his punches, crying like a baby, and promising to do better. Another time, Richard and I forced our bodies between Father's fist and Mother, thinking he would stop rather than strike his own children. Oblivious, he rained hurtful, bruising blows on all of us. It was heartbreaking to see our gentle, caring, and hardworking Mother being beaten, and so we took the hits.

Sometimes, what started as our play could shift surrealistically into terror as when he lifted us high up over his head in anger and threw us down like sacks of potatoes, slamming us onto the mattress in punishment. These slams pained us mostly in mind, for we would bounce unharmed. He never so lost it that he would slam us onto the floor, as if Good Dad would always thwart Bad Dad. A loving father who fell into places of anger so intense he could barely control himself was confusing.

But because his abuse was sporadic, I remember Father more as an upbeat, caring man who not only provided us "three hots and a cot," but tutored us nightly in reading, 'riting, and 'rithmetic. In grammar school, because the apartment lighting was dim, he set up a naked bulb over the dining table, exclusively for our use at homework hour. Mother and Father delayed their activities during our study time, staying as quiet as vigilant mice until our bedtime.

Saturdays were Market Street matinees and Sunday morning was American food brunch, as he cooked up huge meatballs in tomato sauce over spaghetti, ham and cheese omelets, macaroni with cheese, and sliced hot-dogs in ketchup and onion sauce over white bread.

In the second grade, for my first current affairs assignment, Father taught me analysis by carefully picking apart the news story's key points, and then reassembling them into a beguiling narrative. He patiently coached me that first time until I memorized my report. The next day, standing with my feet slightly apart, delicately holding the news clipping in front of my chest, I confidently described the inventor in the photo, a young man proudly holding his prototype of an atomic-based device that looked like a Flash Gordon proton-cannon. The teacher raved and, after a few more successes, I joined Father as an inveterate reader of the daily paper. Soon, Richard too excelled in current affairs, and daily, we sat with father on the sofa as he passed sections to us, pointing out stories of interest.

Ever so gently, Father guided us to earn grades of "Excellent" in every subject.

Over time, he fixed a singular goal in our minds: college on a complete scholarship that we both could and would earn through good grades. You see, he explained, as a poor family, he could never afford to pay for his sons' college education. He never said this as a shameful thing, or as a judgment upon himself, but matter-of-factly. Life was clear— Father worked, Mother took care of the house, and his sons studied to earn college scholarships.

This became such an article of faith for Richard and me that we never doubted that, one day, the grand prize would simply float into our embrace. Born here. Raised here. Succeed here. College, our American birthright, would deliver us from life as a restaurant worker, even if Father had resigned himself to this.

Father's favorite movie star was Humphrey Bogart, and late at night, when he thought we were all asleep, I could hear him singing "As Time Goes By" softly to himself. Why Bogart and not all the other tough guys crashing across the screen in all those Market Street movie palaces? Because Bogart was the only white Hollywood star that a Toisan-featured man could possibly identify with. John Wayne, Gary Cooper and all the others were too impossibly tall, too barrel chested, too fair skinned, and too blonde, brown, or redheaded. But Bogart—well he was shorter, of slender build, with a slightly receding hairline, swarthy-faced, and with strong cheekbones—exactly like Toisan men. Amazingly, his hair was black, as black as Chinese hair! And his suits hung loose, as Chinatown men wore them.

More than appearances, though, it was Bogart's roles that resonated deeply for Father. In *"The Maltese Falcon,"* Bogart the loner hero walked the streets of San Francisco, ambushed by rough men and waylaid by cops and DAs, but still and yet, seized his living against a cast of unknowable, twisted customers. Father too, walked the same streets every day, and, along with many Chinese men, risked unprovoked attacks after dark. He daily confronted the sneak-attack, racial, attitudinal whippings and verbal haymakers from white bosses, customers, and casual passers-by. In *Casablanca*, Bogart was himself an immigrant, betrayed by love, and stranded in a hostile, foreign land, far from family and friends. Like Bogart, my stranded Father somehow made lemonade out of lemons.

And finally, in character, they were both reliable like an unstoppable train, always on schedule. Father often repeated that his boss at the Meteor Restaurant considered him indispensable, "Oh, Lee, if I only had a few more workers like you," or "You'll always have a job with me." Wryly, Father remarked that perhaps he should be made a partner, knowing that would never happen.

Yet, he never missed a day of work, turning his earnings over to Mother every Friday night. Every Saturday night, they handed the landlord his cash, for, as my parents taught us, it was important to pay bills on time. Father's industry brought home the apartment building's first television set, an Emerson, and then, the first washing machine, from Sears, a whirling tub with a hand-operated wringer to the squeeze water out. Father strove to stay moral and, hopeful, to doing the right thing by his family and himself: always by his bedside was a well-thumbed copy of Dr. Norman Vincent Peale's *The Power of Positive Thinking*.

In retrospect, Father felt he had failed Mother when she suffered a nervous breakdown shortly after Richard's birth. What was surprising was that she made it so far intact. Nor was this caused solely by Father's periodic rages. The decade of terror of the Japanese ethnic cleansing, the trauma of her older brother's suicide after the Communist victory, her adaptation from life as a working farm girl to one in a completely modern society, her attempts to master a difficult language in months, the sharp severing from the support of her loving mother and Clan Sisterhood—all this left Mother completely traumatized.

Over the years, I had seen that Father's tenderness towards Mother prevailed more often than not. In his calmer moments, he felt guilty about letting her down, about not protecting her. That's why he paid for a babysitter for Richard even as he ranted about every unaccounted for nickel and dime. He loved her, always had, and always would. When we were around seven, he made the biggest demonstration of love a man could possibly make in that day.

This feat began when he became business partners in an auto repair business with a man named Kai Yep. We called him Yep Sook -- Mr. Yep in Toisanese -- or Bob, his American name. Eventually, we called him Bob all the time. In smaller, delightful ways, Bob was more generous with Richard and me than Father was, treating us to potato chips, sodas, and comic books and giving us his spare change. The business tanked, but Bob stayed in our lives. He was my Father's best friend -- a jovial, verbose buddy who openly admired Father's grasp of politics and world affairs. In fact, Bob was the only friend Father ever had.

Bob also had a car although he didn't have a job. With his freewheeling schedule, Bob helped Mother with shopping, picked up Richard and me after school, or drove us to the beach, the Zoo, and Golden Gate Park. Mother and Bob spent so much time together that the Cheong kids started to insinuate that something more than friendship was going on. Evidently more was going on, for I caught them *en deshabille* several times, although as a kid I did not fathom the implications of partial undress in the middle of the day.

Father undoubtedly suspected, but despite his potential for rage, he never expressed jealousy, or accused Mother of unfaithful behavior, or in any way cut Bob off from the family. In his own way, I think Father knew he couldn't meet all of Mother's needs, socially, emotionally, or financially. And so, like all good Toisanese, he accommodated, so long as minimal appearances were maintained. He genuinely wanted Mother to be happy, and if happiness was an unspoken triangle of sorts, well, so be it. Besides, Bob met so many of his own needs. Perhaps, as with like so many other immigrant fathers, compromise was part of survival. He had no choice but to absorb the blows of the outside world to keep body and family together; now what could he do but accept this unkind cut of his own uneven marriage. One can only fight so many battles.

For his part, Bob did not seek to take Mother away from Father, nor did he try to commandeer our affections through his treats. All of our adults held it together for the entire family unit, now 4+1.

In many significant ways, Father exercised a good, strong influence, including this remarkable instance of Toisan flexibility and pragmatism. But he could not pass onto me the subtler, more potent Toisan ways. Summoned by his father at the age of thirteen to America, a society for which he had no preparation, he had to assimilate as quickly and as completely as possible. The price for this desperate bargain, one that his father forced upon him, was to jettison his Toisan ways.

In this way, it ended up that Mother, and not Father, was always our connection to the Toisan sensibility. Having reached adulthood before she left the village, she retained the inherent Toisan characteristics of compassion combined with industry and perseverance.

Father was only half-formed and, perhaps because of this, he was Toisan interrupted, broken by his recruitment into America. He worked hard and persevered, but denied compassion by his own father and struggling always to survive, his compassion slowly dribbled away over the years.

So, too had his beatific visage, as I realized, as I stood in mid-stride in his childhood stairway, gazing at his teen-age face.

Mother was our quiet *yin* influence, just as Father was clearly our *yang* influence. Mother embodied China while Father personified America.

But as young boys, Father's *yang* was always more eye-catching, thrilling and desirable. Going forth into the larger white world, hitting home runs, wise-cracking, graduating from college with a good job, and moving to the suburbs into a nice house with a yard, just like Dick and Jane's, that was graspable and doable. Brewing suspicious smelling chi soups, having the patience for new-baby speaking-round-and-rounds, endlessly sewing and shopping, and repressing all bad thoughts during Chinese New Year's were not congruent with the messages we received in public school and through the television. So Richard and I took our lead from Father.

Father also sparkled in ways that other Chinese-American fathers did not. He was a freethinker, a radical. He told me about a white classmate, a girl, who initially tutored him during his houseboy days, and then sought his company outside school, often inviting him to bike with her to a matinee on his rare Saturdays off. This was a brave kind of crush, for in the 1930s, interracial liaisons, even puppy love, were illegal, against all social sanction, acts that justified violence against any male of color, regardless of age, throughout America. It took bravery for a Chinese houseboy to be seen with a white girl so often at school and then in the town. If he could have done so, he would have married white, I am sure. Or for that matter, any color he was free to choose.

Atypically, Father had turned his back on Chinatown society. This was radical in the 1930s and 1940s. It wasn't as if he had other options, like signing onto the Social Register, hanging out at the local Irish tavern, or joining the Union Square Optimists Club. He refused to tolerate not only the exploitation of himself and other Chinese-Americans, but too, the petty politics, egotistic airs, vicious gossip, and exploitation of their own by so-called Chinatown leaders. Father preferred striking out on his own, even if it meant being without a community.

Father was also unusually well read—*Time, Newsweek,* and *Life,* books on history, politics and self-improvement, and the daily paper. He often returned home describing a rousing political discussion at work. In time, his co-workers bestowed on him a respectful title, "The Professor," for his grasp of history, politics, and current affairs—and his relentless argumentation. Often, after a Saturday matinee, we'd stop at Union Square and listen to the spontaneous, noisy, public debates that were so much the life of the Square then. A speaker would stand on the concrete rim of the raised lawn and launch into oratory. Someone else would jump up alongside him and argue the other way. Audience members would hoot, cheer, hiss, and clap, and hollered out their own broadsides. Always rousing, sometimes caustic, and oftentimes comic—regardless, the debates invariably ended with a handshake and the applause of an appreciative audience. Later, Father would explain the issues to his perplexed but enlivened sons.

As a union man, he spent Saturday mornings manning picket lines in support of strikers at other restaurants. He also passed out campaign literature and went over sample ballots with Mother. Passionate political views and picketing were second nature to him and, by extension, comfortable to me. Later, in school, the teachings about the First Amendment guarantee of speech, press, and assembly seemed obvious—my father lived them for me.

My father's teachings remain alive, healthy, and active in my life today. But I, and his other two sons, owe him a different debt than we owe to Mother. Father assumed we had just better get on with the business of being Americans, and the sooner the better. He taught us American values and the American way; but he also taught us we could be patriots without being parrots. Our Americanization came quickly and soon. Only over time have I have come to prize equally what Mother gave me—wisdom that I couldn't see, didn't grasp, and denied as a child, under the rush and crush of assimilation. Beneath my father's larger-than-life American example, my mother's immutable Toisan ways eventually seeped through, making me the person I've finally become.

Chapter 154
Two Buses Daily

Why did I visit you every day at the tuberculosis ward for nine months? Because I'm your mother, that's why.

In Toisan, we say that only a mother can love her children the best they can be loved. We don't trust childcare, like they have in America. Leaving your children with a stranger makes me go "ugggh! What kind of a mother would do that?" In the village, if a mother is working in the field, she will come home several times, even if her own mother is watching the children.

A mother must be with her children every day, and throughout the day.

Yes, I took the bus from Chinatown all the way to San Francisco General Hospital in Potrero Hill. Every day—rain or shine, chilly or warm. One hour each way and had to change buses, too. Yes, our visits were only an hour long. Two hours on the bus every day, just to see my son for one hour. Sometimes our visit was shorter when the bus was slow. One time the bus broke down and I could only see you for five minutes. Then, it was back to the bus stop. But this is what a mother should do for her children. I never thought of it as a sacrifice. I was always happy to see you, to know you were fine, ate enough food, had a good teacher, and that the nurses were nice to you. That's what makes a Toisan mother happy—that her children are happy.

It wasn't such a bad bus ride. Quite safe in 1962. Everyone was nice and no one ever bothered me. I passed all the neighborhoods on the way to the city hospital. Mexicans, white people, black people. So interesting to watch all the people. So different and yet so the same. After a few months, I met a Chinese janitor who worked at the hospital. He gave me rides home and in exchange, I food-shopped for him, which he couldn't do because he worked during the day. Nothing special—roast duck, barbecue pig, some vegetables once in a while. Sometimes Bob came with me. By then, his car had broken down or he would have driven me every day I am sure.

There was no question that I would visit you every day—no matter how long they kept you. Originally, you were only to stay two months. But still, I didn't want to let you go. I said we could take care of you, But the doctors insisted you had a serious case that needed lots of attention. Also, they were concerned we might catch it.

Finally I agreed. And before you knew it, nine months had passed. But it didn't matter—I would have visited you everyday if it was nine years. That's what it means to be a Toisan mother.

Chapter 165
Visitors Must Wear Masks

In 1962, I unexpectedly found myself in a new village, the tuberculosis ward of San Francisco's General Hospital. The residents were a cross-section of the children of San Francisco's working class - Mexican, Irish, Italian, Chinese and black - all from families who could not afford to pay for private long-term care.

The nursing staff comprised the elders of this village. The white Registered Nurses (RN's) were nominally in charge, but I soon found that the African-American nurses' aides, assigned to menial chores like changing sheets and cleaning up after meals, had equally important roles in the village's life. The only men were the Irish-American school teacher, "Mr. Sullivan," and the African-American maintenance man, "George" (their workplace names reflected the class and race structure of the times).

The time I spent in Ward 75 turned out to be an early rite of passage. At the age of eleven, I was unexpectedly wrenched from a comfortable home and community and exiled into an unknown environment. This alteration, on a less drastic level, was not dissimilar from Father's move to America at age thirteen, or Mother's as a rather young twenty-year old. As if I were caught in a family pattern, I was cut off from my parents and brothers and set adrift in the company of strangers. Fearful initially, I took comfort from the promise made to me by the public health doctor that I should be home in two months – shorter than a summer vacation, I thought - and Mother's promise to visit me daily

In the tradition of my Toisan parents, I discovered that unanticipated, wrenching change drew out the best in me. Schooling was my main responsibility, as I knew well. In my letters to Donald Soo, my best friend and classmate, I grilled him on his subjects, tracking his responses against what Mr. Sullivan was teaching me, to make sure he taught me the same subjects at the same level of difficulty. I built model airplanes—gifts from Mother; devoured a donated childhood collection of Tom Mix comics; learned to sketch from Ron Nagy's "Learn to Draw" series on the local PBS television affiliate, Channel 9; drew my own comic strips; and faithfully watched the College Bowl question-and-answer contest every Saturday night to test and increase my own knowledge of the world.

Mother visited every day, rain or shine and she was the only parent who visited daily. Her clockwork appearances anchored me safely to the outside world, assuring me that this was only a temporary limbo. Every day, I eagerly waited for her to come. We didn't always have a lot to say, but I was always happy to see her smiling face. Every day, she brought me a gift of comic books or airplane models. At Christmas, she delivered my gifts, and on Chinese New Year day's, she passed on my relatives' red money packets. Eventually, we fell into a quiet routine of playing checkers. Most of the time I won, or she let me, and after my promised two-months-max hospitalization had long past, I began winning with a vengeance, as if punishing her for committing me to the hospital instead of sticking to her guns about home care. At other times, I badgered her about my release date. She simply smiled through my whining. She seemed to understand--doctors too had delayed her when she was trying to come to America. She never threatened to visit less. She never complained about her two-hour bus trip through rain, fog, or winter's bite.

Father visited every few weekends. Richard and the Soo kids came a few times. Since kids were not allowed into the Ward, Richard and the Soo kids gazed up from five floors below and we shouted our happy conversation. Even from that height, I could see that Richard had changed. He strutted a bit more, seeming more surer of himself, and, yes, definitely more independent. I had been away a long time and perhaps my little brother was no longer so little. I felt sad that he might not look up to me as much. But when he spotted me staring, he laughed gleefully, jumping up and down, and waving so mightily with both his hands, he resembled a propeller hat trying to fly up to touch me.

Over time, I came to trust the African-American nurses more than the white nurses, with the exception of Mrs. Ross, the day head nurse. They felt familiar, loving, and indulgent, like Chinatown mothers. Daytime Dorothy, the big, loving, nurse's aide, became my surrogate mother, as she was with all the children. She held and comforted those who broke down crying because of homesickness. She gently painted red, stinging Mercurochrome onto our scratched knees. She looked the other way when I spit out the beets I hated. She loudly reminded the RN's that we were still children when they became overly picky about rules. George, the African-American maintenance man, reminded me of Father: he was always diligently picking up and cleaning up after other people's messes, just like Father in his busboy job. George daily read to us the news from the outside world, every day, as Father had every evening.

Life in a TB ward is about waiting. Waiting for visits from Mother. Waiting, waiting—for yet another test result from the saliva test, or the x-ray, or the lung-mucous test, where a tube that felt like fire was slid down a nostril into a lung. Waiting for that magic release date. Waiting was hard. Two months passed, and still, I was not to be released. Three, then four and five months passed, and I gave up on a date. Once I broke down crying in front of Mr. Sullivan, sobbing that I missed my friends, my family, and my school. Another family, too impatient, showed up in force, grabbed their son, and fled out the door, they had gotten so tired of waiting.

There were distractions. The most important came the day I heard that a boy about my age was being admitted, and moreover, he was going to take over my bedroom, the sole single room in the ward. My first reaction was visceral dislike, that this was the guy booting me out of my room, even as sympathetically I saw Arthur Woody Hudson wheeled in, flat on his back on a hospital gurney and wearing a face mask because his TB was that dangerous.

Soon enough, Woody transferred out of his room onto the main floor. He spoke a rougher version of American than I was used to. He said he was from Hunters Point, a community of African-Americans that had emigrated for the jobs at the bustling bayside shipyards during World War II.

But in 1962, Hunters Point was the decaying "Dock of the Bay," the object of lament in Otis Redding's song. Woody fell into a fighting stance at the slightest perception of a verbal slight. Woody said he was tough, the best fighter in his grammar school. At first, I wasn't willing to be his sparring partner, but he persuaded me that I should at least learn to take care of myself. He taught me how to protect myself against a flurry of punches, to dance around and to throw quick, hard punches to the head and especially the eyes. He steeled me to take the pain of a blow, to keep fighting and moving.

Mr. Sullivan asked me to tutor Woody. Bit by bit, I came to impress upon him my less dramatic, but nonetheless equally significant skills. Settling back from his larger-than-life street persona, Woody learned spelling and the rules of grammar, eventually writing not only proper sentences but whole paragraphs. He also got a handle on long division and learned to remember dates of discoveries, wars, and statehood.

It was a small jump from learning school subjects to using his hands more constructively. Together we embarked upon the making of model airplanes, battle ships, and statues of Frankenstein, the Wolf-man, and Dracula. Woody learned to attach a propeller through the head of a Hell-fighter plane with one drop of glue dangling delicately off the point of a pin, allowing the propeller to still spin freely. He deftly painted perfect drools of blood dripping from the Dracula's lower fangs. Soon, Woody was drawing and scripting his own comic books, too.

Woody's mother was delighted. Had my mother known what Woody was teaching me, she wouldn't have been as pleased. Besides self-defense, Woody already had a girlfriend. She wasn't his first girlfriend either, only the latest. He talked about kissing and lying on top of girlfriends. He said that was how people made babies, explaining that girls didn't have penises, but a soft, moist opening between their legs. I had heard something about this from some kids who played at our project playground, Dan DelCarlo and Roland Young, two Italian-Americans. But Woody was not only detailed and graphic, he had done it.

From time to time, a kid freaked out in a raging tantrum, throwing things and striking out at the nurses. It was usually a boy, and George and the nurses would grab him, subdue him, and strap him down to his bed. A few times, Woody lost it, too. Since he could really fight, he was a much more deadly proposition to subdue. Inevitably, it was Mrs. Ross, the day-shift head nurse, who was the bravest during these outbreaks. She rushed in and entangled her arms around Woody's arms so he couldn't pull a punch until he calmed down. Yet ,she was also the nicest, spending time eliciting his underlying feelings after the tantrum. She would do her best to soothe him, letting him know that he wasn't a bad child for the tantrum, that she was still his friend.

Not every head nurse was a Mrs. Ross. Among the many rules in the Ward was the strict separation of girls and boys in the evening. Separated by the centrally placed nurses' station, we were not allowed to enter each other's sections after dinner. One Saturday night, the draconian night head nurse, Mrs. Logan set us up by inviting the boys to watch TV with the girls. Mrs. Logan accompanied the boys to the girls' side, then left only to summon the building's supervising nurse who scolded us, turned off the TV, and ordered us straight to bed.

In shock, we still managed to blurt out the truth, but the supervising nurse stuck by Mrs. Logan. A clearly upset Woody, our spontaneous rebellion, broke out—and to my surprise, I jumped right in as one of the leaders. Both boys and girls refused to budge, like in a sit-in. We sat in the girls' section, arms crossed. We even switched the TV back on. We hooted, and accused Mrs. Logan of lying. The rebellion went until 9 p.m., our normal bedtime, when our energies faded out we voluntarily returned to our beds.

Mrs. Logan treachery burned itself deeply into my mind, for it was the first time I had actually been wronged. Yet, this was also the first time I had stood up against something wrong! That was exhilarating, and to know there was a good nurse, Mrs. Ross, to whom we could and did appeal, was comforting. Like *The Wizard of Oz* with its good witch and wicked witch, we knew we had an ally when the bad head nurses went berserk. She could and did set it straight.

This too turned out to be a rite of initiation of an early kind of manhood, an understanding that standing up for right is more important than compliant survival, than even obsequious material comfort. As kids stuck in a hospital ward in the 1950s, we could have been punished in so many ways. This incident also increased Woody's respect for me for he now knew I wasn't a "chicken" anymore, but would stand up to abusive authority. I enjoyed his newfound regard, but I wasn't sure that without his righteous presence, I wouldn't have "chickened out."

Toward the end of my stay, Woody and I were racing to see who would get well first, yet neither one relished being left behind without the other. My earlier admission was no assurance that I would be released first for test results alone decided that. As it happened, I was the first to get the good news. I would be going home at the end of this, my ninth month.

There were rituals to leaving. The most overt was the doffing of the pajama-like clothing of the ward. Everyone watched the mother dress her child in spanking new dress or pants and shirt, a jacket, and shiny shoes. Woody couldn't even look at me as Mother helped me changed. Although he stayed near the checkout counter, he kept his back to me the whole time, not able to bring himself into the goodbye circle. He was the tough guy, and yet he was pushing away tears with his fists. Eventually, I went over to him. I gave him all my models and all my comic books. I told him we were friends, and that I would write him. Woody and I shook hands, said our final good-byes, and I left.

Woody was released two months later. We talked on the phone, but never visited. Hunter's Point and Chinatown were connected by the #15 Third and Kearney bus line, but while our worlds were not so far apart, they were just too different.

The fighting skills that Woody taught me served me well. I was a straight-A college-bound "goody-goody" who ran for school offices, i.e., prime bully material. But those first few times someone fired on me, I fired back and beat them. Thanks to Woody, that established my rep for I was never bullied in junior high or later in high school. I hoped that Woody's scholastics had equally benefited as much from my influence.

It turned out that Woody had transferred to my junior high school to renew our friendship, but one semester too late. Years later, Ruby Soo from the old neighborhood described an African-American student from Hunters Point who had inexplicably transferred into our Chinatown junior high. He was always singing to himself, moving in a dancing kind of way and wore a hat with a feather on one side. He didn't make any friends and disappeared at the end of the semester.

After grilling Ruby about his description, I knew that Woody had come searching for me, his friend. He knew my junior high school from my earliest letters, but had not figured on my graduating when he transferred. By then, I could not track him down.

Much later, in 1976, when I was clerking at the Employment Law Service of San Francisco, it turned out that our receptionist was from Hunters Point. I mentioned I had a friend from there, an Arthur Hudson, whom I called Woody. Did she know him? She looked at me with a look that shouted out "You can't be for real?" Then, she told me Woody was her older brother. I gave her the same look back, then my home number and a message for Woody. But she was always vague about Woody. Yes, she had given Woody my phone number, that first message, and all my messages. She didn't know why he didn't call. Didn't have his phone number or address either. Didn't know what he'd been up to.

One day she quietly informed me that Woody had been found dead, drowned in the bay. He had apparently been involved in "some foolishness" was all she would say. Later, she mentioned Woody died a heroin junkie. How our lives had diverged. If only he had arrived at Francisco Junior High one semester earlier. I'm sure his mother sent him there in desperation, hoping I could influence him again. Might Woody still be alive today, if I had been there for him? He had come looking for me. I felt loss and guilt for not being there for my friend.

But by then, my own life had taken such an unexpected, tragic turn that it was all I could do to keep it moving, stay alive, and reenact a stand against abusive authority. But this time, on my own.

Chapter 18
Right Feeling

Nom kee—*right feeling*—*we had that from the start. We liked each other*—*enjoyed each other's company. He took care of me. Would I have married him had I met him first? Yes, of course, because we had* nom kee. *Yes, I loved him. But I loved your father, too. Still do. They had different qualities. They were different kinds of men. You know, there were other men who wanted to spend time with me, asking me out to eat, buying me clothes. But I ignored them. You remember Mr. Lai, with the green car, he used to drive us on weekends when we lived on Kearny Street? Well, after a while, he used to ask me out all the time. Just him and me. During the week, when your father was working. Treat me to a meal, go shopping downtown, and so on. I never went with him or any of the others- no* nom kee.

He was introduced as Kai Yep, and Bob was his American name, and that's what we called him. Bob came at the right time. I was still shaky from my nervous breakdown. It was around 1956 or 1957. For a long time, I hadn't been all that well. He treated me to coffee and cake in Chinatown. He helped me with food shopping. Just little friendly things that made me feel good, alive, and fine.

Did your Father know him? Of course he did. That's how I met him—*through your Father. Bob was his business partner in a garage. The garage failed, but they stayed friends. Bob, too, read the newspapers avidly, and so they spent hours yakking away. You know how your father likes to talk about World War II, how Stalin tricked Roosevelt, how Communism wasn't that bad for China, and all that? Bob didn't know as much and would listen to your father for hours. That made your father happy, to have someone like a student. Sometimes, they went to movies together, or fishing at the piers with fishing poles made of bamboo, just like in the village. In time, Bob became part of the family, sleeping over on our couch.*

Bob was a rogue. He didn't like to work a regular job, but he made money. He had spirit, wasn't afraid to go anywhere and talk to anyone about anything. He had his own car then and took me everywhere, places where most Chinese didn't go in those days. Bob didn't dress dull, i.e., Chinatown-style, but was very "sport," wearing cowboy boots, bolo ties, and dark sunglasses. And he was big for a Chinese. Broad chested with strong arms, strolling with his head and chest forward, like a bull, and afraid of no one. People respected him on the streets without knowing why. Even white people would make room for him. In those days, Chinese had to make way for white pedestrians coming their way, but not Bob. He stood up to rude people, including white people. He wasn't a troublemaker and he didn't look for trouble. But he got a lot of respect.

Bob did do some work for the tongs, those so-called Chinatown businessmen associations. Some of them are hok seah woy—*underworld, you know. But Bob did little tasks. Drive around the big shots. Watch a gambling house door in case of robbers. Pick up an order from the restaurant for the bosses. That kind of thing. Oh, there's some stuff he wouldn't tell me about, because sometimes, he had "business..." then disappeared for a few days. He told me he used to drive down to Los Angeles* to pick up a car-trunk load of marijuana from Mexicans. But that was a long time ago, he claimed, in the early 1950s, before we met him.

No, he was not really a gangster, but a runner. He never hurt people. He hated violence, because Bob's own father was a very violent man. One time in China, his father smashed a chair over the head of Bob's younger brother. That brother was injured for life, spending many years in a mental institution. Bob was so afraid of his father that he learned how to please him, to calm him down so he would never have his own head broken in like his poor brother. And he escaped from home as soon as possible, through an arranged marriage while a young teenager.

His family had money. Oh, his grandfather was some kind of big shot with offices in Beijing, Hoisin, Guangzhou, and Hong Kong. But the Communists executed him. He had treated the common people badly and the Communists did that—executed a lot of brutal, rich people. Some of the family's money left China with Bob's father. His father had that liquor store on Stockton Street near Broadway, around the corner from the housing project. You know, where the 30 Stockton bus used to stop on the way down to Market Street. Bob helped out once in a while, too. He always had some money. Enough to enjoy life.

He was very different from your father. Bob didn't work eight hours every day and come home tired, unlike your father. Bob didn't mind spending money for treats, unlike your father, who would always make silly excuses never to eat out. "The MSG isn't good for you. You cook better than the restaurants," your father would say. Bob lived like a free man. He spent money on me. Drove me to Golden Gate Park, to the ocean, or to visit friends.

And Reno, oh yes Reno. For a few years, we went to Reno a lot, to gamble the night away. Reno was magic. I could forget about everything—housework, your father's temper, worrying about my sons, trying to get my mother and brother to America. In the 1960s, it was cheap. The buses cost only $6.00 and gave you back the fare in chips plus tickets for a buffet dinner and breakfast. We saw the shows—happy singing, fancy dancing, and pretty lights. Stayed up two or three days without sleeping, spent $20 or $40 at most. Win or lose—didn't matter. Sometimes even your father joined us. Then one year, I lost a lot of money. I was hurting the family. So one day, I stopped. I just stopped and never went back.

You know your father had a mean side, from when you were little kids. Very mean. He got angry about little things, usually money. "Neah-neah-neah" as he muttered about this and that spending. "Jah-jah-jah" this and "jah-jah-jah" that as he shouted at me. He even beat me. That's another reason why Bob and I got closer. Bob wasn't like that. He treated me like a lady. Remember, Bob hated his own father's temper.

One day, I just got fed up with your father's temper. I didn't want to be hit anymore. We were on Kearney Street then. Bob was in the room that night when your father started in. You know how he gets. Hunching forward. Index finger jabbing. His face reddening as he talks talked faster and *louder. He threatened to hit me and rolled his fingers into a fist. He's so strong from his work that he could really hurt me.*

So that night, I took a risk. I told him to shut up, that I was tired of his complaints and his "neah-neah-neah this" and "jah-jah-jah that." I called him all kinds of the worst Toisan names—"leen how (demented), fook (brainless)," and so on. He called me the most horrible Toisanese names you could call a female, mostly the kind you say about women's sex, so I won't repeat them. This was really the angriest argument between us. I picked up a chair, and held it over my head, ready to hit him. I knew he would get angrier, for I had spent weeks thinking this through. Now everything was going along exactly as I had planned, and I was counting on Bob to step in and stop it, before it got out of control.

That's exactly what Bob did. As your father lunged toward me, Bob stood between us. He placed a palm against your Father's chest and the other in my direction, separating us. He urged us to calm down. Please stop arguing, the children are sleeping, they have school tomorrow, and the neighbors will hear. Do you want the police to come and take you to jail? He said many things like that in his calm, soothing, reasonable voice, the same voice he must have used to calm his own violent father. Well, eventually your father did calm down, and when I knew his rage had passed, I put down my chair. After that, your father never hit me again, or ever raised his fist again.

Well, he stopped hitting me, but he never stopped picking on every little thing. Still "neah-neah-neah" and "jah-jah-jah" all the time. When you and Richard were in junior high school, he started in on you and Richard every night. Sometimes, he punished you two by locking you up in the clothes closet for ten or fifteen minutes. Really for nothing. But he didn't hit you. Eventually you two went to friends' houses and the library, just so you could study, returning only in time for bed.

It got so bad, you even told me to divorce him. Do you remember what I said? "Don't ever speak to me of divorce. We are Toisanese. We do not divorce." Had I divorced your father, it would have destroyed him.

You know your father worked very hard for the little money we had. His bosses didn't always treat him fairly either, you know. And the one time he injured his shoulder at work, the one time he needed the union's help, they took their time and didn't process his claim for many, many months. Never sick a day, worked on his days off, and he never went away on vacation, preferring to work for overtime pay when he could. Your father's only entertainment was movies, newspapers, and cigarettes. He didn't complain about any of that.

That's why over the years, when he picked on me at home about this and that little thing, I just ignored him. It's just the sounds he makes, like frogs croaking. I pretend I'm listening, but I'm not. He "jah-jah-jahs," and I answer "yeah, yeah, yeah!" and go about my business.

Did your father and I make a good match? We've been married for fifty years now. We know how to live together, and we will live together until the day we pass over. We were first and we had it the toughest, that's all. But if hadn't been there, though, I think maybe I might have gone crazy. But he made life good for me.

You know, Bob really loved you and Richard. He watched out for you two on the streets in case anyone was picking on you. He bought you snacks and toys. When your youngest brother, John was born in 1965, Bob was as much a father to John as your own father. John was sick a lot as a baby, and Bob watched over him all the time, like he would with his own child. He took him to doctors and ran out any time of the day and night to get his medicine. He stayed over on the sofa if John had a fever, getting up to check on him. He would baby-sit when I went out with my Clan Sisters. When John grew older, he drove John and me everywhere. He treated John to everything kids like.

Do you remember how I took care of my brother's children when his wife left him? She left with a gambler, said she had made a mistake marrying too young and never had any real fun. My brother told her that if she left, she could never return, that she had to give up the children. She agreed, and so Ada, Victor, and David, all under ten years old and about John's age, stayed with us. Well, Bob took care of them too, just like he did John. Those were good days. The streets were still safe. We walked to Fishermen's Wharf to watch the guitar players and the jugglers. John really liked the Man in a Juke Box. You put in a quarter on a hand that stuck out of this colorful box, the size of a phone booth. The man inside made some warm-up sounds, asked your name, and then joked and sang silly songs about your name. There were summer art and music fairs in Washington Square, and carousels and Ferris wheels at Portsmouth Square during Chinese New Year's. We drove to the zoo, the beach, Golden Gate Park, and to drive-in movies. In summer, when it was warm and still light, say around 9 p.m., Bob walked us down to Clown Alley on Jackson and Columbus Street for hamburgers and French-fries. What a treat that was!

Yes, over the years, Bob was very much part of our family. Sometimes, he lived with us. Other times, he had a hotel room. That's how it was for over thirty years. He was your father's friend. He was a second father to all my kids, and he was my boyfriend, a constant companion until he passed over in the early 1990s. There has never been another one.

SECTION III INITIATIONS (1964-—1972)

Chapter 18 Speaking in Tongues

Our new twelve-story, a half-a-city-block housing project became a vertical Chinese village. Just as new car owners are time-and-again uplifted by their new car smell, we were enraptured by our new "no-smell" apartment, for Chinatown was redolent with the century-old odors of too many peoples, restaurants, and food stores sharing tiny quarters in sunless buildings. North Ping Yuen (Peaceful Gardens) was subsidized housing with million-dollar views. How delightfully miraculous for a third of the apartments, including ours, looked out onto vistas of the Bay and the East Bay hills. The remainder faced south, sunny all afternoon long. But best of all, each family had its very own kitchen and private bathroom, rare for Chinatown. "First class," as Mother put it, and we woke up every morning smiling for few months on end in our new home.

We washed our clothes in a rooftop coin Laundromat and hang-dried them on adjacent rows of shiny, metal cables. Culturally sensitive wash-and-dry as while Chinatown mothers smiled at the convenience of machines washing, yet they loved the fragrance of sun-dried laundry.

On the multi-level playground and courtyards, little kids gleefully shimmied up monkey bars then jumped from ring to clanking ring, seniors danced tai chi in the sun, and housewives watered bok choy in their private garden patches. Teen-agers played endless hide-and-seek, using all twelve floors, running hunchback along the balcony ramparts, our presence given away only by the slapping rhythm of tennis shoes and muffled titters. All summer and way into the evenings, rival teams thwacked endless baseballs, stopping only when our mothers, craning over sky-high balconies, called away too many players to dinner. In embarrassingly but loud Toisanese, of course. For recalcitrant ones, mothers shamelessly hollered our rarely used Chinese names as a call to dinner. Sometimes it took resorting to the threat of a spanking with the ubiquitous chicken-feather duster, visibly shaking them from on high.

But underneath this calm surface, our parents' widening personal differences strained me severely. These were not the first cracks in our family life. Mother had suffered a nervous breakdown when we were children. Although he stopped his sporadic beating of her, Father's abuse switched to emotional pummeling, putting her down for spending a dollar or two more here-and-there, and asserting that but for him, she and the children would be out on the streets, tirades we could not and did not miss hearing. He never praised her for our always neat-as-a-pin home, delicious, nutritious four-and-five course meals night-after-night, or the special chi soups that took so many hours to prepare.

Somehow, my parents had wrought a tolerable solution in their love triangle with Bob, as Mother's consort, as Dad's best friend. My parents' differences festered battles did not end, but Bob's presence extended the peaceful intervals that probably saved us all from deeper emotional damage and neurosis. My father managed to bite his hurtful tongue during our study times, at least through junior high school. Thus, he kept his commitment to his sons' goals: college by scholarship. Gratefully, I buried myself in book until bedtime: endless study equaled endless quiet.

Then at other times I couldn't stand their triangle. Yes, I grew increasingly distressed at the continuing presence of Bob, an arrangement that disturbingly did not fit the nuclear family pattern. At times, I lashed out at Mother: "Tell Bob to leave. I just want normal parents." I wanted my family to be perfectly nuclear, like the Nelsons in *The Adventures of Ozzie and Harriet* and the Cleavers in *Leave It to Beaver.*

"Make Bob leave. He doesn't belong here."

But Mother could not respond, as she had in my Ward 75 days, as she had in so many ways for so many years. For in those psyche-shocking years, still recovering from her war-time years, managing both a raging husband and a complex triangle, she fought for her very psychic survival. She sucked up every ounce of her spiritual reserves, energy that use to flow to us, to keep her own spirit alive. Our abiding spiritual connection to her and that mysterious Toisan source of power was pinched, then ruptured.

Unconsciously, in my thirteenth year and Richard's eleventh, we began searching elsewhere for this implicate nutrient.

In the 1950s and early 1960s, you couldn't walk through Chinatown without tripping over a China missionary, specialists in saving the souls of heathen Chinese. Expelled en masse by the Communist government in the 1950s, many relocated to America's Chinatowns. By my eleventh summer, an indulgent Richard and I had been saved so many times by so many zealous ministers of so many denominations that we could have sold time-shares in heaven.

We found ourselves momentarily adherents of an Assemblies of God mission.

Hands raised in the air, eyes aimed at the white-painted ceiling of our basement chapel at the Assemblies of God Chinatown mission, I beseeched the Holy Spirit to descend upon me. Donald, Ruby, and Carol of the Soo family were already speaking in tongues. Soon Warren from the sewing factory and then Paula from the Lee family restaurant were mumbling "lubba-lubba-dek-dek-dek" with their tongues. I could pick out Richard's voice as he joined this eardrum-hammering cacophony. Reverend Mrs. Baird placed both of her hands on my head, then my own tongue exploded, uncontrollably darting into unused corners of my mouth, shoving out whatever sounds it made. I fell to my knees, entering the timelessness of a blessed grace. After trying so long and hard, the Holy Spirit had finally entered my body.

Perhaps others within the urban village of Chinatown might have filled in when my parents could not. For younger kids, the women of North Peaceful Gardens became a nurturing an amalgamated Clan Sisterhood, transferring the old village ways of community life to watching over this vertical, concrete village.

But my journey was further complicated because I had started to disconnect from Chinatown. For me, public school's relentless assimilation policy had succeeded too well. I had become a living conundrum, "Chinese-American," one who wouldn't and couldn't be Chinese and, by the hyphenation, was at best a qualified American. My first personal act of Americanization was to wrangle my way free of Chinese school. I considered myself as American as my white teachers and as all the white suited-up professionals who streamed past my home to San Francisco's Financial District every day, and to whose ranks I aspired. Physiognomic features to the contrary be damned. I limited Toisanese dealings to my mother and Chinatown merchants, and competed in public speaking contests, honing my American enunciation to a fault.

There was a brutality to this choice— Americanization is not itself a damaging choice, but the mid-twentieth-century brand of assimilation was also about rupture: the repression of one's ancestral history, culture, and first language, an ongoing act of dismemberment. It was this that damaged our psyches. Assimilation brought with it shame at our racial origins, our culture, our parents' ethnic ways, history and, finally, of our community. We were not white, like "real" Americans. Yet, as a youth, I could not put my finger on this unrelenting pressure to my spirit. I drugged the pain of this psychic tug-of-war in the daily workaholic mastery of school subject. Now I emotionally released it within the new drug of the bliss of the Holy Spirit.

With our new "family," Richard and I made the rounds of Assemblies of God youth camps, country churches, skid-row soup kitchens, and nearby Bethany Bible College revivals. My spirit now freshly stuffed, nascent talents blossomed, and soon I organized the Friday youth night services, preaching in our whitewashed basement chapel, reciting from memory long passages from the King James Bible, and finishing the night by laying on hands, imbuing others with Holy Spirit energy. Before long, the Bairds turned me loose on the Assemblies of God Northern California circuit, as a pulpit pounding teen-preacher sensation. Here, I honed my leadership skills even further, confidently sermonizing to white audiences in suburbs and farm communities, and learning how to schmooze after services, as we raised money for the mission.

Embracing a Christian life relieved me of the burden of making sense of it all. Born again, I became "right" in the eyes of God, blessed while alive and called to perfect heaven at the end-time. The palpable descent of invisible energy into my hands or through the crown of my head confirmed the truth of the gospel, the actuality of God's trinity of Father, Son, and Holy Ghost, and thus the unquestionable authority of the Assemblies of God in all my affairs.

In the mid-sixties, my life outside of school was this mission church. I organized the Friday youth night services, preaching in our whitewashed basement chapel, reciting long passages from the King James Bible committed to memory, and finished by laying hands on people, imbuing them with Holy Spirit energy. Before long, the Bairds turned me loose on the Assemblies of God Northern California circuit, a pulpit pounding teen-preacher sensation. Here, I honed my leadership skills even further, strengthened my public-speaking confidence addressing audiences, white audiences, in suburbs and farm communities, and learning how to schmooze after services, as we raised money for the mission.

Richard too became an enthusiastic convert but embarrassment followed Richard here. Preaching for the first time at the Friday night youth service, in his enthusiasm for the gospel he came off more like a tongue-tied teenager with a bad crush than the silver-tongued evangelist we each aspired to be. A few in the audience started to snicker and, towards the end, many erupted into outright laughter. Richard remained silent, even sullen, the rest of the evening. I knew what had happened: he felt betrayed, for implicit in youth night, the denomination's version of amateur hour, was the promise of nurture and the gentlest correction. As close as we were, I was sure I was his inspiration, his role model. I was as hurt by this betrayal as deeply as he was. He finally sat down, hunched over, sadness across his face. Richard was my only brother, the closest human being in my life, and I hadn't protected him this time, on my turf, my Friday night youth service. I was too young to know how to stop it when the ridicule gathered force, but the Bairds should have set the catcalling straight, and hadn't. We walked home together as always, but from that night on, I returned alone.

It wasn't long before I followed Richard out of the church. Over time, the mission's elitist, exclusionary religious and social doctrine became evident to me. Initially, we were indoctrinated to believe that everyone else had got it wrong, that only a few Pentecostal Christian churches knew the truth. The Assemblies of God would be among the 144,000 saved souls to ascend to heaven at the Second Coming of Christ, as foretold by the Book of Revelations. Since the denomination numbered 500,000 members nationally, the math was a little tight. But that was okay with me, for I was sure I was on Christ's A List, an ascension kid who would make heaven at first call, missing the seven years of trials and tribulation prophesied in the Book of Revelations.

But it was the social gospel of Brother Fife, a visiting minister, who stepped in when Mrs. Baird took a leave of absence due to poor health. One day, the visiting Reverend Fife preached that the Bible mandated the separation of races. "The Book of Ruth says so...right here!" he snarled when I questioned him, his fingers jabbing at his authority. This teaching contradicted every aspect of daily life evident in our multi-ethnic neighborhood. It ran against the ways of our parents, who accepted everyone. Disturbed, I carefully reminded Brother Fife of the words of one of our favorite old-time gospel songs: "Jesus loves the little children, all the children in the land—red and yellow, black and white, they are all precious in his sight."

Brother Fife's eyes enlarged, his nostrils flared back simultaneously and then he barked at me. He insisted I was wrong, wrong, wrong and in a tone of maniacal authority cited several more verses from the Book of Ruth. The absence of the grace of the Holy Spirit in this last teaching broke the spell of the mission.

Shortly thereafter, Richard quietly left the mission. I followed when Brother Fife commandeered my pulpit one Friday night, when I questioned the church's infallibility in all things. Yes, I had grown from the Ward 75 Saturday-night kids rebellion. This night, I stood up alone for the first time in my life.

Assemblies of God ministers were never challenged, and so I had kept quiet counsel with my growing doubts, sharing them only with a few close friends. Someone must have passed them on to Brother Fife, for he began to monitor me. One Friday night, my team enacted a play called "The Man in Black," a French existentialist drama in which a man dressed completely in black conceals himself behind his mountain of possessions. The play ends with the chapel descending into total darkness. I knew the play's theatrics were disturbingly modern for the Assemblies of God, but the moral fitted in—material wealth shuts out the saving light of Christ, leaving us in Satan's darkness.

Underneath the surface, Reverend Fife and I had been on a collision course. But I was so impossibly entwined with the church that I could not release myself despite my revulsion at stone-hearted political and social teachings that violated the teachings of Gospels. In my choice of drama, I was throwing down a gauntlet against the church's social doctrine, and, by extension, to the new minister, Brother Fife. Perhaps he too was seeking an opportunity to establish the authority of his own tenure.

When the lights came back on, Brother Fife commandeered the pulpit from me, announcing that Satan had seized possession of my soul. He shouted that another Man in Black, the devil himself, was present in our church, that I was Satan's tool, and then swiftly moved the assembled into the mob mentality of group prayer, calling upon the same Holy Spirit to come down and save my soul.

Brother Fife had literally demonized me.

As well-indoctrinated Assemblies of God members, my friends knew what they had to do in the presence of Satan, which was to freak out and pray frenetically for their souls. It surely wasn't to stand up for me. Imagine my shock as thirty-five of my closest friends, including my dearest childhood friends, shunned me as evil incarnate. No one would look at me as I stood in the side aisle, pleading that I was the same William they had known for years. Instead, in a kind of Pavlovian reaction, their faces stayed focused on Brother Fife, praying louder and louder, hands fluttering to the ceiling as they gave themselves over to a collective roar that blew away reason and ripped apart a decade-old friendships with hurricane force.

Wounded in spirit, unable to move, yet somehow I dragged myself, leg by heavy leg, up the stairs. Like the songs of Ulysses' sirens, the familiar, comforting strains of speaking in tongues almost pulled me back into the mission and plea for redemption. But, as I slowly drew the front door shut, their chorus faded to a powerless hum. I am not sure of the source that powered me to walk out of that cultist basement cave. It was definitely from another channel than their Holy Spirit, perhaps the energy that surged through me years later, from the native soil of Toisan.

I had grown from the Ward 75 Saturday night kids rebellion, when it was Woody's character and leadership that help me stand against the night nurse's shenanigans. This night, I stood up on my own, by myself, and although traumatized, I left intact in body, mind and soul.

On my measured walk home, pain alternated with exhilaration, for as something old died, I felt something new birthing. I never went back, despite anguished personal pleas and special prayer meetings called by the congregants on my soul's behalf. For although I at first felt lost without this community and bereft at the chilling break of childhood friendships, I had already discovered the rich cultural and political milieu of North Beach.

In my Odyssey, other tongues, intelligible voices, had been speaking to me and I was listening. Those voices included the Committee Theater Improvisation Troupe, City Lights Bookstore, the San Francisco psychedelic counterculture, the anti-Vietnam War movement, the counterculture, and most importantly, as it would turn out, Martin Luther King's Southern Civil Rights movement.

No doubt, part of my nomadic search was part of any young man's "checking it out." But it was more desperate than that, for I was searching for an "answer," a new "tribe" or "village," the proverbial balm of Gilead.

I was fifteen when a few friends and I first wandered into the Committee Theater's black-painted lobby, mesmerized by enlarged reproductions of Jules Feiffer-like editorial-page cartoons hanging like banners from the high ceiling. There she was, the slender, leotard-clad dancer pirouetting in her ode to spring. And more shockingly, a towel-draped Uncle Sam and Nikita Khrushchev of the Soviet Union awaiting their turn to ravish the globe, a Mercator map etched on the behind of a barely clad and curvaceous female posterior. There they stood in the background facing each other: a skinny Uncle Sam in star-spangled top hat and stringy beard, undressed except for an American-flag towel wrapped around his torso, and Nikita Khrushchev, then the premier of the Soviet Union, with his trademark paunch, holding tightly the corners of a hammer-&-sickle-flag towel wrapped around his waist. The conversational caption read "First your turn, then mine," unmasking the Cold War as a convenient partnership "fucking over the world." I got the message: capitalist or communist, the weaker nations and peoples suffered in the Great Game.

One of the staff, openly surprised and pleased at the sight of Chinatown teens, invited us in *gratis*. After that first night, I simply couldn't stay away, and over time, became a fixture, sitting in back, off to the side on the high stools where the cocktail waitresses rested during skits. Relying on suggestions from audience members for their spontaneous skits, the troupe tackled the hot issues of the mid and late 1960s and became my private seminar on race relations, sexual freedom, drugs, religious hypocrisy, and the Vietnam War. In time, I enrolled in their student troupe, the Wing, and unexpectedly became a member of a family of kindred spirits who guided me in my curiosity, commiserated with my occasional confusion, and laughed heartily at my pithy improvs.

Mother encouraged my theater participation; perhaps she was pleased that Richard and I had finally left a church that wanted to control our every waking moment--a criticism voiced with increasingly frequency--but more likely because she trusted our instincts to ultimately select the right people and experiences from our rich neighborhood smorgasbord.

Soon, I expanded this first theater experience and my worldly vistas through volunteer ushering at the American Conservatory Theater, a delightful immersion which introduced me to the plays of Eugene O'Neil, Arthur Miller, Ibsen, Shakespeare, and other playwrights of the Western cultural pantheon. Mother cooked dinner a little earlier on ushering nights, and earlier dinner nights grew in frequency as I adding ushering ed at pop concerts, forgetting myself in the harmonies and the thought-provoking lyrics of Peter, Paul and Mary, Simon and Garfunkel, Joan Baez, and Joni Mitchell. I floated away on the lush cascades of sitarist Ravi Shankar, flautist Jean Pierre-Rampal, and classical guitarist Andres Segovia.

When I wasn't at the Committee, I was a half-a-block away, at City Lights Books, the book-stuffed narrow townhouse of a store, historic home of the Beat poets, a center of contemporary writers and depository of obscure poetry journals and Old Left periodicals. City Lights became my new library, offering writings, an intellectual atmosphere, and a cool, bohemian attitude that the Chinatown branch of the public library could not.

The clerks, often lost in their own reading, didn't mind that people spent hours without buying a single book. I did buy books from City Lights, books not part of the high school curriculum and suggested to me by an English teacher, Robert Winkley, including a collection of short stories by Ernest Hemingway and *Brighton Rock* by Graham Greene, books by two authors who had roamed and experienced the world. Had Mr. Winkley detected a certain restlessness for knowledge and, possibly, travel in my daily journal assignments?

But these books seemed detached and cold to me. What captured my imagination were the books on black America—and City Lights had them all. Alex Haley and Malcolm X's *The Autobiography of Malcolm X*, Ralph Ellison's *The Invisible Man*, Claude Brown's *Manchild in the Promised Land*, and Richard Wright's *Native Son* all fascinated and horrified me with the bleakness and terror of life in urban black America. Stunned me, and I felt a call to action—for America wasn't supposed to be like this.

Yet, because only a few black families lived in our neighborhood, America's black-and-white race problem had been a distant one for me. But the daily news of Martin Luther King, Jr. and the courageous Southern Civil Rights struggle beckoned me. I had cherished Christ's own idealism, a lover of all humanity, a non-violent rebel, someone who did not quote the book of Ruth to justify racism, and a rebel. The Civil Rights movement suggested that I could join something, go somewhere real and do something good. But in 1967, there were few black Americans in Chinatown-North Beach, the movement was in the South and there wasn't a recruiting station, in North Beach, certainly not for a fifteen-year-old kid like me.

Anti-Vietnam War activities, on the other hand, abounded. I often woke up on Saturdays to the chants of marchers in the distance. I passed a churches where draft resisters chained themselves to the front gates as scores of supporters stayed with them in vigil, guitars "twangin' and singers "sangin" in the warm glow of solidarity and lit candles. At City Lights, star spangled banner–peace symbol pins were sold next to buttons urging "Tune in, turn on, drop out."

But anti-war protests did not immediately speak to me. My mother had fled Communist China: the Commies were the bad guys. Besides, I couldn't imagine that our nation would ever send us into an unjust war, nor one America could not win.

Father did not agree with my naïve views. Having volunteered for World War II, he recognized that Vietnam was not a just war. Father pointed out that America had broken its promise to the Vietnamese people of democratic, national elections. It had become clear that Ho Chi Minh, the popular freedom fighter and a communist, would win hands-down. He highlighted articles and editorials from *Newsweek* that disagreed with the official policy in Vietnam. But at fifteen, I didn't the war didn't seem to be a real part of my life. I stayed focused on my studies, perfecting my Motown moves, getting to "first base" with girls, and running for school office.

I was more drawn to a third movement of the hippie counter-culture, marked by multicolored psychedelic announcements for human be-ins, free psychedelic concerts in Golden Gate Park, and weekend triple bills at the Avalon Ballroom, the Fillmore Auditorium, and Winterland. The bands were outrageously named—Grateful Dead, Jefferson Airplane, Sly and the Family Stone, Janis Joplin's Big Brother and the Holding Company, Quicksilver Messenger Service, Big Mama Willy Mae Thornton, Moby Grape, and It's a Beautiful Day. Everyone was welcomed and a "light show" was promised at every show. Every week, I picked up a new psychedelic playbill from City Lights and slowly wallpapered my bedroom into a psychedelic mural.

One day the Gallyot Brothers, Richard and Raoul, my schoolmates and offspring of North Beach Beatniks, invited me to my first psychedelic happening. Jimi Hendrix, John Mayall's Blues Band, and Albert King shared the Winterland billing. In the cavernous stadium interior of the old Winterland ice rink, the three hundred or so concertgoers who would have created a tightly intimate crowd in a nightclub were scattered, dancing freely throughout the arena, "grooving" on one another, wandering about freely, often with their backs to the bands and the massive light show. The band stage was simple, built on the same kind of amateur, rickety risers of found at school gym dances, barely two feet above the ground.

Nothing had prepared me for any of this and especially not for Jimi Hendrix, three feet away, eyeball-to-eyeball. Freak, I thought. He's faking it, he can't play, I thought. But I stood directly in front of Jimi, mesmerized as he sang "Foxy Lady" and then "Purple Haze." When Jimi paused in the middle of "Purple Haze," he crooned that soon-to-be-world-famous signature line, "Excuse me while I kiss the sky. " And then he did as he pursed his lips upwards to the ceiling and kissed the air.

I was close enough to kiss his magic guitar and almost did. Jimi challenged everything about me, and yet he seemed to be whispering to me alone, "Young brother, check it out...check it all out."

I did check it out, at the Summer Solstice Festival of 1968. That sunny day, an inner voice whimsically whispered "Go to the Haight-Ashbury. TODAY!" Upon hopping off the #7 Haight Street bus, I discovered everyone was streaming down Haight Street into the park for a Summer Solstice festival, a "Human Be-in" gathering at the Polo Fields with free music and free food. Someone said they were celebrating the Summer Solstice, the longest day light of the year.

A documentary film crew picnicking on a lawn invited me to join them. David was quintessentially hippie, a longhaired and bearded blonde, wearing tattered jeans and a tie-dyed T-shirt. His girlfriend, Diane, more smartly coifed with her Dutch-boy haircut framing her patrician face, wore a clean white blouse and tight tan pants that slid into a pair of perfectly shined riding boots. They nonchalantly lit up a marijuana cigarette. Then David started to dance without warning or inhibition, as Diane sat nonplused, pulling on the joint. I asked Diane, obviously from a well-off family, why she had become a hippie. I thought that becoming a hippie was a kind of a religious conversion experience, like becoming a Christian or a Hare Krishna devotee. "There's no real love in my family," she replied, without drama. She and David were tired of materialism, tired of the phoniness and expectations they had found in their well-off Chicago families and their high-priced university education. So they had just dropped out to just "be."

The stadium-size Polo Field was awashed in a sea of humanity. I quickly lost my new friends but made others. Wandering about more observer than participant, I felt a heightened state of awareness, suffused with feelings of happiness, peace, curiosity, and excitement. This was how we should all live, in mutual love and respect, sharing and looking each other in the eyes always. This was certainly the way my mother lived— generous and accepting of others. Despite my father's vocal miserliness, he, too, often surprised us by his giving acts, his spontaneous kindnesses, and his unrelenting commitment to housing, feeding, clothing, and educating his family.

In the late afternoon, the stage announced that a group called the Diggers was serving free food outside the Polo Fields. Hungry, I wandered off in search of these Diggers. The Diggers were grilling chicken over an open fire pit. Potato salad, bread, cheese, and pies were spread out on a side table, free for the taking. Nearby was a rack of shirts, coats, pants and dresses, also free. Everything was free, as much as you wanted, no questions asked, and no one looked to see if you were taking too much. No one cared. A bearded guy was sizzling chicken on the huge, ground level grill. He asked for volunteers and soon I too was stoking the flames, grilling, and serving. There was only this one Digger and people like me popping up and helping. Like Jesus at his Sermon on the Mount, we were inspired to feed all hungry and clothe the partially naked as the late afternoon ocean breezes started to move in.

As in Mother's Toisan village, we pitched in to take care of one another.

The crowds started to stream down to the beach, to ritually watch the sunset together on this longest day of the year. Knowing how chillingly damp San Francisco could get at dusk, I reluctantly caught the bus home. But the day left me warm inside. Exalted, my world had been rocked to the core. In spirit, these hippies reminded me of the motley, peaceful multitudes who had gathered spontaneously around Jesus, listening to their era's gospel, for we too were tuning into the good news of our time, a zeitgeist of personal and social liberation. This was the part of Christianity I still treasured, Jesus' actual uninterpreted life. This was the harmony that had dropped out of my own family's household, cast off from Toisan, adrift in America. In some indescribable way, I knew that what I was missing could be found within this tribe even though I wasn't quite sure just exactly who they were. My spirit vibrated, my heart exuded gratitude, and a contented fatigue settled in my bones.

Chapter 19
The Chinese Six Companies

I didn't have much to do with the Chinese Six Companies, the "city hall" of Chinatown. They didn't have speaking round-and-rounds, nor women in the leadership. I didn't even know much about their them when I first arrived except what I picked up from my Clan Sisters. In the 1850s, when Chinese first came to San Francisco, there was no Six Companies, but six separate ones. Each company represented their own clan, and each clan came from one of six districts of origin in the Pearl River Delta, where all the old-timer Chinese came from. That's why a company is sometimes called a "district association."

The first thing newly arrived immigrant did was to registered with their own district association. The association fed them, got them housing and jobs, and kept letters from home for those working far away from Chinatown. We Toisanese belong to the Say Yup District Association because the Toisanese dialect is also referred to as the Say Yup dialect. Cantonese belonged to the Sam Yup District Association, because their dialect is also known as the Sam Yup dialect. Each district association built its own headquarters, those three story buildings with red balcony pillars wrapped in dragons and with large gold-leaf Chinese characters carved into dark marble walls. They bought large cemeteries, just south of San Francisco, a long time ago, when many Chinese could not make enough money to go home. Father has already paid for our burial plots, so you make sure we rest there. Later, when the white people turned on the Chinese, the six district associations combined into one group for greater influence. Their official name was the Chinese Consolidated Benevolent Associations, but every one calls them the Six Companies.

Then every Chinese belongs to a family association, known by their family name, like Lee Family Association, Wong Family Association, Chan Family Association, Fong Family Association, and so on. As long as the family name was the same, we were considered relatives no matter which district you came from. We went more to the family association events because they take care of families.

Summer picnics out of town. Easter and Christmas parties for toys and candy. They lent us money when American banks wouldn't or charged higher interest rates. That's how we bought our first television and washing machine—with loans from the Lee Family Credit Union, then the largest credit union in the United States.

And they sponsored banquets every Chinese New Year. We always ate at the three biggest Chinese New Year's banquets—I was a Chun by birth, but also Lee and Wong since my sisters and I married into those families. The tickets were so cheap, almost free, for a fancy ten-course banquet on plates so large that everyone took home leftovers. My sisters and I took turns taking the Johnny Walker Red bottle home. With so many banquets, our husbands always got a bottle and then spent a whole year finishing it. We saw all our relatives from the old village at those banquets, especially those who had moved out of Chinatown. Everyone came back to Chinatown then, to show off their babies, brag about their kids in college, tell who got married to whom, shake their gold watches and jade bracelets to show how they're doing well, and just catch up on everything. Some years, the banquets were so huge, we took up three floors of the largest restaurants, even closing the downstairs to tourists.

That's about the only time I ever saw anyone from the Six Companies - in front of the banquet hall, making speeches and smiling for Chinese newspapers. They loved being in the newspapers.

Then there were the business groups known as the tongs. Restaurant owners, food markets, souvenir shops, import-exporters and professionals belong to the tongs. Everyone knew some of the tongs were hok seh wui, *dark side organizations— "shadow people" who operated gangster businesses like prostitution, gambling, and smuggling. Our village didn't have "shadow people." They're Big City kind of people, and best to stay away from them. Bob worked for them when he was a young man. He told me a few things, but I'm not going to talk about it. I was glad when he quit.*

You know I used to play poker, and I got to be a pretty good judge of character. If I could have played a few games with those Six Companies men, maybe the tong bosses, I could have figured out what kind of people they were.

Oh, yes, I learned poker at that hotel on Montgomery Street we lived in when you were first born. At first, it was just a way to pass the time, but I got good, and started to win a few bucks every game. By the time we moved to Ping Yuen, I was really good. There were several games in the neighborhood, mostly women players although a few men were regulars. I was in demand to play, because of my fast shuffling and dealing of the cards. I was always called in especially if out-of-towners from Sacramento, were in for a fun weekend in Chinatown. Those ladies always brought a lot of money and they wanted to go up against Chinatown's best. I was happy to give them a few card tips and a good time... and win their money.

By the time you entered high school, I was winning thirty dollars to fifty dollars a night, several times a week, for a few hours of play. Now that might not sound like a lot of money nowadays, but in the 1960s, that was good money. Steak was only twenty-five cents a pound, rice was twenty dollars for a fifty-pound bag, a 100 percent virgin wool sweater cost fifteen dollars at Macy's, and a brand new bicycle was only thirty dollars. I was earning more than a Chinatown restaurant waiter working twelve-hour days. I was making as much money as your father on many a day. Anyway, I didn't end up saving any of it. Spent it on treats, clothes, books, and toys for you and your brother, and sending money to my family in Hong Kong.

I'm a conservative gambler. If I have a strong hand, I push it. If not, I lay it down right away. Too much bluffing is dangerous, and that's how I win, because a lot of people think they're smart enough to bluff their way through the night. But if you watch people carefully, you see through them. Be patient, watch for the clues. It's just the littlest things that will signal if they're relaxed, content, and confident. Other times I can feel the stress of a bluff. Or if someone is betting aggressively, I'll follow, matching their bets twice, usually, until I get the signs. Then I either drop out if the signs are they've got the cards, or I bet aggressively until they drop their hand. I always ask to see their cards either way.

Also, you learn to spot strategies because people use them over and over. For example, some players come on too strong to be telling the truth. They'll announce like a complete surprise, "Oh, what a good hand!" I watch for the signs. Do they have one pair or two? Another common strategy is to place piles of money in front of you at the start of the game, and bet so high that the other players drop out. Watch for the signs. If I had the cards and, after a couple of bets, was sure they were bluffing, I'd call them. This kind of strategy—intimidation by a show of money—usually works only two out of eight hands. You can beat this kind of high roller on the other six hands, and soon enough, their piles of money disappear, and they leave the game.

Poker helped me to read people in life. That's why, although I never learned to speak a lot of American, I have no trouble going anywhere. I can read people and find the ones who will be kind to you, who will help you. If I judged wrong, I know how to drop and move on. That's why I made good husband-matches for my two sisters, and when I get husband requests from Toisan, *I always find good ones.*

Yes, maybe if I had been able to play poker with the Six Companies' elders and tong bosses, I could have figured out what their game was. And the Kuomintang, the Nationalist Party officials, too. They came over in the 1950s, just like me. Landed in Chinatown with their money, rich relatives and corporations. Always telling us to keep America on the Taiwan government's side and attacking the mainland Communists. They seemed one and the same with the Six Companies. Play a few hands and I would have known how to talk to them, too, about my sons, and their desires to make everything better for all Chinese-Americans. But they didn't want Chinese-Americans to ask too many questions or point out bad things about Chinatown. They wanted us to bee men, to *give them face, so America would never doubt it was on the right side, the side of the good Chinese.*

America loved Madame Chiang Kai-sek, the wife of the President of Taiwan. President Chiang was too Chinese. He was only educated in Japan and Russia and couldn't speak American. But Madame Chiang was an American university graduate who spoke perfect American and a Christian who attended their churches. She was small, pretty, and wore cheong-sams, those long silk gowns with the slit up one thigh. When Americans saw her, they felt protective towards Taiwan, like the Communists were barbaric Mongols who had taken China away from them. That's what the Chinatown papers called the Communists you know, barbarians and Mongol invaders.

That's the way the Six Companies told us to be, like Madame Chiang. But I was no Madame Chiang. I never owned a cheong-sam and would probably tear one squeezing it over my head. In their eyes, I was just a poor, stocky village woman. A Toisanese who didn't even speak proper Cantonese and not a word of Mandarin. Madame Chiang wouldn't listen to people like me.

She was one of three famous Soong family sisters. All very beautiful, very intelligent. I wish I could remember more, but each sister married a man who represented a different side of China's future. The oldest sister married a rich banker. The second sister eloped with Sun Yat-sen and after his death, became a Communist and after liberation, a part of Mao's government. Maybe she would have listened to the Clan Sisters. Maybe she would have joined our speaking-round-and-rounds.

When I was still a little girl back in Toisan, our parents gossiped about how rich the Chiangs kept getting, even in the middle of the Japanese war. I didn't know one thing from another. Just a kid and I still don't know for sure. But that's what the villagers said, that the Chiangs were corrupt, getting rich off American aid while the rest of China suffered. You know Chiang Kai-sek wouldn't fight the Japanese, he kept retreating and retreating until he ended up way in the lower backside of China, so far back he was almost in Burma.

Yes, my older brother the teacher was a Nationalist member, but not because he believed in them, but to keep his job. Still he wasn't an official, just a member. Only rich people could buy an official position, so they could get even richer. No, we just went along. The smart ones, the intellectuals, they left Toisan to understand the larger world before deciding which side was better - Nationalist or Communist or some other way. You couldn't know one way or the other living in Toisan. Get along, take care of the family, and harvest the crops - that's what we knew.

The Six Companies used to announce parades and rallies in support of Taiwan. President and Madame Chiang would ride down Grant Avenue and speak at Victory Hall, or something like that. Yes, my Clan Sisters and I lined the streets, but it was out of hospitality for another Chinese person visiting America. Yeah, they had those baskets we were suppose to throw money into to fight the Communists. Everyone lost interest after a while.

President Chiang was smart in this way, he knew how to keep the Six Companies loyal to him. He gave them seats in the Taiwanese legislature - overseas Chinese seats he called them. He gave them exclusive deals to import Chinese food treats to sell in every Chinatown: black mushrooms, bird nest and shark fin for soup, dried fruits and herbs, ginseng, and lots of stuff you can't find in America.

Those Six Companies heads made millions. No wonder they ended up doing more for Chiang Kai-sek and Taiwan even though their main job was to help Chinese-Americans. They wanted Chinese-Americans to be good, not make noise or ask for too much, just mind our own business and take care of ourselves. That was okay with me - I was raising my sons to grow up well mannered, to stand on their own two feet.

But in the late Sixties, everything started changing. You spoke out against the school principal, said Chinese should have equality. That's when I wish we could have spoken to the Six Companies and the Nationalists.

They're powerful, so powerful still to this day. And the entire Clan Sisterhood was just like me , weak within Chinatown. The Six Companies and Nationalists wouldn't have recognized the ideas from a speaking round-and-round. If we were to try to shame these men into right action, like we used to do in the village, where would we stand day after day to scold them? Which was the right district, family, or tong association headquarters building? Who in the Nationalist Party headquarters on Stockton Street would care? That's one thing about those elders, they sure made it hard to figure out who really was in charge. Maybe it was an old-time survival strategy, but Chinatown was just too complex. People didn't care as much about one another anymore.

Chapter 2019
New Yellow Peril

The genesis of what is often referred to as a political awakening, i.e., on my part, was not by desire or by choice, or a need for excitement stemming from idleness, but prodded by personal circumstances, and fueled by a feeling of offense that under my very nose, there existed societal agreements that dared to proscribe my personal choices, and thereby desecrate the ideals of America's democratic scheme under our Constitution.

Perhaps that's what it takes to catalyze anyone to spend exorbitant energy and time to understanding one's own political environment, to know it in the same way we understand the lay-out of neighborhood streets, which areas are safe and which can be dangerous, which times are optimum to drive around to shop, see the dentist, and pick-up the kids, and thereby avoiding traffic jams, the greater likelihood of accidents happening, and the vigilant traffic police who lay in wake during rush hours.

While there may be wealthy families who teach their children not to take their privilege for granted, but to understand and keep in place the political system that protects that status, as a working class son, and of an immigrant family, I certainly did not receive any such clear instruction from family or our otherwise able public and Chinese schools. I did not know that an awareness of one's history and political fabric is as essential to doing well and right in life as the college education I was groomed for. For those of us similarly situated, and from the point of view of the hindsight of my years, I would only suggest that it is important that all Americans not only understand the theoretical fundamentals of our system of government, so aptly taught in our civics classes, but also the historical forces, and the more current politics, which may have shaped your community and most likely, affected the quality of your family's life. I believe that this is the "eternal vigilance" that is often cited as the price of cherished liberties.

And so I started to ask about the origins and of the history of my community. How had Chinatown literally, economically, and psychically become "our place" in American society? Had we ever struggled back, like African-Americans in their Civil Rights movement at that very moment, the mid-sixties?

That summer, the civil rights movement did come to my San Francisco, as the spark that lit the tinderbox of festering discontent. Unexpectedly, it wasn't about black and white America. It was about equal rights and political power for Chinese-Americans. As I read the books from City Lights and the headlines from the South, I saw parallels to what Father had taught me about the early history of Chinese in America.

In 1967, I knew that San Francisco Chinatown was not the singing, dancing, syncopated idyll of the stage and movie musical, "The Flower Drum Song." Yet, the Chinatown of my youth was indeed safe, comforting, and nurturing. But a protective baby crib is still a crib, and once protective sides can slowly become prison-like. In my mid-teens, I discovered that Chinatown was in fact an involuntary community, a protective refuge wrought into being by anti-Chinese ethnic cleansing during the 1880s and continuing intermittently into the 1940s. Like a psychic crib, there were invisible bars: Chinese-Americans, even third-generation American-born ones like me, could step beyond and freely aspire to all that is the birthright of every American. Very simply, as I entered my later teens, I started to receive messages from Chinatown adults and my school teachers to lower one's personal and professional ambitions. Don't think of Harvard, but maybe some local college, well possibly State College or UC Berkeley, maybe. Perhaps you should major in medicine or accounting, or start a small business. Chinese are quite mercantile in that way, you know, but don't think of rising to CEO role in a brand name corporation. Consider it an accomplishment to move into a safe suburb not too far from Chinatown and on weekends, stroll Grant Avenue with your kids, visit friends, and eat dinner with your parents. Politics, big business, the high arts, Hollywood, and pop music – forget about it.

Until this growing realization, my personal political environment was not of any particular importance. Oh yes, Father discussed President Eisenhower and Vice-President Richard Nixon endlessly. He had been openly enamored of John Kennedy's candidacy, glued himself to our Emerson television set during the First Lady Jackie Kennedy's White House tour, and had repeated to me over and over, with a far-away look in his eyes, as if he were addressing the adulating crowd himself, "Ask not what your country can do for you, but what you can do for your country." That made me consider the Peace Corps as a goal and not city government, for national politics was a faraway story that did not explain Chinatown's place in San Francisco, or assuage the feeling of the growing constraints in my life.

President Kennedy's vigor and idealism could not explain to me, for example, why almost universally, the teachers in the multitude of Chinatown serving schools, all the firemen and almost all of the police department, were white Americans, even those serving the Chinatown community. And I might add, they invariably did so nicely, responsively, and with daily dedication. Yet, even with my straight A grades, teachers' recommendations, and superb physical fitness, I couldn't realistically expect to join the Fire Department or the Police force, even if that were my heartfelt answer to President Kennedy's rhetorical admonishment to ask what I could do for my country instead of for myself. If I were to become a teacher, another public servant profession, I couldn't ever hope to become a principal, regardless of skill and dedication, or some future graduate degree earned at nights and on weekends.

Yet, in my Father's youth, even these limited career paths would have been welcomed. After her war-torn youth, Mother was ever grateful for Chinatown's pacific if small cocoon. But for me, born and raised American, indoctrinated to believe in, and did personally view, the Declaration of Independence and our Constitution as the major breakthrough of political philosophy of the human experience in modern times, I was not so willing to be too readily deprived of my birth right. I wanted to know that America could work for me all the way, and if not, to do something about it.

Perhaps its not so uncommon to wake up one day and wonder why reality is the way it is, why either your choices are boundless or circumscribed. How is it that you ended up living on the right side, or wrong side of the tracks? Why can't you dream of becoming a national TV news anchor, or alternatively, at best to hope for a union job as the night janitor cleaning up after that anchor. Or why the only industry in your town is a paper mill or a steel mill is about to close, and what happened to the fishing industry and independent farms your two sets of grandparents remember aloud with such prideful nostalgia?

And so I wondered more and more in my mind, and then aloud. Who could tell me how Chinatown had come to this and why Chinese-Americans were less than white Americans?

No surprisingly, it was Father, from the experiences of his own life and his continuing self-education, who initially informed me of what I needed to know when he realized I was ready – no, when I desperately needed to know.

When I was seventeen and casually mentioned over dinner that J. C. Penney's on Market Street had hired me as a part-time sales clerk on their main floor men's department, Father said, "When I was your age, I couldn't even shop in Penney's because I was Chinese. And now, you work there as a salesman." Unsaid was Father's deeper approval that I was not limited by my race to a lowly backroom job like stock boy or janitor, but had a highly visible, public-contact position as a salesman on their main floor.

Father became the first to tell me about the history of racism against Chinese-Americans: the burnings, lynchings, and mass murders of Chinese pioneers up and down the West Coast that began in the late 1800s; their chilling ethnic cleansing war cry of "The Chinese must go!"; and the anti-Chinese exclusion laws that remained in force until repealed in the mid 1940s. Chinese pioneers, once 15 percent of California's population, fled America or retreated to a few Chinatowns in major cities, where the larger society waited for old age to finish what the mobs had not.

Even up to Father's time as a young man in the late 1940s and early 1950s, Chinese-Americans caught out after dark were fair game for a beating. Father carried a restaurant butter knife when he walked home from work late at night. "Just in case." Like pre-World War II Jews in their European ghettoes, we could only live, own property, work, and socialize safely within the confines of Chinatown.

From Father said, I learned that the Six Companies faithfully protected and served the besieged community during those horrific decades from the 1880s and through World War II - not surprising given our common millennium-long village tradition of mutual aid. They built Chinese Hospital, the Chinese language schools, and the employment centers, (where Father found his first job as a houseboy in Marin County and other work before he joined the union). Then, anticipating the pernicious rapaciousness of racism, the Six Companies, the along with the family associations and the tongs (ostensibly merchant guilds) wisely bought up much of the property in Chinatown, and then devised a clever, interlocking, labyrinthine ownership structure that boggled corrupt politicians and sly developers alike. This was part Toisanese cultural imperative, buy land for future generations, and part modern pragmatism as Chinatown sat on prime downtown holdings coveted by developers, father explained.

But then, Father intoned somewhat ominously, the Six Companies struck a deal with the white San Francisco establishment. The Chinese community must stay within Chinatown's borders and out of city politics. In return, the white power-structure stayed out of Chinatown affairs and delegated political power over Chinese to the Six Companies. This was our own separate but equal pact. This was why the Six Companies were commonly known as Chinatown's City Hall. For decades, this segregationist pact was responsible for the psychic bars I was starting to feel.

For in 1968, that Jim Crow deal was as solid as the day it was forged, but as ruthlessly enforced by the Six Companies elders as by white city fathers, and exemplified for Father by the refusal of the Six Companies to pressure white-managed unions to better defend Chinese-American union members against ill treatment. "The union takes our monthly dues and penalizes us if we're even one day late, but doesn't stand up for Chinese," said Father. But there was a *quid pro quo* for the Six Companies looking the other way, the unions agreed to a hands-off policy on organizing: in the most unionized city west of the Mississippi, Chinatown workers remained unorganized, adding to the wealth of the new Chinatown establishment restaurants, garment shops, and retail stores. The once Benevolent Associations were now predatory capitalists.

One day it all came together for me: "Chinatown or no Chinatown, we Chinese-Americans have our own Civil Rights struggle to fight." In that realization, I felt connected, complete, and on the right track. Perhaps whatever was missing in Chinatown and in my life were one the same.

It started at my high school, Galileo, located near Fishermen's Wharf, a building with a view of the Golden Gate Bridge. By the 1960s, Galileo was a Chinatown high school: we comprised 75 percent of the school's population of 3,000. Yet, Galileo High was also a richly inner city school: diverse, cosmopolitan, and surprisingly harmonious. We streamed in from all over the city: African Americans; white military brats; Mission District Chicanos; wealthy, white, private school outcasts; middle-class Italian, Irish, Jewish, and WASP kids; artistic beatnik offspring and neo-hippies; and of course, Chinatown youth on foot, by bus, hanging off cable car railings, on motorcycles, in cars, and even in chauffeured Cadillacs.

The school felt as safe and nurturing as my housing-project home. Packed into one four-story building ringing a small courtyard, we got along remarkably well despite our differences. We puzzling over homework together, visiting each other's homes on weekends, and generally obscured the social, racial, and class barriers of our parents' generation. The school felt as safe and nurturing as my housing project home. The teachers behaved the same way as our mothers, teaching us, watching us, and reprimanding us. Just another urban village--it seemed that the American experience was a serial movement from one safe environment to another.

In the spring of 1968, I sought to win the student body presidency on an unusual platform - Civil Rights for Chinese-Americans including promoting Chinese-American teachers into the administration, support for the fledgling Black Student Union, a detailed history curriculum on minority Americans, and my personal doubts about fighting in the rightness of the Vietnam War. I had stopped thinking of winning student body school offices as another gold star for college, and expected to be jeered off the stage. Instead, I was elected on the first ballot by a 75 percent plurality.

"What I had gotten myself into?" I thought, for on that last day of spring semester, a vicious rumble broke out between the white athlete clique and a group of smaller Chinatown students whose martial arts training more than equalized the disparity in size.

All was not well at Galileo, nor, as it turned out, in Chinatown. I needed more guidance, more than Father could provide, and found it, ironically enough, in the heart of Chinatown. One afternoon, as I wandered along Waverly Place, a 2-street long alley parallel to Grant Avenue, the high-strung strains from the balcony of the Chinese classical music society's afternoon rehearsals clashed with, and then wrestled with a cascade of lyrical European classical western. The source of the symphony, an airy, well-lit European style beer and cappuccino bar, newly opened, named Il Piccolo. Co-owners Richard Barkley and his Chinese-American wife, Alice, chose its alley location to harbor it from the tourist trade of Grant Avenue. Il Piccolo was a perfect place for private rumination, sharp exchanges of new ideas... and plotting change. I was thrilled to discover this secret intellectual oasis percolating within Chinatown.

Chinese-American intellectuals gathered here over coffee, iced Il Torino liqueurs, and English and German brew to organize against both the larger white power-structure and the conservative Chinatown community. Unlike our elders who dressed in bland colors and oversized, pajama-style suits, these intellectuals stood out strikingly, refreshing prototypes of Chinese-Americans of the future.

Alice Barkley, a recent graduate with a master's degree from UC Berkeley's School of Architecture, was thin, small, and barely five feet tall. Her telltale mane of black hair streamed down below her mini-skirt and, on some days, was braided in a queue. She clipped-clopped about in her three-inch heels, a cigarette in one hand, as she pumped cappuccinos, uncapped beer, and poured wine and all the while firing off a baker's dozen of incisive and comical *bon mots* into our free-flowing brainstorms for the new Chinatown. Having heard of my civil rights speech, Alice adopted me and introduced me to this cabal as the precocious high school activist.

A half-century later, when the pages of entertainment magazine are stuffed is rich with ethnically Chinese stars, celebrities, financiers, and power-brokers, it's difficult even for me to imagine my generation's parched-throat thirst for acceptable Chinese-American role models. Back in the day, surrounded and hemmed in by look-away-when-a-white-man-looks-at-you uncles and grandfathers in flapping, nondescript brown and gray suits in our daily lives; chop-suey English mincing by Charlie Chan, and mute, rat face, sexually ambiguous Fu-man Chu in the media, the fey loser, US dependent President Chiang Kai-sek of the Republic of Taiwan and the fashion challenged, remote, Godless, fanatical dictator Chairman Mao Tse-tung on the world stage, the best we had was an early model Bruce Lee incarnation in a television role even he hated, the role of the Green Hornet's television sidekick (literally). My survival tactic was to not even think about it. I didn't need Supermans, just a few reasonably, slightly different guys would have done the job.

At seventeen, Il Piccolo gave them to me - abundantly - a cornucopia of role models. Bespectacled with salt-and-peppered bristle-cut hair and goatee, Reverend Larry Jack Wong was the steel-eyed leader and intellectual visionary of the bunch. The jovial Alan Wong, a minister and Larry Jack's peer, was the director of the Chinatown YMCA. Wicked-sharp Dr. George Mu, a Ph.D. and an official with the State Department on home leave from the US Embassy in Singapore, unfailingly attired himself in starched shirts, pressed ties, and perfectly tailored herringbone suits. An American-born Chinese with a Ph.D. from the Oriental Studies Department at UC Berkeley, Mu was literate in both classical and contemporary Chinese, fluent in Mandarin, Cantonese, and Toisanese, and a native-born American speaker. George complained the Foreign Services' unspoken bias: Chinese-American patriotism was inherently untrustworthy.

Like me, Larry Jack Wong, Alan and George Mu were Chinatown born and raised in Chinatown.

Mason Wong, the Americanized son of a Hong Kong movie star, and George Woo both had emigrated from Hong Kong and were student leaders at San Francisco State University (then a State College). Mason, a recently discharged Vietnam Vet invariably wore his green fatigue jacket and lace-up combat boots. He reported that the war was so unpopular with the troops that units had refused to fight, and, instead, worked out private truces with the Viet Cong. He told me of "fragging," of hated white officers being shot in the back by their own men.

George Woo, also Hong Kong born and a State University leader, tall, broad-shouldered, and yet rotund, was a Chinese scholar whose words and voice shifted seamlessly between dispassionate analysis, fiery rhetoric, passionate-to-even angry speechmaking, and ironic humor. Bristling with a thick black beard, he resembled the fierce Chinese God of War, Kwang-kung, his intimidating visage was unsoftened by thick scholarly glasses and puffing pipe. He typically wore a silky blue, traditional Chinese cotton jacket, the *men nop,* all four jacket pockets stuffed with American and Chinese newspapers and books.

And of course, Alice Barkley was their equal and very respectfully called the Dragon Lady of this cabal centered at Il Piccolo.

Despite my age, I won their acceptance with my sincerity and eagerness. Increasingly, they solicited my opinions and views to test my grasp of the issues, and eventually elevated me as the "youth voice" of the group. I was the younger brother to the elder brothers of this Clan Brotherhood and elder sister Alice. The group delighted in filling in the gaps in my education, and correcting my naiveté of the world. They also enjoyed corrupting me slightly, acquainting me with the superior qualities and higher alcoholic content of foreign brews over American beer. Their camaraderie not only gave me not only a historical and social context for my fledgling intellectual insights, but emotional support. I no longer isolated. I did not have to act alone.

The Il Piccolo intellectuals slowly provided me with additional history that would have suggested to a less naïve youth the desperate power struggle that was about to erupt in Chinatown. Mother's Toisanese values of compassion and group harmony weren't the only strand in the Cantonese cultural tradition. When oppression reigned, Cantonese were among the first to rebel in China, that in great numbers, we joined the Taiping Rebellion to redress decades of oppressive taxation by the Qing Dynasty. This rebellion swept through China in the late 1800s, established China south of the Yantze River as Taiping territory, and almost overthrew the monarchy.

Of course I knew that Overseas Cantonese had largely financed the 1911 Chinese democratic revolution of 1911, led by Dr. Sun Yat-sen, himself a Cantonese. I had proudly recited his Three Principles of Democracy in Chinese school so long ago, but it was my Il Piccolo friends who explained them to me.

The first was the Principle of Nationalism - majority rule of Han Chinese with equal protection for national minorities, including even the Manchu people who had oppressed Chinese for three centuries. That sounded like Civil Rights to me!

The second was the Principle of Democracy - elective government with constitutional separation of powers, but with a Chinese twist of two additional branches, a fourth branch to oversee national exams for ministerial posts on the basis of merit and a fifth branch of censorship to root out the corrupt and the incompetent. That sounded like government of, by, and for the people, I happily noted!

Finally, the third was the Principle of Guaranteed Livelihood - state ownership of land; regulation of economics to prevent extremes of wealth and poverty; and policies which ensured a thriving middle-class of farmers, craftsmen, and merchants.

Sun Yat-sen's vision sounded just like Benjamin Franklin's ideas of self-sufficient livelihood, I thought. Dr. Sun, it seems, clearly envisioned a responsive national party, like Sweden, a democratic socialist nation, not one dominated by the rambunctious two-party system and unfettered free-market corporate capitalism of America and widens gaps between rich. No surprise that the good Doctor Sen's, political institutional values were those of the Chinese farmer: inclusivity, village based, fairness, honesty, opportunity, and protecting the little people against abuses of the wealthy and state to guarantee livelihoods for all. No wonder Mother treasured Dr. Sun Yat-sen as fervently as Americans cherished George Washington and Thomas Jefferson.

And so my cabal of political parents moved to the same democratic tune as me. Reverend Larry Jack Wong, and others who dropped in and out of Il Piccolo, had been inspired by the Christian non-violence of Dr. Martin Luther King, and so I felt assured of their tactical scheme, a commitment to debate, non-violent demonstrations, and change through transformation, not violence.

But shortly after his death, these elders told me, Sun Yat-sen's Nationalist Party was taken over by the same kind of corrupt, incompetent, self-interest groups that plagued the imperial system overthrown by his revolution. This corrupted Nationalist Party now reigned in the halls of the ornate Chinese Six Companies headquarters a mere half-a-block away on Stockton Street. Unlike

Although Asian-Americans veterans in Hawai'i aggressively ended Jim Crow in Hawai'i by entering politics and wresting state and federal political offices from entrenched white politicians, Chinatown's own veterans buckled under to the Six Companies and the ironclad Nationalist Party policy of not rocking the local political boat, and whose only political goal was propping up Taiwan as the legitimate government of China. Thus, squeezed into the strait jacket of "model minority," we added the virtue of patriotic anti-Communism to our Christianity, and the quiet workaholism of stay-in-our-place professions and businesses.

These were the unspoken constraints the Il Piccolo regulars chafed against.

And who were the enforcers of this fealty? My friends explained: the enforcers were the local tongs, including Bing Kong Tong, whose headquarters loomed ominously across the alleyway from Il Piccolo. From the 1850s to the early 1900s, the tongs openly ran Chinatown's slave-girl brothels, gambling parlors, and opium smoke-easies, and regularly paid off cops and politicians. Because of their tongs' roots in China's underground revolutionary societies, those of the defeated Taiping rebellion, within each tong was a secret society, no longer revolutionary but criminal in nature. This was the originals of *hok seh wui,* the dark-side organization, or the "shadow society." With established ties to branches in China and Southeast Asia, they resembled the Mafia with its roots in Sicily. In the 1950s, the tongs trashed pro-Mainland Chinese newspapers and chased their editors and supporters out of town. By 1968, most tong members operated legitimate retail business. Still, my Il Piccolo friends portentously warned me to not discount them.

And so I signed on. I dropped out of The Wing, the Committee Theater's improv training troupe, consciously moving those improv skills off the stage and into my own ground-level real life, i.e., the improv of political change. Those social insights from hours of reading at City Lights and the intellectual excitement of the possibility of change--well, I was about to deliver them home to Chinatown, too. And in my heart I nourished my spark of inspiration from Martin Luther King's Civil Rights movement, to help ignite the cleansing fires of non-violent social change, reform that doesn't require destroying anyone, not even the bad guys.

My parents welcomed my somewhat edited report that I had found some college-age friends at Il Piccolo. "They are reformers." I admitted. As to these friends' desire to change Chinatown, Mother only advised me to be careful. In truth, my parents had never forbidden me to explore new ideas, make my own friends or foray outside Chinatown to museums, theaters, opera houses and symphony halls. Unlike many Chinatown parents, they never insisted on the stunting Hobson's choice that I work every free moment to bring home money instead. So too, they also did not now prohibit me from joining this movement for equality. Besides, I was a good son, even brought home our first color TV on installment plan, paid for by my Penney's Department store paychecks.

Mother became more alarmed, however, when I told her that a group of young Chinese-Americans known as the Wah Ching, or "Young Chinese," also convened at Il Piccolo. The Wah Ching were delinquent Cantonese-speaking immigrants from Hong Kong who had descended into petty criminality against their own community: shoplifting, small burglaries, and extortion. At Il Piccolo, the Wah Ching forged an unlikely confederation with my Il Piccolo friends. The Wah Ching were a smoking gun against the Six Companies' assertion that all was well with the model minority. In turn, the liberals could help the Wah Ching move away from petty crime by helping them obtain government grants for job training and youth programs.

In actuality, these intellectuals had so very little in common with the Wah Ching. Except for George Woo and Alice Barkley, they didn't speak the same language and their connection was at times as tenuous as that of well-meaning white liberals helping inner city street gangs. But in the intoxicating, rosy idealism of the day, and with the persistence of George and Alice as bridge builders, the alliance held, even reached common political goals.

As I got to know some of the Wah Ching leaders, I couldn't help but admire the pragmatic caginess within their idealism. Like the Sharks in the musical *West Side Story*, they cheekily grasped that casting themselves as a "social disease" had already produced not only public sympathy, but also real city dollars for picnics, dances, and music shows and several well-paying youth worker jobs. With their politicized, intellectual allies, Wah Ching youth might well indeed receive language and vocational training with entrée into union jobs, hitherto unthinkable opportunities that could change their lives dramatically and yes, move them away from crime. Sure, why not with nothing to lose, they could always fall back into street life.

Yet, another locus of activism buzzed several blocks away, just below Grant Avenue. A group of young adult American Born Chinese ("ABCs"), in and out of juvenile hall veterans, organized a non-profit organization, Legitimate Ways, Inc. -- or as they called themselves, Leways -- as an alternative for younger ABC at risk street youth who did not fit into the churches, the Y's, and the family associations. The founding Leways members exuded an American sense of high style merged with ethnic pride: I envied their *Easy Rider* motorcycles airbrushed with flowing dragons in reds, greens, and purples. I spotted them, and danced to blues, soul, and the psychedelic music at Winterland.

Many Leways members were "Ping" kids, i.e., Ping Yuen Project raised like me. Soon, I too proudly displayed Leways two identifying lapel buttons; a bright yellow button in bold black letters that blared out "New Yellow Peril" and a second one that declared "Leways—Unity," encircling a sage clutching the telltale Taoist staff of divine wisdom. At Leways, I learned to shoot pool and to jam a mean, noisy, and high-scoring game of pin ball.

As 1968 wore on, some older members of Leways organized into a militant, leftist cadre, the Red Guards, named after Mao's youthful vanguard army, but styled after the Black Panthers. They marched through Chinatown screaming, "Political power comes out of the barrel of a rifle." Quoting directly from Chairman Mao Tse-tung's Little Red Book, they waved it dramatically in the air as vigorously as street preachers waved Bibles. Setting up business in the Soda Fountain of Youth storefront, next door to Leways pool hall, they displayed poster-size portraits of Chairman Mao, piles of the Little Red Book, the multi-volume *Selected Writings of Chairman Mao*, and a constellation of red and gold Chairman Mao buttons.

In 1968, in the Chinese Nationalist stronghold of San Francisco Chinatown where fluttering Chinese Nationalist flags defiantly dominate the roofscape to this day, this open display of Maoist paraphernalia was heresy and provocation. The Chinese Six Companies could tolerate Leways, but a base for Chairman Mao—never!

Mother had left China to escape Communism and, for her, the advent of Mao's Red Book in America reignited disturbing memories. While I was not drawn to the Red Guard as I had been to Leways, their fervent presence was a wake-up call to rethink my views about China, the United States, the world, a reevaluation encouraged by Father.

In the summer of 1968, Chinatown may have struck the discerning observer more as a breeding ground of insurrection rather than a protest movement in the making. It was both as our tightly knit urban village was unraveling and I somehow had wandered into its vortex.

There were now several militia-style uniforms: college students favored George Woo's blue and brown Chinese cotton jackets; New Leftists paced about in their Vietnam Vet army fatigues; Leways' younger members wore dark Derby-brand, zip-up jackets with Ben Davis jeans, resembling squads of Viet Cong; the Wah Ching draped colorful Superfly style knit sweaters over their black peg-leg pants; the Red Guards settled on surplus green Army fatigues topped by a dashing red beret; and everybody wore very dark sunglasses.

Although committed to Dr. King's non-violent tactics, the Il Piccolo leaders knew that in the collective DNA of our collective Chinese philosophy of governance, we implicitly understood that the Six Companies and the Nationalists had lost the mandate of heaven, that living balance of righteousness and harmony, of duty and reward, between ruler and ruled. Chinese history taught that the oppressed inevitably rose in protest and rulers reflexively retaliated with violence, then rebel forces would violently establish a new order under heaven. I felt it coming, the operation of this inexorable Chinese social law of reordering, but couldn't, or wouldn't, accept its inevitability. I only hoped that the sophisticated Il Piccolo liberals would effectuate non-violent change before the Wah Ching with their street instincts and Leways' youth, injected with the virulence of Red Guard righteousness and Black Panther militancy, could trigger the counter-attack.

Yes, it never crossed my mind that these new ideas and calls for change would not sit well with the entrenched Six Companies. I was naïve in my implicit assumption that our Chinatown was a tightly knit community, that we would work things out for the good of all. I assumed that the Chinatown elders who had suffered exclusionary traumas would welcome this next generation's commitment to removing all barriers to the American dream. I assumed that our differences would be worked out *en famille*.

"Why wouldn't the elders welcome our renewed campaign for the full equality they had always craved?" the idealist in me argued. "After all, that was how it was in my family. That was the Toisan way, and the Chinese way - work it out for everyone."

I could not have known at that time that these old men had grown so craven and so preferred the status quo, their vested, profitable way of life, and as events would later demonstrate, would do almost anything to protect it. "By any means necessary," so said a popular Black Panther militant slogan.

It was against this polarizing backdrop that I finally threw in my lot with the Il Piccolo activists to organized the first Chinese-American Civil Rights march along Grant Avenue. Perhaps we could keep the lid on, change the community without violence. At that time, Grant Avenue was best known to America as a stage set for "The Flower Drum Song," a popular 1960s musical portraying Chinatown as a sunny, halcyon middle-class dream of a shiny, smiling, singing and tap dancing "model minority." We expected the street to be filled with ABCs visiting from the suburbs and tourists that sunny Saturday, and were not disappointed.

A small but lively group of around forty of us filed up the steep sidewalk alongside Portsmouth Square and onto Grant Avenue, our boldly lettered, bi-lingual picket signs held high: "Equality for Chinese," "Chinese Representation at City Hall," "We've been here for a hundred years!" "We want unions," "No more sweatshops," "Chinese for Mayor—About Time."

Then, I saw the old-timers. They had turned out to watch us, these old men of another generation who had lived under the Six Companies regime. Gathered in clumps of two, three, or five, they idled curiously on street corners, entryways, or hunched over the ornate balconies of association headquarters. They tried to appear nonchalant. As we marched block by block, they seem to number in the hundreds, watching us in silent amazement, with the neutral body postures they had learned to wear, like the drab suits they put on in the morning, to slip safely through another day. These were not the well-fed leadership, but the bent, wiry, wage earners—the survivors. I had expected them to boycott the march, but at that moment, I felt our connection, they had built this Chinatown for us, their next generation. They recognized we were picking up their long-dormant fight for full acceptance by America. Walking tall already, I arched my spine higher for them and chanted louder for them, as if compensating them for their quiet, shuffling dance, their tongues bitten still during a harsher time, so that we could be born to fight another day.

On that warm summer afternoon, Chinese-Americans actually outnumbered tourists on Grant Avenue. It was the only moment of that tumultuous time that I felt we were one community, one village, united by our common craving for full acceptance, facing each other in the silent exchange of a non-speaking-round-and-round. Would our march swing them openly to our point of view, and transform the Six Companies from the grassroots up? Could we work things out: the Wah Ching and Leways youth trained for real jobs and the old leadership accept the new vision of the Larry Jack Wongs, Alice Barkleys, and George Woos of the new generation. Could we live together harmoniously as one Chinatown?

We marched past these quiet sentinels of another time, pass the Empress of China Building, Grant Avenue's tallest building, with its bay views, oriental pavilion rooftop restaurant, and posed owner-photos with stage and screen stars, governors, presidents, and foreign dignitaries feted there. We stomped pass the souvenir shops where I had worked summers since the age of ten —China Bazaar, the Empress of China (where my old boss, Auntie Francis Wong, smiled and waved at me); past the Sun Sing Theater where, as a child, I had lost myself in Cantonese movies; and finally, we turned at the corner of Jackson Street, dominated by Lun Hing Supermarket, the only Chinese owned and operated supermarket, and the Italian market, where Mother bought her live turtles, live chickens, and live fish. Chanting as we marched, we exercised the power of our voices, pressing our community to reclaim its own voice, and its rightful place in America.

Tourists reacted openly, some smiling as if amused, pointing curiously at our signs, and snapping photos with their boxy Instamatic cameras. A few drew back in repulsion, as if to say, first the Blacks and now the Chinese! What's America coming to? This definitely was not the Grant Avenue of Flower Drum Song.

At the rally later in Portsmouth Square rally, my friends vehemently attacked the Six Companies, in both American and Cantonese, for exploiting their own restaurant and garment workers at what was termed "slave wages." In a derivation from the turncoat appellation "Uncle Tom" that militant black leaders hurled at moderates, they scornfully branded the Six Companies "Uncle Tongs." No one was reaching out to the Six Companies; instead the crowd attacked them mercilessly.

I, too, picked up the microphone, but avoided harsh attacks, instead advocating change in the secondary schools: more Chinese-American administrators, firing of openly racist teachers, and instituting Chinese-American history curriculum that honestly portrayed our history. But most controversially, I demanded the immediate hiring of a Chinese American principal. Galileo needed a principal who ate with the common people in their homes, not just at the banquet halls, which of course was an indirect swipe at the Six Companies, and that principal should be from our Chinese-American

Triumphant, we reconvened at the community center basement, and then adjourned to Il Piccolo. "First round of beer on the house!" shouted Alice Barkley, as we roared, more alive than we'd felt in a long time.

The ante was quickly and mightily raised when the Big Money rolled into Chinatown that summer in the form of the War-on-Poverty's multi-million dollar program grants. It was during these community meetings to allocate funds when I finally understood that the chasm in our community was unbridgeable. Six Companies loyalists and my new friends entered meetings screaming at each other, barely restrained by the few calm ones from bashing each other's heads in with the metallic foldout chairs set out for every meeting. Distressed, I stopped attending them.

The Six Companies hated us young upstarts, "outside agitators" we were termed, challenging their franchise over the lucrative War on Poverty dollars that would have automatically passed to them under the old Jim Crow system. My colleagues railed back at them as "poverty pimps" and *fan hung,* or walking rice containers, for their nightly social habit of gorging themselves insensate at self-congratulatory, ten-course banquets.

The standing Il Piccolo joke was that you could always tell a seasoned Six Companies' *fan hung's* stomach from that of a *nouveau fan hung.* A seasoned one's stomach delicately arched out from just below his sternum, and then curved like a huge teardrop into a perfectly round belly, the product of years of slow, careful banqueting. In contrast, a mere overeater's stomach gracelessly flopped over his waist belt, the proverbial male spare tire. The consensus was that George Woo had a ways to go, despite his already formidable girth.

Late that summer, we discovered that a contract had been placed with hit men from New York's Chinatown targeting four of our leaders: Mason Wong, George Woo, Alice Barkley, and Larry Jack Wong. By chance, an alert security guard at San Francisco International Airport detained the triggermen after puzzling over their sharply tailored, pin-striped, double-breasted suits, so unlike those of drably dressed, local Chinese-Americans. The guard uncovered guns in their luggage, and then alerted the police department to their final destination—San Francisco Chinatown.

My reformist friends survived…at least for the time being....

Chapter 22
The Troubles

I was very proud of you when you were elected the president of the student body of Galileo. Why wouldn't I be? You were the one chosen out of three thousand students. All kinds of other races there —white, black, and Mexican from all over the city. And you were from Chinatown, from a working-class family, too. Everyone congratulated my relatives. "What a good son your sister has, to be selected." Why did the students pick you—because you were very smart, that's why.

Of course I was very worried over the trouble with the principal. Very worried. You were a good student, and when he suspended you from school, I was shocked, confused at the news because only bad people get suspended. My son is not a bad boy. You looked so hurt, then lost. My first thought was that we should apologize right away, try to get back along with him again, and just stay out of trouble. We're poor, and in America just like China, we could not protect you. If we had money, he would have phoned us, and everything would have stayed okay-okay. No trouble at all.

But you were an intellectual at heart, with a strong sense of right and wrong, not a real troublemaker. If something were wrong, you would say so, do something about it. That's your character and I could stand with you. But it was about power. He had the power. We did not. In Toisan, principals have power and it was the same in America. I didn't want him to hurt you in any way, especially your chances to go to college. I wanted you to learn the American way from college, then build influence to come back and fight another day. When you could win. You were just a student, a child. You couldn't beat a principal.

Everyone in Chinatown knew about the Galileo troubles anyway. Many agreed with you, said that we should talk about Chinese not being treated fairly, that it was time for a chang. Said you knew the history, were very reasonable in your criticisms. Even some Chinese newspapers defended you —The Chinese Pacific Weekly, East-West Chinese-American Weekly. Now my eyes can't read so well, but in those days, I read Chinese newspapers all the time. I knew what the community was thinking all the time.

But the Six Companies would never help. They're good only at settling trouble in Chinatown—and only between Chinese. A white person, a school principal—forget about them standing up to a white official. Go hire a lawyer, they throw in your face. With what —burnt rice crust? Like poor people had money for lawyers.

I was very worried when we went to the meeting with the principal. My thought was to let him lecture us first. Then I would calm him down, talk softly to him, like in a speaking round-and-round, and let him know you're a good son, a smart boy who's going to college, someone he would even be proud to have as a son. I wanted him to know that we were a good family, hardworking, honest people, that we could all be friends. Then, if I had to, I would have dropped to my knees and begged him to please let you back into school. Yes, I would shame him, just like we use to do to bad men in the village, to make them take back their wives. He would think it was his decision, but that was okay with me. But would a white principal even listen to me? I would go to the meeting even if I didn't understand American. I would have your father translate word for word, even if he wouldn't hear my words. I would do my best.

A lawyer came with us, and the principal got angry. Then he met with just the family first, and I started to speak, to calm him down first, and let him know William is a good boy. But the principal got up from his desk, charged at Father and started to scold him like a child, his fingers pointing at his face. Oh, he was big, this principal, but that was the wrong thing to do. Father, who was agitated but calm when we got there, jumped up from his chair, and with his own fingers jabbing back like in a sword-fight, scolded him back. The principal retreated behind his desk. Father chased him, speaking faster and faster, circling the desk, his face getting angrier. The principal sat down. He stopped talking.

Chapter 22
All American High School

Mr. Kearney was easily a full foot taller than father, twice as broad in the shoulder, and at least fifty pounds heavier. But Father sprung forth from his chair, stretched his back and neck upward, squared off eye-to-eye, and started in. "The old days are gone. Chinese are no longer second-class citizens. My son stands up for Chinese rights. He speaks for me and I am proud of him." Then Father let loose an impassioned recitation of all the wrongs committed against Chinese-Californians, a venting of the ills of his own life in the guise of history. Like the longest string of Red Devil firecrackers, he cracked and boomed out all the unspoken pain from the underpaid, underemployed, wretched labor that had kept his family together.

In that moment, I understood my father's rage: he had never been angry at us. He just took it out on us, and forgave him all his transgressions.

To Mr. Kearney's credit, he listened calmly to Father's soliloquy. After a pause, Mother gently stressed that I was a good student, not a troublemaker but college-bound. Mr. Kearney did not refute that, but said that my activities could be detrimental to my success in life. Well, at least all the adults were united in their concern for my future. Then our attorney, a Mr. Sidney Wolinsky, head of the local Neighborhood Legal Services Foundation, convinced Mr. Kearney that rescinding the suspension was in everyone's interest. Mr. Kearney walked me over to the Dean's office, handed me an eraser, and I rubbed out the suspension from my record.

Jubilantly.

That was how it was, those last six months of my final high school semester, like being strapped into the latest, extreme theme-park thrill ride. Each tumultuous personal confrontation ran into another, and my emotions spiked and soared and dipped hour by hour. Only this ride had no terminus. Literary commentators say that exact dates and locales, and facts that have been cross-confirmed by official documents, letters, photos and multiple interviews result a good biography. In contrast, a memoir is at its best when it is a narrative of emotional memories; the cold facts themselves are not to be too keenly exalted; and the better practice may be to regard confidently recited facts with skeptically.

Yet I remember the factual flow of the events of 1968 all too well, including how Mr. Kearney and I became archetypal nemeses. Against our better natures, he came to personify old, institutionalized racism, and I, the first of the new generation of outspoken, reformist Chinese-Americans. We were both caught in a larger drama, the birth pains of an emerging zeitgeist. As for trustworthy emotional memories, well, 1968 was undeniably an emotional maelstrom. In that storm, I often couldn't tell who was a friend, how to do the right thing, even what motivated me at times, or what my feelings were. So it is the emotional memories of the time that I recall with some suspicion: it is the cold hard facts of events that are trustworthily and clearly branded onto memory. And, yes, there are many emotional memories--they still flare up in my psyche, are confusing still.

Had I known how to look back then, I might have dwelled on the training-wheel emotional ride of my Ward 75 rebellion against an unjust nurse. We were punished anyway, a penalty that was never openly revoked, or amends made. I might have connected with the lessons from the emotional bloodbath of the night my entire Assemblies of God community simultaneously expelled and shunned me. Because I dared to think differently, ask questions. But, no, although thoughtful I was not as yet reflective. I might then have been better prepared, as I considered change to be a procedural, purely a mental process: what's right is obvious and everyone will agree without much resistance. I had no foreboding of the contortionist forces of the emotional blastoff to come, that it could be like torture.

In the fall of 1968, began my final semester and as the civil rights student body president. In a few short months, January 16, 1969, I would turn eighteen. The Vietnam War was escalating, and the draft boards were calling up the newly 18s of the world, including yours truly. What does a patriotic young man do when he discovers that America is on the wrong side of a conflict? Many demonstrated, and anti-war protests marches dominated the 1968 presidential elections.

Like I needed another pressure front and I'm sure it only agitated my righteousness.

So, I remember being so angry that I dressed down San Francisco's new Superintendent of Schools at a televised town hall after he short-shrifted my questions about long-delayed maintenance at Galileo. Then surprise the next day, when he sent a chief assistant to survey my complaints, and two weeks later, even more surprised when workmen built out private counseling offices. Finally, a feeling of awe as I observed the shock and pleasure of principal, teachers, and students alike.

I remember happily internalizing a new lesson: that speaking out made the system work. I remember that day's triumph and then later, how fleeting triumph can be.

The presidential candidates swung by Chinatown, as they did every four years: Chinatown was then the nation's grandest media symbol of anti-communism. That was why the Chinese New Year Parade perennially attracted Richard Nixon, his trademark grin and skinny arms suspended up in the air like a "V."

That summer Vice President Hubert Humphrey also dropped by the summer American language program where I tutored immigrant kids. As my charges clustered in the schoolyard, Humphrey's visual backdrop for the nightly news, his entourage stormed through my kids, like a football team's defensive line. I was already disappointed in him for not coming out against the war, and here he was, absentmindedly knocking my kids down. " Just like we're coldly killing Vietnamese kids, " my mind leaped. I hollered a clear, nasty protest, and the Vice President turned around, and the strangest silence hung for a moment, as if the film reel had stuck. My kids started crying, hugging my knees, but Humphrey turned on his heels, as I sheltered them in my arms.

Bobby Kennedy's motorcade streamed through Grant Avenue. This time, it was Catholic school kids who became the photo op for the nightly news. I shook his hand and a shock bolted through my body. A mere thirty hours later, Bobby won the California primary, only to be assassinated by Sirhan Sirhan.

I remember feeling hypocrisy as I started my last semester, assuming that the unwritten rules of school life still held. Show school spirit and you will be accepted. Use the opportunities of school life as a steppingstone to success. The main rule was say what you like, do what you like, as long as you played fair.

"But the times they are a changin'," as Bob Dylan's anthem reminded us daily on AM radio, and our beloved principal Dr. Moreno retired to be replaced by a new principal, Mr. James Kearney (pronounced "Kar-nee).

Galileo's biggest annual ritual, was the "Song and Yell" contest which was, a group ejaculation of school spirit. All three thousand students gathered in devotion on the football field for the single purpose of screaming their heads off for a football team. The team was introduced and we screamed some more. Then the newly elected homecoming queen was announced and we screamed some more.

Emotional memories resurfacing.

Hypocrisy at the pernicious, unspoken underside to the "Song and Yell." Outrage at the predominately white football team disdain of Chinatown kids, considering themselves enrolled in a racially inferior school. Anger that they officially endorsed as one English teacher opened the first day of each semester with the stark statement that Galileo's reputation plunged when Chinese students became the majority. Stupefied that he was never admonished. Loathing that the white superiority students clique stuffed ballot boxes to ensure a white Homecoming Queen was always elected. Pride at how many of us worked so hard to keep the balloting clean that year and then focusing on a single Chinatown candidate. That year, Millie Gee, a Leways girl won. As I crowned her, Millie's unbelieving joy as her tears streamed down her face mirrored the feeling of honest victory well-fought in the cheers and smiles of the entire school of 3,000 students assembled in our football stands.

Fear again when, after the rally, the retiring principal accompanying the new principal, Dr. Kearney, mentioned my speech at the Portsmouth Square civil rights rally, where I had criticized him. Relief when he said there had been truth in what I said, that perhaps he should have spent as much time in the housing projects as in the gilded banquet halls. I was totally touched, but should not have been surprised at his thoughtfulness. Gratitude for Dr. Moreno had always set the tone of fairness for Galileo, despite the apartheid system of San Francisco.

Unfortunately, the same would not be true of the new principal, Mr. Kearney, who rapidly came to symbolize the racist, uncaring power structure. My own role became similarly polarized: I was the first of the emerging, outspoken, new Chinese-American generation.

My first confrontation began with my dressing down San Francisco's new Superintendent of Schools at a televised town hall after he short-shifted my questions about long-delayed maintenance at Galileo. The next day, Mr. Kearny introduced me to one of the Superintendent's chief assistants, to give him a tour of the building's needs. Two weeks later, workmen came to build private offices in the counseling room. I walked in as they put in the finishing touches. The counselors tried on their new offices for size, pleased at the miraculous speed with which this long-ignored request had been answered. Yet, they could not openly admit that a mere student had accomplished what they had not.

As for me, I saw that speaking out made the system work.

Our second confrontation more archly epitomized our symbolic roles. Chairing the weekly Student Council of homeroom representatives, my agenda increasingly highlighted outside activities of community fairs and dances, War on Poverty jobs, civil rights marches, and antiwar rallies. We discussed integration, the lack of Chinese-American administrators, and the need for a curriculum on the true history of America's minorities. Each week, homeroom representatives faithfully reported these discussions within minutes, making this a very effective communications system to our three thousand students and of course, to our teachers, but to their growing alarm.

Yet events were outpacing the student government's polite discussions. Groups of Chinatown street kids were taking direct action, a code phrase for vandalism of property, seizure of administration offices, and battling the police. Early that year, I arranged a truce between the Chinatown street kids and the black gang from the Fishermen's Wharf housing projects, two groups that typically rumbled with each other. The terms of the truce defined the common enemy as racist teachers and administrators, as well the white athlete clique. Perhaps that accounted for the attack on the white athletes the previous semester.

Emotional memory flashing up again. I remember mixed feelings at hearing of the slashing of the car tires of the English teacher who berated Chinatown students with impunity. Slashed time again and again, as if avenging each one of his despicable put-down rants. Horror at an arson attempt that left burn shadows marks on an already dilapidated rear hallway wall, an item on the Superintendent's to-do list from that triumphant encounter so long ago. Despair when one lunchtime, students rioted in the courtyard, setting fires to garbage cans, and smashing a number of office windows. Confusion and Hurt when a history teacher branded me a rabble-rousing "Adolph Hitler unleashing his storm troopers."

Clever when I placed on our Student Council agenda an item to discuss a one-day student strike, as a way to channel the growing violence turn into a peaceful protest. Disbelief when the tone of the administration understandably hardened. Ironically, the three main administrative leaders were all Irish-Americans, in an almost karmic repeat of the 1880s conflict between the Irish and the Chinese.

Although I was schooled year after year in civics by history teachers that open, unbridled, and even harsh speech was our birthright, and mentally embraced this, yet when the words were raining on you, it was a hard rain.

I remember many, many moments of fear that brief five months, of feeling misunderstood, of more standing up than I could have ever imagined, and yes, of more standing alone than I could handle.

My Il Piccolo friends laughed jovially at my hurt feelings, flat out telling me to expect to be misunderstood time and again, and branded with worse names.

Devastation as jours after the morning discussion of a one-day strike, Mr. Kearney summoned me into his office. He wasn't interested in anything I had to say. He simply suspended me, all within a half-an-hour. I was to return with my parents in four days for a meeting. Now a suspension may not sound like much of a punishment, but for a college-track "A" student who lived for academics, it was a college-stopper, a blemish that could deny me admissions and jeopardized my scholarship chances. Shock and Humiliation, I slunk slowly back home, the culprit who had single-handedly sabotaged our family's aspirations. Shame, for I had flushed away my father's years of hard work.

Father was reflective, not condemnatory at all. Mother wondered why we couldn't meet immediately and talk it out. In America, she found out, there was no speaking round-and-round, only the power of a principal to order parents into a meeting without regard for their work schedules.

During my suspension, I visited Benny at his Smoke Shop, reminiscing about simpler times. I walked pass our old apartment on Kearny Street where I bumped into Charles Wong, a Chinatown born and raised attorney and an Il Piccolo regular. He inquired in the watchful way of Chinatown elders why I wasn't in school. I blurted out the story and my worries about college. He suggested that my first amendment right to free speech might have been violated and invited me to his office, the Neighborhood Legal Assistance Foundation, a legal unit of the War on Poverty that defended poor people. As a housing project family, we qualified for their services. Charlie and Sidney Wolinsky, his superior, met with Father. Father wanted to fight back.

And now I should share more of the details of that meeting when I father's anger forced Mr. Kearney to sit back in his seat. So many loose ends tied themselves up neatly that meeting. Then, too, I got a new insight, something about lawyers, and the respect they commanded, the power they had.

When my parents and I entered the Principal's office with our lawyer, Sidney Wolinsky, Mr. Kearney flew into a rage, refusing to meet without his own lawyer. After some more loud exchanges and hand waving, it was agreed that Mr. Kearney could meet first with the family—alone.

As soon as my parents sat down, Mr. Kearney charged at Father, shaking his right index finger before Father's face. "Now Mr. Lee, your son is in trouble and you should never have brought a lawyer into this..." Mother quickly said something in Chinese, in gentle tones, as if tone alone could becalm the situation.

To my surprise, Father did not cower, but rose to his full height, managing to square off eye-to-eye with Mr. Kearney, who was a full foot taller, twice as broad in the shoulder, and at least fifty pounds heavier. Father jabbed his own index finger back, a fencer crossing swords. "The old days are gone. Chinese are no longer second-class citizens. My son is standing up for Chinese rights. He speaks for me and I am proud of him."

Mr. Kearney stumbled back behind his desk. Father pursued him, circling the desk as he angrily lectured him on the litany of wrongs against Chinese-Americans. His impassioned outburst addressed a general history, yet was a venting of his personal frustration, of a life relegated to second-class citizenship. Like a long string of Red Devil firecrackers, he cracked and boomed out all the unspoken pain from the underpaid, underemployed, wretched labor that had kept his family together.

In that moment, I understood the source of my father's rage. He had never been truly angry with us; he just took it out on us. In that same moment, I forgave him a whole host of transgressions.

To Mr. Kearny's credit, he listened calmly to Father's soliloquy. After a pause, Mother gently stressed that I was a good student, not a troublemaker but college-bound. Mr. Kearny did not refute that, but said that my activities could be detrimental to my success in life. Well, at least all the adults were united in their concern for my future. The meeting ended in an amicable settlement. Mr. Kearney walked me over to the Dean's office, handed me an eraser, and I rubbed out the suspension from my record.

Jubilantly.

As with speaking out, I saw that lawyers, too, forced the system to work.

But as with that night when I fled the Assemblies of God mission, the deepest cuts were inflicted by my classmates, some whom I had known since kindergarten, others from junior high school to now.

Sharp betrayal at the unkindest of cuts as my classmates' whispering campaign, that I was a power-hungry and a tool of outside agitators.

Stoicism as recognizing, if painfully, that they were the last of the true-blue assimilationists—and "model minority" mentality to the core of their beings. I never confronted them. Having been one of them, I could not be angry with them nor had any need to explain myself.

Tranquility in the knowledge that I had simply moved on ahead of this last of the model minority.

Victory, as the younger students welcomed the changes, signing on for the ride along the mutable curve of history.

Protective towards Richard, who entered Galileo during my last semester. He had not been interested in the counter-culture, improv theater, or City Lights Bookstore. But he knew all too well the deep wounds of Father's thwarted ambitions. The campaign for Chinese equality made sense to him. We walked to school together, a brisk twenty-minute stroll we executed without a sweat given Father's training in power walking. But with all my student activities, Richard was on his own after school and on weekends. And, too, I sought to protect him from the ire of the administration by concealing our sibling connection. I was aware that with two-and-a-half years more at Galileo, he could easily end up as the surrogate whipping boy for my activism.

Guilt's looming weight if that were to come true.

Satisfaction, that in less than six months, we had shattered the racial stereotypes of Chinese-Americans held by many Americans at the time: indirect, inscrutable, and conflict adverse, who spoke in abstruse fortune-cookie sentences. But actually, we had recovered those ancient Toisanese qualities of direct, plain, and loud speaking.

Skepticism towards all politics, but especially the presidential candidates swinging by Chinatown, the nation's grandest media symbol of Cold War anti-communism. Puzzlement as Richard Nixon zoomed through Chinatown with his trademark grin and arms pushed in the air like a rabbit-ears TV antenna. Disappointment when Vice President Hubert Humphrey marched through the American language program where I tutored: my immigrant kids served as his visual backdrop for the nightly news. Guarded hope as Bobby Kennedy's insurgent motorcade streamed down Grant Avenue, and this time, Catholic school kids did duty as the nightly news backdrop. I touched his peeling hand--and felt numbness at first, and then destiny, as a bolt powered its way through my body. Thirty hours later, I remember an unnerving, miserable paralysis at the news of the *déjà vu*-like tragedy--and then despair--for Sirhan

Despair as Sirhan Sirhan had assassinated our last national hope, Bobby.

I remember all these events so clearly, and all the emotional memories too. It's just that because there were so many all the time, I'm not sure I remember them in their right order.

I was seventeen going on eighteen and I was zapped out.

Chapter 23

The Golden Gate Bridge Makes Grandmother Smile

I don't remember whether my mother arrived by boat or plane?...hmmm, neh... well, it was the mid-Sixties.... So it must have been by plane. What I remember is my nervous anticipation, trying to hold back my happy tears, standing there impatiently. She was around seventy then and I was in my late thirties, but I was acting like a little girl who had so missed her mother. She cleared immigration, then customs. We stood and looked at each other, our eyes locked. We held each other tight, both of us crying. She whispered my name, "Jen. Jen. Jen. It's been so long." I whispering, "Ah mah. Ah mah. Ah mah."

Grandmother, my brother Wah, and his wife squeezed in with us in our apartment for the first few months. When word got out on the Chinatown grapevine that Grandmother Chun was in America, all the old Toisan Clan Sisters dropped by. Those first few weeks were so busy; they brought her fruits, candy, food, and red packets with money. Just like Chinese New Year's. Spent hours talking about so-and-so of the village, where they lived, how the kids were doing. Every morning someone took her to dim sum and every evening someone else honored her with a banquet. Your father helped Wah find an apartment in East Ping Yuen project across from us. Grandmother moved in with him.

Maybe because I was so happy because of my mother. Maybe because all the Clan Sisters encouraged me. They said that with two grown boys, enough time has passed that for sure, the next one is guaranteed to be a baby girl. I really wanted a girl and soon, I was pregnant again.

I still remember when I got pregnant. You kept remarking, "Mom, you're getting fat!" I didn't say a word, just "yeah, yeah." Then when I was seven months pregnant, my stomach sticking out like a ripe winter melon, you said quite emphatically, "You're really too fat. Time to lose weight." Your body froze and your mouth dropped when I told you, "I'm not getting fat. I'm having a baby." Well, John wasn't a girl, but I was still so happy when he was born. You really loved John, too, offering to baby-sit him when I played poker. I always gave you money from my winnings.

Grandmother baby-sat John when he got a little older, along with Wah's three kids, Ada, David, and Victor, all around John's age. That's the way it was in Toisan, elders watched the kids while parents worked. They fed the pigs, chickens, and ducks while we worked the fields. Elders tended the vegetable garden, too. And all three generations lived in one household. We had to because in China, the government didn't take care of old people. And there wasn't food everywhere like here in America. If left alone, elders would starve to death. We had to share the simple foods we had with each other. Still, living together was good. Someone was always home to watch the kids after school, clean their scrapes when they fell down. And kids always fall down! Make rice soup when they're hungry, or take a nap together in the afternoon.

Grandmother tutored John, Ada, Victor, and David in Chinese, spending hours going over every word until their pronunciation was perfect. She helped them perfect their calligraphy and memorize Chinese characters. That's why, even today, John's Chinese is better then my first two sons'. And all the children loved her, always laughing, hugging, and climbing over her while seated in her favorite sofa chair. She looked like one of those Buddha statues with one kid on a shoulder, another hanging off an arm, and still another curled up in her lap.

My sisters and I cooked elder soups for her. Lots of lamb soup because lamb is very nutritious, but more importantly, lamb helps is "bow hoot" "or warms up the blood. And birds' nest soup. Also, pig liver soup.

We added the herbs gee-doo, bok kee fong, and ginger to a ⅓ to ½ pound of lamb. Ginger is a great source of heat. In the special chi-soup pot, slow boil everything down to about 3/4s of a rice bowl. Eat after dinner. Made this soup every other week.

For the weeks in-between the lamb soup, we made birds' nest soup for her. Very expensive, around $1,000 to $1,200 a pound, but we use only an ounce each time so the birds' nest lasted seven or eight months. Add some white-meat chicken to sweeten the broth, and then the same slow-boiling technique as the lamb soup until you have 1-½ rice bowls worth of soup. Serve ¾s of a bowl with dinner and the rest first thing in the morning. You know birds' nest is the stuff certain birds chew up and regurgitate. They take it out of the birds's beat and then dry it. That's why it's so expensive!

And pig liver soup. Very easy to make. Boil it for half an hour in about a rice bowl's worth of water. Then, let it cool down for five minutes. She'd drink it like a tea.

Also, the chi energy of elders is not as strong, so don't feed them too much vegetable soup. Vegetables are yin, lowers their blood strength. That's why we made Grandmother lamb soup so often. We cooked her lots of fish dishes, because that's also good for elders. And steamed pork hash with shredded ginger topped by salt-preserved fish from China. But mainly fish dishes with her meals.

Grandmother had become sick in Toisan. The Japanese invasion, then the civil war put too much pressure on her. She was a little healthier in Hong Kong, and then got well in America. There's so much food here and it's cheap. Only 50 cents for a pig liver. In China, you think we could afford lamb and pig livers? No, animals were few and far between and the rich always got to the good stuff first. And Grandmother had bad blood pressure, 160 over 95. But a doctor gave her some pills. Between our soups and the medicine, her blood pressure went down to around 120 over 80. You know that's a very good blood pressure.

Grandmother liked Bob, said he was a good man, saw right away that he made me very happy. She knew he was kind of like my boyfriend, of course. Many Toisan elders are like that: they see things clearly right away. They look in your eyes and face and they know what kind of person you are, how intelligent and hardworking, whether you are kind or mean, honest or tricky. You know she just accepted everything about me, that I was a grown woman now, had raised two kids and about to raise a third. She didn't act like she was a mother and I was still her little girl. She never told me how to raise my kids or that I could have done better, like making the older boys stay in Chinese School for example. She gave me respect, or, as we say it, bee men, i.e., gave me face.

Not all Grandmothers are like that, you know. Like your father's mother. When he first came over, she tried to boss everyone, tell us what to do and how to behave. She insisted that we better believe in Jesus or we'd end up in hell. Tried bossing everyone until her dying day, saying whoever was nicest to her, she would leave them her savings, and then always playing one relative off another. It wasn't that much money, but she used every little hook. It got to the point where even your father avoided even though she lived upstairs in an apartment he secured for them.

No, Grandmother Chun wasn't like that. The only advice she ever gave me was to try to understand why my husband was so grumpy after work. He goes out to earn the money; he puts up with demanding people all day; maybe he has mean bosses even, she said. It's not personal, he's not angry with you. So leave his dinner for him to reheat and ignore his noise as his home is the only place he can let it out. That's the way it is in Toisan households. People get mad, say mean things, and clear it out of their system. Then it's over. Forget about it. Don't bring it up again. That's true for everyone, parents, grandparents and kids. The home is the place to drop your frustrations. We don't divorce, so we say mean words if we can't hold it any longer, but we learn to let mean words pass, too. But today I say that if a husband beats his wife, she should divorce him even if this was unthinkable in Toisan.

Grandmother Chun wasn't curious about traveling to Los Angeles or New York. Not even to Oakland and Sacramento, the second city that Chinese historically settled in. She was happy staying around Chinatown with her daughters, her grandchildren, and the Clan Sisters. This is kind of a Toisan way once you're settled. Even today, my brother, sisters, their, their children, and their grandchildren live in the Bay Area. I like it that everyone's close by, even though we may not see each other for weeks or months.

Yes, we showed Grandmother the sights. She especially loved the Golden Gate Bridge, commenting what geniuses Americans must be to have constructed such a beautiful bridge. She smiled at the brilliant orange, an auspicious color reminding her of gems. She thought white people were friendly since they seemed to always be smiling at her. Maybe they smiled because she looked so much like a traditional Chinese grandmother. Short and a little chubby, a black cap with green oval jadeite in front, a traditional black outfit, Chinese cloth shoes, and a soft, warm smile. When she saw her first black American, she commented that America must be a real big country and a kind one to let people from all over the world come and live here, including her own family. My mother never had prejudices about anyone. She taught us only to discriminate on the basis of a person's character but never on race, money, or religion. Even in America, despite so many difficult years, Grandmother never scolded, gossiped, nor said anything bad about anyone.

Her time in America was good, very joyful. She was much happier in Chinatown than in Hong Kong. Of course, I was deeply sad when she crossed over. But at least we had reunited and spent her last decade together. I was the one who sponsored her immigration over to America of course, my silent promise to her during our mother-daughter Lucky Day.

Chapter 24
Tremors

Grandmother Chun left a frayed China behind only to land in a community in fragmentation. But age, unawareness, her daughters' love, and Clan Sisters' attentions shielded her.

Despite our family's joy at the birth of John and our reunion with Grandmother, my eyes were on the streets. In early 1969 the discerning observer may have viewed Chinatown more as a breeding ground for insurrection than as a non-violent Civil Rights movement in the making. Groups of youth favored one of several militia-style uniforms: college students stuffed leaflets in their George Woo-style blue and brown Chinese cotton jackets; New Leftists paced about in their Vietnam Vet army fatigues; Leways younger members rendered themselves indistinguishable in dark Derby-brand, zip-up jackets with Ben Davis jeans, resembling squads of Viet Cong; and the Red Guards marched in surplus green Army fatigues topped by a dashing red beret. Only the Wah Ching high-styled, strutting about in colorful Black ghetto Superfly-style knit sweaters over their black peg-leg pants. And everybody but everybody wore very dark sunglasses.

That Chinese New Year, the year of the Monkey in Chinese Astrology, the seething youth rebellion spilled out into the streets in an attempt to gut the community's biggest model minority PR event, our annual two-week long celebration. Leways and Wah Ching youth alike, resentful at overbearing tourists, taunted and harassed them along Grant Avenue. Increasingly, random fistfights broke out over the two weeks ticking down to the grand finale, the Saturday night Chinese New Year parade, America's largest night-lit parade, in prime time on Grant Avenue. On parade night, I witnessed scores of fights erupt up and down Grant Avenue, climaxing in a shooting battle as retreating youth shot at and pinned down policemen from the balcony ramparts of one of the older Ping-Yuen projects, mere yards away from festive Grant Avenue. The quasi-revolutionary admonitions to "pick up the gun" and to "seize the day" had won over those advocating discussion and cooperation. The leveler heads of the Il Piccolo activists had not won out: the militants now set the tone.

Meetings with city and public school administrators rapidly deteriorated into chaos, with officials forced to flee for their safety. Tom Wolfe, the pioneering new journalist, arrived in Chinatown in his trademark three-piece white suit and shoes to hang out at Il Piccolo and Leways. In his book, *Mau-Mauing the Flak Catchers,* Wolfe describes our local devolution from peaceful Civil Rights movement into violent confrontation One night, a school board meeting in Chinatown ended abruptly when the impaneled School Superintendent and his staff fled after a cherry bomb blew up in front of them.

Soon, the Barkleys announced that Il Piccolo would be closing, that they could no longer subsidize the café as a community meeting place. It was a common belief that the Six Companies had quietly quashed program funding for a Wah Ching clubhouse, and then a proposal to convert Il Piccolo into a restaurant-training facility. That last night, there was a sad but spirited party, as intellectuals, activists, and youth alike paid our respects and full price for every bottle of European beer. One inebriated irregular rambled up to the Six Companies headquarters and, in a fitting but futile symbolic act, tossed beer bottles through its ornate windows. Wah Ching as a movement for social change was dead, and everyone, activists and youth, dispersed into the streets when Il Piccolo closed forever.

The tongs had already been quietly wooing Wah Ching members, perhaps predicting that the demise of Il Piccolo would show the youth who really held sway over the community.

Some Wah Ching youth had already hedged their bets. Always more a pragmatic federation than an organization, each faction remained loyal to its own charismatic leader. In those final days, from the sidewalk tables of Il Piccolo, we watched several Wah Ching move their personal belongings into a nearby tong building on Washington Street. They refused to look at us, in part out of shame, and in part defiant.

"Who are you to judge me? We tried it your way and got nowhere."

One faction, led by a leader named *Sun Ngeen Look*, or Crazy Six, had joined Suey Sing Tong in Oakland. Other factions had allied themselves with Hop Sing Tong and Bing Kong Tong in San Francisco. Why were the tongs, quiet for so many years, now recruiting so heavily? How could we have know then that youth we had come to know as friends would soon be hunting each other down in a deadly game of urban assassination?

It was also the beginning of the end for Leways. One spring night, while shooting pool at Leways, I was detained in a routine police sweep while shooting pool. Although I was outspoken and confident of my rights, this solitary confrontation with an armed, uniformed policeman in all his authority terrified me. He demanded my name and address for "crime prevention ID cards." Along with others, I was so intimidated I never returned to Leways. These sweeps ways shut down Leways in its doors in a matter of months.

As with so many other movements of the Sixties, the places for thoughtful conversation and non-violent social justice activities were closed downing. With the demise of Il Piccolo and Leways, Chinatown lost the two places that could sway delinquent youth away from crime. The tongs' puzzling but aggressive recruitment foreshadowed a potentially violent fight for control of the community.

The price of change was rising across the board, as I found out when Mason Wong invited me out to a demonstration at San Francisco State College as part of an outreach to community members (later renamed SF State University) to observe the strike and noon rally for an Ethnic Studies College. Student leaders who were demanding an Ethnic Studies College and the strike was now several months old, with no end in sight. Joining the leadership of the Third World Liberation Front, we convened at the Ecumenical Center, directly located across from the campus. At exactly high noon, we marched out into the student commons, the Quadrangle, with upraised fists, defiantly yelling

"Power to the People." I had expected to observe only, not march into the middle of the crucible with the college administration's most wanted. Sucked into the action, I ducked my head, hanging as far back behind the Central Committee as I could without splitting off, raising my right arm in an unconvincing "Power to the People" salute.

And that was when the games began, as the San Francisco Police Tactical Squad charged into the crowd, using flanking maneuvers that split the demonstrators into smaller and smaller groups. For the next few hours, they systematically isolated, then beat to a bloody pulp, the heads of as many leaders of the Black Student Union as they could corner. I watched them swing their standard-issue, long, black, hardwood clubs reinforced in the center with steel pellets like sledgehammers. There were few things to my youthful eyes so violently graphic as the sight of blood pouring down like a thick, red waterfall against the blackness of crushed Afros, the agonized black faces, and the torn, black leather jackets of the unarmed. That infamous day went down in the strike's history as Bloody Tuesday.

Yet, that strike and a similar one at UC Berkeley were settled in 1969 with the establishment of Ethnic Studies programs at both campuses.

In the spring of 1969, I received notification of my acceptance into the University of Berkeley at California, for the upcoming fall quarter of 1969. I was awarded a complete scholarship package. Despite the turmoil of the past year, I had at least fulfilled, this, my family's life-long goal. In 1969, UC Berkeley was then one of the top 10 prestigious universities in the United States, the only California school campus rivaling the Ivy League schools of Harvard, Yale, and Princeton.

As I waited for the fall term, several of the Il Piccolo activists invited me to co-found a new organization, Chinese for Affirmative Action, to be modeled on the NAACP. I felt too whipped by the last year and declined the honor. My head was spinning from the events of the past year. I still suffered emotionally from the attacks of my classmates, teachers and the confrontation with my principal. Also, the closing of Il Piccolo and Leways completely demoralized me.

I felt a personal sense of failure, having misjudged the situation and now accepting that any peace in Chinatown was a long time a-coming. Mainly, I recognized even that a good heart couldn't substitute for my lack of hard political and professional skills. Perhaps along with fulfilling my parents' dreams for a secure future, I might forge the tools necessary towards making a decent society a great one. I was ready to leave Dodge. No commuting for me to Berkeley and straddling two worlds. I'd live in a campus dorm there full-time and where I hoped to meet, understand, and engage people from all over America. Maybe one day I might return with the knowledge and connections that could change conditions.

Or not.

Like my parents, I knew when it was time to leave the village. And now it was my turn to sally out into the larger, unknown world of America, and university was but the first stop, as far as I was concerned.

Chapter 25
First Son Leaves for University

I withdrew. Pulled down all the shades in the house. Sat in my armchair, not speaking except as necessary that fall of 1969. Your father didn't know what to do with me. Bob did most of the shopping and the chores. Everyone thought it was because you left home for university, that I was sad because of that.

Not because of that. You were supposed to go to college. That's what your father and I wanted for you, especially your father, because that's the only way you could get past his restaurant jobs. You know, in my village, we had lots of middle schools and high schools and Hoisin had lots of colleges. There were even famous universities in Guangzhou and Hong Kong. Children's education was important for Toisanese. We believed that children shouldn't have to worry about making money until after college.

I was sad, not because you left home, but because I had failed you in this duty as a parent. When a Toisan boy goes to college, a Toisan family is supposed to give him money. For books, housing, and food. For new clothes for the first day of school. For a car to drive. But no, not a red cent did we give you, we were so poor. We couldn't even drive you to Berkeley because we had no car. Instead, one of your own friends took you there.

I failed you as your mother.

The few times you came home for dinner, you pulled up the shades. Said you didn't like the dark. Tried to cheer me up. But no use. I pulled them down as soon as you left.

You sent us a letter, trying to cheer me up. I remember that letter, thanking us for teaching you well. You said there was a larger world out there, one we knew very little about. You asked us not to be sad at your leaving. You said that we could trust you to find your way, even if it meant making mistakes, that we could not always protect you. You said you always would honor and love us, and you would be home for Christmas and Chinese New Year. You mentioned nothing about receiving no money for college. I guess you didn't know this was our parental duty.

But when Chinese New Year's 1970 came around, I pulled myself out of the sadness. Chinese New Year's—always a time to let go of the bad stuff from last year. Always a time to think ahead into the New Year for all good things. That's the way it's been for over five thousand years, ritual and celebration. Pay your debts. Make peace with your enemies. Put away sadness. Clean the house. Cut your hair. Wear new clothes. Adorn the house with plum branches bursting with blossoms by New Year's Day, and pyramids of shiny tangerines topped with living green leaves. Then, bless children with shiny red envelopes of money, coconut candy, sweet ginger candy, and all kinds of delicious dried fruits. Every one of the ten days has a special significance. There's a best day to have a start-the-year dinner. The lunar calendar tells each family that. There's a "everybody's birthday" celebration, when everybody becomes one year older, celebrating that once again, together as a village, we made it through another year successfully. That's why we rarely celebrated your personal American birthday—the community's collective birthday is the time for our traditional celebration.

But the most essential practice is no bad thoughts, no bad words, and no negative feelings of anger, sadness, and envy. For the whole ten days. Forgive everyone who offended you or harmed you in the past year. Pay off your debts, can't let them linger into the New Year. Always maintain a positive attitude, because how you think, feel, talk, and treat people during the first ten days determines how things will be during the next year. This positive attitude affirms the good of the past year and continues the flow into a joyful and provident year ahead. This is how difficult situations change for the better, enemies become friends, and misfortune turns into abundance.

You were so happy when you returned home for Chinese New Year's Eve dinner. The shades were up, the house was bright and clean, the plum blossoms were flowering, and your red envelopes sat on bowls of shiny tangerines. I was my old self, soaking vegetables, cutting up white boiled chicken, and snapping orders at you for last-minute purchases.

You gave little John his red envelope money, then tickled him silly and finally swung him around and around like you used to do.

I guess you knew your mother's spirit was back for you practically leaped in the air for joy when I barked at you to go get the crackling skin pork. "Make sure the skin is crackling—lok, lok, lok," I reminded you, like when you were a boy. You never seemed so pleased to be ordered out to jostle with the last-minute lines of New Year's Eve shoppers. Like us, they must have the tastiest two pounds of the last roasted pig of the day for this, the closing meal of the old year. Steaming fresh out of the oven, chopped while still too hot to handle with bare hands.

Yes, you were happy and so was I... again. Gung hay fot choy. Sun neen fai lok. *All good fortune in the New Year.*

Chapter 26 Clouds

My strongest memory of my first year of college is of clouds.

Clouds of tear gas blanketing protesters throughout the year, like my first day in Berkeley, when I almost changed my mind about UC Berkeley. That first visit, I joined thirty-thousand People's Park demonstrators herded along by armed National Guardsman, bayonets at the ready, with half-tracks revved up for mayhem. We reached People's Park, ringed by chain-linked fences, and defended by National Guardsman in formation with their bayonets pointed out at us. Even under their helmets, they looked more scared than brave, as we on the other side went through our fears at armed guns in our face. The funny thing was that we were both of the same generation, that in a different situation, we might share a joint or a beer. Then something happened, female protesters stuck long stems of sunflowers into rifle barrels, and the National Guardsmen let them stay.

At a second visit, a noontime anti-war protest, through clouds of tear gas, rag-tag groups of anti-war students battled *mano-a-mano* with fully armed, helmeted police all afternoon long. Tear gas invisibly drifted into classrooms, libraries and the student union, wispy remnants that clawed at our eyes and throats for hours after the campus police had time-punched out.

Caught somewhere between abject terror and shame at my fear, I forced myself to stay through both visits. It's one thing to be intellectually courageous or to speak one's truth in calm, safe assemblies and public rallies as the worse that can happen is to be booed off the stage. But the physical act of marching into well-armed soldiers and police who, days before, had wounded scores and blinded one bystander, or witnessing people beaten in front of you, is "really real." Yeah, I was scared shitless both times, but I stayed until the end.

In my freshmen year, cumulous clouds glided over the spacious campus, more clouds than I had ever seen in my urban upbringing. Clouds burnished Maxfield Parrish beautiful by the neo-classical columns, wide peaked roofs, and marble steps of Berkeley's buildings and as afternoon drew to a close, the golden light of the setting sun.

Clouds of marijuana smoke in the rooms in Davidson Hall, our co-ed dormitory, as America's middle-class children gathered in our generation's version of cocktail hour, listening to the Beatle's *Abbey Road* album, exchanging stories of our upbringing, flirting, clucking our dismay at the War (always the damned War), exchanging rumors about Professors, and asking who wanted to carpool to Altamont, where the Rolling Stones were giving a free rock concert.

Clouds of mental confusion as Marxists, Conservatives, Liberals, the Spartacist League, the World Law Federation, the Esperanto Society, Hare Krishnas, Jews for Jesus, Students for a Democratic Society, the Christian World Liberation Front, L. Ron Hubbard, street characters like the Soap Bubble Lady and General WasteMoreLand, and our outnumbered professors competed for our attention, our allegiance, our lives, and our souls.

The UC Berkeley campus, circa 1969, was obviously was not my family's life-long notion of bucolic academia. Had I told them that the university was an armed camp, they may well have insisted that I attend another campus.

So, I didn't tell them.

Beginning with my Il Piccolo friends, I had started to edit my reports of my doings to Mother and Father. But with Berkeley, I went beyond editing, I hid truths from them: the dangerous demonstrations, my lifestyle experimentation, and the many fleeting liaisons. When and why had I started this concealment? By my third quarter, I was barely visiting my parents' home, afraid to reveal how much I had grown and grown away from them.

My evasions started that day when my Mother's soft words and mediating style failed to soften my high school principal, and I thought, bless her heart, but she doesn't get this America. Recognizing it was Father's aggressive soliloquy on my behalf and our attorney's confident power that persuaded him to rescind my suspension, I concluded that these were the tools of influence and success, not mother's ways, not her Chinesey "Why can't we all get along? We're all friends here." Her gentleness looked like weakness, her soft words came off mute, and her patience easily mistaken as surrender. So much for her old Toisan ways. At a deeper level, my turn away from Toisan ways had started at thirteen, when pinched by life's circumstances, Mother was no longer able to pipeline to me the energy, the connection to Toisan. I had too long been weaned off her spiritual mother's milk.

My Father's repudiation of all things Toisan had already pushed me away from him. I vividly remember the day when I turned fifteen, when he raged, "I will pay the rent, put food on the table, and buy clothes for you until you turn eighteen. After that, you're on your own. No more help from me." From his perspective, it was a good offer as I would ha e five more years of family support then he did. Dad was on his own at thirteen. But he didn't present it as a traditional passage into independence but as a punitive edict, a threat even. He snarled it in my face.

In Toisan, parents proudly supported scholarly gifted children: even a poor family would sacrifice greatly to put a son through college. Had mother been present, she would have sharply remonstrated the coarseness of his words, the error of his threat. But it was just the two of us in my bedroom.

Father's words didn't hurt me so much, as shook me awake. I didn't like what he said as who likes discovering that his father considers him a financial burden, who kept him chaining to frustrating jobs? I simply took it as his truth from his own childhood and now and my truth from him. So, I continued my turn away from Mother's nurturing soft Toisan perspective to Father's harsh view of life, his "roughing it" immigrant viewpoint. Okay, I will be on my own at age eighteen, and I silently upped the ante, and free of you too. You won't hear from me, and you better not be telling me how to live.

As we counted down to lift-off date, I felt a decreasing responsibility to let my parents know of my whereabouts, thoughts, and friends, and yes, my explorations and experimentations of a kind that would trouble them. I prepared myself to honor my father's eviction notice.

So it was that with a portion of the same courage that brought my father, and then my mother into an unknown and equally daunting America, I checked into Unit II, Davidson Hall, UC Berkeley's first co-ed dorm. Finally, I was on my own, paying my own way through a hard-earned scholarship and a part-time campus job planting and then cleaning up hundreds of tomato plants at the Genetics greenhouse. I opened myself to used this time to enter a larger American, aware that the intimacy of Davidson Hall would help me decipher the unspoken social mores, cultural codes, and implicit rules of mainstream America.

Although I had been better exposed to America than my parents and in a cosmopolitan way, better exposed than most Americans, my San Francisco was not Middle America, and so mainstream Americans remained a mystery to me. My first insight was the discovery that Jewish Americans were not 100 percent white folks, even if they were indistinguishable in my eyes, but a kind of category within white folks. Davidson Hall introduced me to this new category of Jewish-Americans, who looked white to me, but not to WASPs, who considered them off-white.

Nothing personified this split more than the relationship of my floor-mate John, later the editor of our nationally regarded *Daily Cal* student newspaper and subsequently an investigative reporter for the *Wall Street Journal*, and his dorm girlfriend Alysha from Los Angeles' West Side, an upper class Jewish-American enclave. Free to fall in love with a non-Jew within the liberated zone of co-ed Davidson Hall, Alysha soon succumbed to lifelong social mores and family pressure to marry within the Jewish community. They spent the rest of that year as "friends," but John's heartbreak was constant in his downcast eyes.

I surmised that, similar to Chinese-Americans, Jews had faced prejudice, found strength in five thousand years of their own recorded history, and fostered strong communities to overcome the obstacles. Sounds a lot like the Chinese-American community, I thought. Ironically, a philosophical dispute arose as to whether Asian-Americans, the model minority, were really people of color, as true-blue an oppressed minority as others in the Ethnic Studies department as African-Americans, Chicanos, and Native Americans unquestionably were, even as we Asian-Americans had carved out our own department within Ethnic Studies. Many viewed us more as "off-white," not than "off-color," a position of ethnic ambiguity akin to that of Jewish-Americans. Were we one of those endless variations of lustrous not-quite-whites with underlying yellows, blues, or grays that only home decorators truly appreciate. Despite the history of anti-Chinese ethnic cleansing, we also ended up being the "model minority," and still suspect as the supplicant ally of the majority society.

The second surprise was that not every Rockefeller was considered of equal peerage: hierarchy existed within elite, wealthy white families. Peter, a Rockefeller, explained to me that children who were direct offspring of Rockefeller men enjoyed higher status than those of men who had married

Rockefeller women and joined the family. Peter's father had married in, mandating that Peter and the other men and women in his category wore blue tuxedoes or cocktail dresses at the annual family reunions. This color lessened them from the "authentic" Rockefellers, who as the preferred lineage, wore formal black. Peter chuckled that the "blues" had all the fun at these clan events. My fondest memory of Peter, a son of privilege despite his misgivings, came about one afternoon as I rushed off late for work at the Genetics Department greenhouse on the other side of the campus. He agreed to retrieve my clothes from the impossibly slow dryer. Not only did he do that, but he also neatly folded over ever so neatly every pair of underpants, socks, jeans, and T-shirts into piles, and then arranged them in a neat row on my bed. A Rockefeller fetching and folding my laundry! Father, once a houseboy, would never believe it. Warm feelings welled through my body, renewing my faith that most people, at heart, were intrinsically kind.

Unfortunately, the hardest lesson of Davidson Hall was that too many of my white dorm mates lacked this second-nature *tai-chi* balance of give-and-take within relationships, a balance so intrinsic to my upbringing under Mother. Perhaps it was the difference between the communal-village sensibility of my Toisan heritage and the individualistic focus on acquisition, ownership, and privilege that constituted the upbringing of most of my white dorm mates. Over the year, I increasingly felt ripped-off, then increasingly dishonored. I waited in vain for the natural rebalancing, but to my surprise, the more I shared, the more I was perceived as a soft touch, a pushover, a weakling. I had to pull back, not be so generous with my records, books, notes, limited funds, and marijuana stash. This withholding was not an easy transition for me, but I learned to harden as a first response, and then to soften only when sure.

By spring of 1970, settled, but at times disappointed with life at Davidson Hall, I turned back to activism. I started by switching jobs to work at the new Asian Ethnic Studies program, as the inter-departmental liaison to Black, Chicano, and Native American Ethnic Studies groups, a role well suited to my multicultural urban upbringing and as the sole male clerk-typist there (thanks to my typing classes in junior high school). Interestingly, in their community service orientation, Asian Ethnic Studies offered Conversational Cantonese in direct contrast with the classical Oriental Languages Department which offered Mandarin exclusively. An improvement, but a puzzling choice to me, more like a bad compromise, as Toisanese remained the predominant dialect of the Chinatowns of America. I wasn't surprised. Most of the activist campus Asian-Americans were middle-class, raised in white neighborhoods, with little if any fluency in any Chinese. Thus, this decision to offer Cantonese was well-intended, but from the head and not from the 'hood.

Later, inspired by Mao's Cultural Revolution exhortation to go down to the country and learn from the people, the department moved all its offices and classes into the community, which coincidentally meant San Francisco Chinatown. Intellectuals could both serve and learn from the people if based among them. Despite it's Red Guards "correct line" imperative, I discerned that the real and unconscious motivations were personal: these fully assimilated kids craved an Asian submersion to feed the starvation of cultural isolation; to heal wounds of assimilation, and eventually, to feel bone-deep good about being Asian-American. I piped up, that since I just came from the "hood," I'd gladly hold down the scaled down campus office. "You know, like answer the phones, pick up the mail," to the chuckles of my sympathetic fellow clerk-typists.

On May 1, 1970, President Nixon sent in B-52s to carpet bomb the neutral country of Cambodia, escalating a war he had promised to end. Immediately after that day's morning news, students truck and shut down the entire UC Berkeley campus by noon. Then clouds of tear gas once again roiled through the campus, and over the streets as our growing ranks spilled into the community. Over the next three days, other campuses followed: 536 of them, to be precise. On May 4, National Guardsman shot and killed four students at Kent State, Ohio. On May 15, law enforcement shot and killed 2 and wounded 11 students at Jackson State, Mississippi, an African-American college. While unrelated, somehow, we conflated it with government's counterattack against the national student strike.

In response, students were more resolved than ever to keep the campuses shut down. To what purpose, since it was our own education at risk? Again clouds of confusion of practicality colliding with ideals, for no one wanted to lose a term's worth of academic credit. Several Berkeley faculty members lead us beyond striking for the sake of striking by proposing "Reconstitution," a complete reorientation of the University's teaching purpose towards spreading the truth of the war into the larger community.

If ever a speaking-round-and-round took hold at Berkeley, it was during Reconstitution. Department by department, then college after college, Reconstitution was adopted. Everyone was equal, professors, students, men, women, people of color, whites, even campus workers who cared to join our discussions. We spoke, shouted, quieted each other down, and planned the next day's anti-war activities. Those final two months were the most comfortable of my freshmen year, with its bonds of community and the exhilaration of acting together for the common good.

Along with other students with Bay Area roots, we rode out like a brigade of Paul Reveres, to our old high schools, churches, and community centers. I alerted friends at Galileo to an upcoming anti-war march. At a previous San Francisco mobilization of over 150,000 marchers, I had spotted many Galileo students, pleased to see that the pioneering activism of my Chinatown days had taken root and spread to other issues. Soon, I was recruited to join an antiwar tour addressing Asian-Americans at nearby campuses. Apparently, I was one who offered a different perspective: Chinatown born-and-raised and working class.

After a packed, contentious but, and rousing presentation at UC Davis, an agricultural sciences campus an hour from Berkeley, Jerry Chong, from the old Kearny Street apartments, introduced himself. I was puzzled when he asked if I remembered him. Of course I did for he was the older brother I never had, whom I admired for his brains, athleticism, leadership, style, and leadership.

In the chaos of my first year at Cal, Jerry was the embodiment of sanity, harkening back to our simpler, halcyon days in the Kearney Street apartments. We reached out, shook each other's hands. In the grab of our handshake, I felt as if I had reached back onto the safe shores of that stable epoch, of my first home, our apartment building cum village.

Jerry filled me in on his time in Vietnam, as the respected leader of a marine squad that fought the Viet Cong nightly in the Mekong Delta. Night patrol was the deadliest patrol, a nervy game of hide-and-seek and search-and-destroy among the quiet waters and darkened reeds.

On too many mornings, white American GIs had stood in his way, staring him down, and demanding to know, "Who's that gook? What's he doing, wearing commando stripes?" or "What is that doing, carrying an M-16 like he's worthy?" Never wounded in combat, yet these bursts of racism wounded him as deeply as bullets. Still, Jerry returned home a hero to a job at IBM, earning rave performance reviews and promotion after promotion. But when he and another valued IBM employee, the only other Vietnam veteran, wore black armbands on a national day of silent opposition, the rave reviews and promotions stopped, the personnel counseling sessions increased, and soon he was out of a job. Jerry was in his second year of law school at UC Davis.

My main point that day, that at home Asian-Americans suffered from the same mentality that considered Vietnamese aspirations unimportant and their lives cheap had struck home to Jerry. It was white Americans, not his Vietnamese enemies, who had spat words of hate at him and, most spiteful of all, questioned his American birthright, Jerry ruefully recalled. His words penetrated more deeply than any well-written anti-war editorials or stirring orations. In small moments, I had wondered whether I was cowardly, or unpatriotic, or ungrateful for opposing the war, but no one could challenge Jerry's medals. Jerry and I were the same kind, and but for a few years difference, I would have blindly fought alongside him. Those doubts now disappeared for good, grounded in the reality of Jerry's rejection of the morality of the war.

We had been hooked by an angst of finding ourselves at odds with the country we were raised to love and serve. Were we ingrates whose actions shamed our parents, since they had found economic and political refuge here? But Jerry had paid his full price of admission in night-patrol and I'd paid mine in the streets, was still paying it as we spoke. We were the only ones who could, and did, provide each other absolution from what had felt like a sin.

When President Nixon announced America's's withdrawal from Vietnam in January 1973, Cal students danced wildly on Telegraph Avenue and Sproul Plaza, chanting "Ho, Ho, Ho Chi Minh, NLF has won again!" The campus quickly shifted into a more-or-less normal rhythm of study, play, final exams, and quarter breaks. I hitchhiked home for dinners and holidays, and family was only a phone call away. But I progressively drifted from the closeness of my family, coming to relying on my familiar if temporary "families" in Davidson Hall, Asian Ethnic Studies, and campus activist circles. I was living out the pattern set by my parents, and of centuries of independent Toisanese pioneers, casting out onto the seas of the larger world. My father, as if in instinctual accord, checked on me less. Mother, though, continued to insist on my presence at family gatherings, solicitations I patiently but frequently declined.

In the same way, Richard was already making his own life. In early 1972, I knew enough of the surface facts to conclude that Richard was walking along a similar path to mine, but not in my footsteps. He co-organized a student walk and march from Galileo to the Board of Education, protesting the same issue of a Chinese-American glass ceiling in the public schools. Where I had merely raised this issue, they succeeded. Stanley Tong, my Geometry teacher and a popular sports coach, was eventually appointed principal. Richard, too, served on the Chinatown–North Beach Youth Council, organizing youth dances, street fairs, and other community events. Yet he never visited me at Berkeley and wasn't interested in applying there.

He won a scholarship to attend State University that coming fall, planning to continue his summer teller job with Wells Fargo Bank on a part-time basis while enrolled. Richard, too, was becoming his own man, and I was happy for him.

We had grown up as close as two brothers could, running the streets of North Beach, Telegraph Hill, the waterfront; walking to and from the same schools every day; avoiding or fighting off the same bullies; chipping in to buy the *"Down Memory Lane"* record collection from Reader's Digest; jointly collecting Spiderman, Fantastic Four, and X-Men comic books, and in our last collaboration, Playboy magazines. As the older brother, I often overshadowed him in strength, reputation in school, the streets and the mission, and of course, priority in our parents' traditional eyes.

Richard didn't seem to mind my first-born ranking, since I wasn't a mean older brother. In critical ways, we were equals, made joint decisions, some very important ones. Once, when I was around ten, after our Boy Scout troupe wound down, one older neighborhood boy, a newcomer and a teenager whose father owned the local rice store, drew us momentarily into his "Rebel Without a Cause" juvenile gang. We started with a short spell of shoplifting toys from downtown department stores. Then, he began to talk of "rumbles," the 1950s slang for fistfights with kids from other blocks or what he now called "gangs." His pitch sounded fun in a dangerous kind of way. But one Monday, our teenage would-be leader of the pack gleefully reported about his recent weekend in a place called "Juvie," the local Juvenile Hall incarceration facility. At that point, Richard and I looked at each other, went home, and talked it over. If shoplifting and rumbling led to

"Juvie," this would cause a lot of trouble and distress for our parents, not to mention the punishments we'd suffer for weeks. One of us offered, "I'll quit if you quit." We did, convinced others of our old pals to stay away, and then wisely spent our evenings, once again, in our apartment building, studying and playing with the Cheong kids, and our weekends with Father at the Saturday matinees and family Sunday brunches.

Like most brothers, we had our tussles, but they were rare and fought fairly, never to inflict damage, and at any sign of surrender we stopped and went on to the next thing, grudge-free. Harmoniously sharing the same small project bedroom for eight years, happily tolerating the beat of top-forty radio, the mysterious sounds of my French or his Spanish lessons on our tinny record player, the smells and noise of raising guppies, hamsters, and lizards, we ended many a night falling asleep together sharing stories, life's lessons, and tomorrow's plans.

Our later conversion into the Assemblies of God church was in tandem, too. True, our old Kearny Street pals had joined *en masse*, but we now lived blocks away in the new Ping Yuen projects, with our own playgrounds, the Cheong kids, and scores of new friends. If either of us had hesitated, or wasn't interested, that would have been the end of it. But we went for it, and although Richard left first, without consulting me, his departure actually quickened the process of my own exit.

Richard's abrupt solo departure from the Assemblies of God mission was his first major step into his own life. From that moment, we slowly drifted apart, at first imperceptibly, and then by strides during my two remaining years in high school, as my interests in theater, music, the counterculture and finally, politics filled my time.

It was during this drifting that we fought our final fist fight. Richard said something that seemed to be disrespectful unnecessary to my older brother lip, or in my unconscious resistance to his developing independence, I took it that way. We threw fists hard and fast, harder than usual, as if we knew the fight was about our growing apart, about Richard freeing himself of my older brother authority. Soon we were on the ground wrestling. Then with a final fury, my last breath actually, I managed to sit on top of him, pin his arms to the ground with my hands, and shouted, "See, I can still beat you. You're still my little brother, and don't you forget it." But we knew that it could have gone either way that day. We never fought again, but between us, he. He was now free now of my traditional first-son authority, but I too was free of having to watch over him.

Then, surprisingly, I repeated this same ritual of emancipation with Father, only our encounter turned quickly dangerous. Although Father had expected me to be on my own by eighteen, he too, didn't had hard time accepting my burgeoning autonomy. One night he unfairly threatened me with discipline. His justification, mirroring my last fight with Richard, was that I gave him lip. He screamed that he was still my father and as long as I lived in his house, I had to obey him. I was seventeen going on eighteen, and full of myself, and refused his command to extend my palms for a chopstick whacking, a sharp, but relatively harmless childhood punishment from childhood. I knew I didn't deserve it and I certainly wasn't putting up with any infantilizing punishment. As with my final fight with Richard, this too, was the last hurrah of Father's evaporating authority. Enraged , Father screamed at me and we ending up shouting for minutes. Suddenly, he scurried into the kitchen, u-turned, and alarmingly armed with a small, Serrated steak knife in one hand, rushed me. I as quickly dashed safely into my room and bolted the door.

This fight wasn't like the one with Richard, where there was never a possibility of serious injury. One of us had to stop, and I knew it would be me. Lost in rage, Father lost control. From behind that closed door, I screamed that I held the stout business half of a cue-stick, whacking it loudly against the door to emphasize that I would defend myself. I screamed that I wasn't afraid of him anymore, that he could no longer treat me unfairly just because he was in a bad mood, that I could really hurt him. *Thwock. Thwock.* He left my door and within a half-an-hour, we had both calmed down enough so that I could leave for some night air. Father was slumped in the living room armchair. He didn't look at me, didn't say not a word, lost in something. He never physically disciplined me again.

So by the time I reached Berkeley, I lived very much apart from these male members of my family. No longer growing up in my footsteps, my little brother became his own man, with his own interests, friends, goals and secrets. We didn't see each other except during holiday dinners. I rarely made it back home, and though I encouraged Richard to consider Berkeley, he never visited me.

I used our separation to avoid the life-long oppressiveness that can characterize the sibling relationship between Chinese-American brothers close in age, where the younger always gave way before the example of the older, and the elder had to live up to a higher standard. Even though my authority had seemingly vanished in a final fight, I wanted to give Richard respite from this still-powerful conditioning, space that he obviously wanted and space, too, that I wanted, to explore, play and grow, to not have to monitor him and advise him on his every activity.

So, with my single-minded focus on Berkeley, my activism refocused back to campus, where I co-founded a very successful campus club, the Asian-American Students Association. My motivation for such a massive undertaking was because middle-class Asians didn't invite me to their parties: I was a Chinatown kid, an undesirable car-less student from the projects who didn't go away during spring and winter breaks. As it turned out, I found the few parties that I crashed to be downright boring, cocktail parties barely buzzing to a kind of soft-volume, soul muzak. I wanted to amp up the happening vibe and create fun, stimulating events where everyone was welcomed, and, yes, that even the coeds who had rejected me couldn't resist. Our student group started with multimedia dances (akin to the early Winterland happenings), then poetry readings, jazz performances, and art events that expressed our long-suppressed Asian-American heritage. Our swiftly growing membership swung the annual campus election to Bruce Quan, a Chinese-American, as co-president of the Berkeley associated student unions and John Sugiyama, a Japanese-American, as co-vice president.

About to complete my bachelor's degree in architecture, I contemplated entering the school's Master's Program in City Planning and Urban Design. The conventional academic wisdom was that public housing projects inevitably devolved into devastated battle zones of drugs and violence, where community spirit and personal self-esteem degenerated along with the buildings. It could be otherwise, I knew, like the nurturing, self-contained community of my own Peaceful Garden Chinatown housing project. Perhaps a new generation of urban architects, actually raised in public housing, could and would design a new kind of safe, decent, and sustainable public housing for all Americans.

That summer, I was about to fly overseas to visit the three faces of China: republican Taiwan, free-market colonial Hong Kong, and then the Communist heartland. The first step of my new career was to return to my family's past. I received a departmental grant to photograph the public housing spaces there in Taiwan, Hong, and China. My plan by was to unite the my past with my future, on a journey combining field research with my search for personal roots.

Now the only clouds over Berkeley were of the cumulous variety and soon clouds in the sky as I jetted off to Asia. Spring was finally peaceful and the lengthening days sunny.

Life was great.

CHAOS UNDER HEAVEN (1972–1978)

Chapter 27 The Speaking Round-and-Round Goes Nowhere

What mother wouldn't want her children to have the best possible future, not to be limited like your father's generation? Despite all the troubles with the principal, everything turned out okay-okay.

And so, Richard followed in your steps, speaking out about Chinese rights. He started by working an after-school job sweeping up and watering the plants on Old Chinatown Lane for the senior citizens of the Self-help for the Elderly Agency. Later, he worked with the Youth Council and Wells Fargo Bank. He was going to State College in the fall.

Those last two years before college, Richard was spending more and more time with his new friends. He went out of town on trips, to Los Angeles and New York. With the summer youth program, he said. One summer, he called to say that he would be a few days late returning home. It turned out that he was in a car accident and didn't want me to know. One summer, he went camping a lot, and then stayed out later and later all the time.

*But you did the same, so I thought this was normal. Everything looked okay-okay for Richard, as far as I could tell. But now looking back, of course, it wasn't. The elders were getting angrier and angrier, calling the young people "bandits" and "lawless elements." Everyone was afraid of the Wah Ching. More kids on drugs. Where did all these drugs come from? So many so suddenly, like from out of nowhere? And guns were everywhere. How did so many guns show up in Chinatown at the same time? There were never shootings in Chinatown before. More and more burglaries, young men robbing old people. Your father was robbed several times, on the stairs of our own Ping Yuen housing project, returning from work late at night. Aiyahhh—*jow gow sli-lah, *chaos under heaven! Chinatown was no longer safe.*

I should have followed the situation more closely. Things were changing from your time. What was wrong with me, thinking events would let him move right along just like you?

You know, in our village, if we saw problems coming, we could talk about it and change the situation. I told you about the speaking round-and-round of the Clan Sisterhood, a way to fix all kinds of problems, even between two angry people who hated each other. Of course, back then in the village, we didn't include men because they didn't listen to women. Especially if a man was part of the problem. But once we decided on a course of resolution, we stood in front of his house and harassed him day after day, talking loud, shaming him, and pleading until he gave in. If it had been like the village, I would have known what to do. There would have been no trouble, no rebels, no war, and maybe Richard would not have, would not have… been jailed…

One day, in the summer of 1971, a warning in Chinese was posted in Chinatown, calling for an end to lawlessness in the community. Bing Kong Tong issued it. The poster threatened that those young people who failed to comply would be stopped by any means necessary. By any means necessary. The warning was published in Chinese newspapers, in three columns across the page. The warning was posted everywhere. Grant Avenue, Stockton Street, all the side streets and dead-end alleyways of Chinatown. Everyone in Chinatown was ji-ji-jah-jah'ing about it for days and days.

Night after night, I stayed up waiting for Richard to come home. Sometimes, he came back home by 11 PM, other nights, at 2 or, 3 AM, and sometimes he called to say he was sleeping at a friend's house. But at least every night, I knew he was somewhere safe. I wasn't the only one worrying. All my Clan Sisters worried every night. Chinatown was dangerous now, with the killings, and something terrible could happen just because your son was in the wrong restaurant, on the wrong night.

I didn't think the bulletin had anything to do with Richard. He was like you, a reformer and a rebel, not a Wah Ching. He was not a lon doi—a broken child, juvenile delinquent. Yeah, yeah, he was a good kid, saved money all the time, starting as a child. He collected rare coins, Lady Liberty head dimes, buffalo nickels, and silver dollars. Worked at a bank, no surprise for he liked money, touching it and having it around. Going to college. It was that girl, that May Tom who testified against Richard, who kept changing her story about what the gunman looked like. She even said the gunman shot with his right hand. Everybody knows Richard is left-handed. Been all his life. Does everything with his left hand.

Maybe I was too busy raising baby John, trying to have some fun when I could. Poker with the Clan sisters. Going to Reno for a few nights. Maybe I wasn't thinking straight. Maybe I didn't watch over Richard enough. Maybe if I had, he wouldn't have gone to jail. That's the one thing I feel bad about, that I let Richard down. I let Richard down. It's my fault he ended up in jail. I just thought he was like William. He's leaving Chinatown going to college and everything's fine. I didn't watch over him carefully enough.

In this way, I failed him as a mother.

Chapter 28 Wailing Wall

On the morning of June 16, 1972, when I read in the *San Francisco Chronicle* that a Richard Lee had been positively identified as the main suspect in the slaying of another young man, Poole Leong, I did not imagine for a moment that our Richard was the suspect. I paused at the coincidence, but with scores of Richard Lees listed in the phone book, I was unconcerned, didn't even call my parents to double-check. End of story, and what else is in the *SF Chronicle* today? I flipped to the *Doonesbury* comic strip.

In the past few months, the media had been reporting an alarming number of sensational murders in and around Chinatown. Police sources blamed a Chinese youth gang war. Yet, it was never clearly substantiated what, if anything, they were fighting about. Was a Chinese-American Hatfield-McCoy personal feud running amuck? Were Wah Ching factions fighting over street rackets or in retaliation for unpaid gambling debts and bad dope deals? The news reports fed the public's growing sense of shock, an escalating feeling of outrage, and finally a desire that something - anything - be done to stop the violence.

Enjoying the trajectory of my rich student life and urban design aspirations, I had somehow compartmentalized Chinatown as the past. I was living large in Berkeley. This was my time, my life and perhaps deep down, I didn't want anything to put on the brakes, to force me to "slip back." I wasn't consciously aware of this filter, but in effect, I was long gone from Chinatown. It was easy enough to ask old friends. Or more directly, to call Richard for his perspective and assure me he wasn't involved in any way.

Inexplicably, I didn't.

Instead, I wryly editorialize in my mind that the Il Piccolo sages had predicted this bitter fruit. Your just desserts, Six Companies— – and I sighed with the smugness of the righteous. Thus, I muffled the alarm bells clanging inside head as the media relentlessly reported gang-style executions in and around Chinatown.

On the morning of June 28, 1972, my sanctimony received a hardcore dose of reality. Over the preceding two weeks, I hadn't heard a word from Richard or my parents. The *SF Chronicle's* front-page headline story reported that Barry Fong-Torres, then highly regarded and dedicated executive director of a Chinatown youth service agency, had been shot to death the night before, when he answered the door to his own apartment. Barry Fong-Torres's murder put a human face on the murderous horror ravaging Chinatown. Unlike anonymous immigrants, he was someone I, and the larger public, could have roomed with in college, befriended at a cocktail mixer, or debated with over a beer. His brother was the famous *Rolling Stone Magazine* journalist, Ben Fong-Torres, a role model for me.

The assassins left a scrawled note "Pig infomer (sic) die yong (sic)..."

This curious note caught my attention, an anomaly in *modus operandi* as no notes in any language had ever been left at any of the preceding ten-plus Chinatown-related slayings. As if youth gangs wouldn't have automatically been blamed anyway, the misspellings blatantly pushed the public, the news media, and investigators to search for no other explanation than the Chinese youth-gang war.

The article also reported that four hours later, mere blocks away from the crime scene, a Joe Fong had been routinely stopped for a speeding violation. Routine that is, except for one thing: my brother Richard Lee, a wanted man, was his passenger and now the police were fingering Joe Fong and Richard Lee for the Barry Fong-Torres murder!

What the hell was going on?!!?

Stunned, I had been away only for three years, yet, I was clueless. The rising crime rate was no surprise. After Leways and Il Piccolo shut down, there were no institutional restraints, no organizational home to refocus youth energy. Insider activists knew that factions of the Wah Ching had confederated with underworld elements and now openly fought each other. But we didn't know why, and the last few months hinted of Byzantine interests making moves beyond our ability to interpret. The general Chinatown community was essentially as befuddled as the general public. For example, who was Poole Leong, the man my brother was accused of killing? Was he a tong soldier in the wrong place at the wrong time, a wannabe Wah Ching who crossed the wrong person, or was he killed because of a personal vendetta? If Richard was the gunman, as alleged, what was their connection? What could have motivated Richard to kill him? As for Barry Fong-Torres' murder, what was it exactly he was snitching about that required him to be silenced? If the police believed that Richard and Joe had slain Fong-Torres, as the media reported, they should have charged them both, but never did. A simple paraffin test that night would have implicated either of them. But neither one of them were charged with this slaying. In fact, no one was ever charged with Barry Fong-Torres' death. That however, did not prevent the police from later assuring the Fong-Torres family that the right people had been put behind bars (ostensibly Richard and Joe Fong), but for other crimes. No one, the media especially and perhaps not even the police department, really knew what was happening, only that it was happening.

Or did Richard kill them? First Poole Leong, then Barry Fong-Torres? I didn't think so, couldn't think so, couldn't or wouldn't imagine that of my kid brother. I hope to God not, but really, I didn't know anything anymore.

Still, I clutched my one sure connection, Richard, and hoped that, like Ariadne's cord, he could navigate me safely through the labyrinthine puzzle of a now unimaginable community, to uncover the facts and ultimately, to prove his innocence, if innocent he was.

That meant reacquainting myself with visited Richard in, of all places, at the city jail, where he would sit until trial. The bail amount was surprising high, although Richard wasn't a flight risk as he had shown up at his bank job every day until his arrest. The young adult facing me through the thick Plexiglas window was not the confident, low-keyed, suit-and-tied, smiling bank teller I had dined with, months ago, at Johnny Kan's, where jackets-and-ties were *de rigueur*. The man in front of me seemed distracted, lost, and disheveled in his prison issued jumpsuit. Then, as he focused on me, he seemed to grow hard, and his two dark eyes glowered into me, as if to strip away all notions of civility. I picked up the phone handset, but Richard carefully batted away my questions.

"What was going on in Chinatown? Is it true what the papers were saying about him? Why... who... killed Barry Fong-Torres?"

His lawyer had cautioned him against talking over the electronically bugged visitor-phone system. Still, he reassured me of his innocence, urging me to talk to his lawyer, James Martin McGuiness instead, for the details of his defense. Some friends had retained him on Richard's behalf.

This was comforting news as McGuiness was one of the city's finest lawyers, a die-hard defendant's lawyer who once willingly spent several nights in jail when he refused a judge's order to divulge confidential client information. If anyone could, surely James Martin McGuiness would rectify this nightmare.

McGuiness' young associate, Patrick Coyle advised me that Richard should never have been charged for Poole Leong's murder. Richard had a complete alibi for that evening -- dinner with friends, and then attendance at a graduation ceremony at Lowell High School, both events taking place on the other side of town at the same time as Poole Leong's slaying. The sole connecting evidence was the uncertain eyewitness testimony of a sixteen-year-old Galileo student, May Tom. Also, Coyle continued, descriptions of the assailant varied and none of them matched Richard's. Moreover, everyone identified the shooter as holding the gun in his right hand, while Richard was 100 % a left hander.

I suggested that Richard might be scapegoated, convicted through guilt-by-association gang innuendo. Coyle was confident he could make a successful motion to prevent this kind of prosecutorial tactic. But in any event, the innuendo could easily be refuted. Richard didn't fit the profile. No prior arrests or convictions. He had a responsible work history and guilty men would not have shown up to work every day, particularly not in the bustling, very public City Hall branch of Wells Fargo serving cops, Judges, and reporters! Another fact that didn't fit the thug profile was that Richard had been accepted into State University for the fall semester.

Coyle felt sure this was a case of mistaken identification, one that would be cleared up soon.

Momentum, personal momentum. So hard to cancel my life in the making, my trip to the three faces of China. Fear of regressing to an old reality. In the Superman comics books of my youth, a villain would trick Superman into a mean, crude, and ugly parallel universe, known one called Bizarro world. To return to normal reality, Superman had to trick the villain into repeating his own very strange name. What charm, what magic name, what strange incantation would deliver Richard and me back home to where we belonged?

My heart was set on leaving for the Far East in a week, but how could I leave with my brother in jail? I discussed canceling the trip until Coyle advised me that the trial date was early November and, that nothing much would happen between now and then, except, perhaps, that the real killer might be arrested during the summer.

Richard felt the same way, that there wasn't much that I could do whether I was in the Bay Area or not. Perhaps in our new non-dependence and autonomy, he felt that his problems were his, and mine were mine, that he had no right to upset my plans. Momentum, faith in your chosen destiny, all too readily, I took him at his word and, too, convinced myself that it was all right to go.

I flew to Taiwan and then Hong Kong with the hope of entering China. I never got into China. China Travel Service kept dawdling on the visa, until finally, in frustration, I gave up. However, the trip turned out fabulous in despite that. I sharpened my Mandarin, and spent hours at the National Palace Museum in Taipei, Taiwan, ogling Chinese art. In Hong Kong, I lived with relatives in a massive housing project named So Uk Choon, but, through Berkeley friends, was introduced to every level of Hong Kong society. How had I thought a few days in Hong Kong was enough? Hong Kong was public housing field work heaven and I stayed in one of hundreds with relatives. I shot hundreds of color slides and black-and-white photos, and received a standing ovation from my School of Architecture colleagues following my presentation.

Still, this journey was nothing in comparison to the journey I was to undertake after Richard's trial.

At summer's end, Richard was still in jail. He lost his bank Wells Fargo Bank job along with his college admission and scholarship. As the November trial date approached, Coyle informed me that, given the weak case, the firm had decided that Coyle could proceed to trial, confident that the trial judge, Judge Walter Calcagno, would dismiss the case on the basis of insufficient evidence.

My parents and I attended the five-day trial until the verdict was rendered on November 1, 1972. Except for watching the Perry Mason series on television, we had no experience of the court system. We simply assumed that, just like Perry Mason, our Coyle would catch a dishonest witness on the stand or the police would arrest the real killer at the last minute, and that *tah-dahhh*--Richard would be free and justice served. That's how naïve we were. We pushed open the high double wooden doors into a cavernous windowless chamber, feeling like little toy figurines abandoned in a huge, spare toy chest. The lack of windows and the overhead fluorescent lights discomforted, as if we were sealed off in a strange universe with its own rules and unpredictable denizens.

Bizzaro world.

As I watched this trial, however, a dense, sinking feeling pressed me further back into the rigid, hard wooden bench of the spectators' section: I recognized the vampires of anti-Chinese racism past rising from their coffins, gathering around for a blood feast, to gorge themselves on the energy of someone at the prime of their vitality. It was as if the national Civil Rights movement were only a TV drama, as if we had never marched on Grant Avenue three years earlier, jump starting our own stalled march for full citizenship.

First, Judge Walter Calcagno disallowed the defense attorney to examine the mostly white jury pool on their racial attitudes towards Chinese-Americans. Then, the prosecutor, Pierre Merle, precluded both Chinese-Americans and African-Americans from the jury.

He then called, as a completely unsure "eyewitness," a teenage girl who had glanced out of a well-lit apartment into a dark courtyard. She couldn't or wouldn't answer a straight yes to a direct question unless the Prosecutor prodded her several times. I had to wonder if she was under coercion to testify.

Then, a white Chinatown police intelligence officer, Sgt. Diarmuid Philpott, testified as an expert on Chinatown, but never mentioned the decades old gambling syndicates' and their pay-off schemes to police and politicians, or the tongs' recruitment of Wah Ching youth, but only speculated on my brother's criminal connection. He diagrammed a youth-gang war between two groups, Wah Ching Youth and something called the Joe Fong Gang, then speculated that Richard Lee was Joe Fong's right-hand-man, who killed without hesitation on Joe Fong's orders. He suggested that this slaying was part of a series that must be stopped to protect the terrorized residents of Chinatown and outraged San Franciscans alike.

If the reader is wondering why I appear more observer than participant in narrating the events of the trial, it's because I often was. I couldn't fathom why the prosecution so aggressively persisted despite the weak, circumstantial evidence. I didn't know Richard in the close way of our earlier years. I had been away from Chinatown events, felt psychologically alienated. My old friends, now fearing for their lives, would not talk to me, nor bring me up to speed of the impact of the closing of Il Piccolo, Leways, and the tong recruitment of Wah Ching factions. So the trial had aspects of a refresher course for me, as well the real-time determination of Richard's guilt or innocence.

The trial concluded with the craven, oppressed, offal of a jailhouse of confession by a desperate convict, in jail under arrest for kidnapping and armed robbery in California He was also about to be returned to a Federal penitentiary in Indiana to serve out an unfinished sentence. This young adult African-American inmate, Thomas Porter, Jr. testified that yes, yes, an otherwise tight-mouthed Richard had inexplicably confessed the crime to him, in gratitude for being saved from an attack by other cellmates. Moreover, Richard had given him a name of an outside contact, in writing, who could help him buy a gun upon his release, and that outside contact, a social worker with a respected youth service organization, was the older brother of Joe Fong.

This linchpin of the prosecution's case was divulged at the last possible moment as are all proverbial "last minute surprise" witnesses, the classic tactic of desperation that miraculously wins the weak case. Coyle strenuously objected and then firmly overruled by the Judge.

Coyle then moved to exclude this testimony. Denied. Coyle then requested a recess, a reasonable period of time to investigate Porter's story. Denied.

Porter further testified that Richard had boasted that May Tom would not identify him, for fear of retaliation from his gang, effectively dispelling the smell of possible pressure put on her by authorities. Yes, he admitted he was a repeat offender, in custody for kidnapping a Bay Area taxi driver at gunpoint, then forcing the driver to transport him and his girlfriend to Southern California, a drive of many hours. He insisted that neither the police nor the District Attorney had approached him, but apparently in a fit of civic duty and good citizenship, he had contacted them of his own volition. He claimed he had not been promised leniency for his testimony this day, nor were any promised made to his co-defendant girlfriend, a Caucasian prostitute pregnant with his child.

Yet, this man who apparently had not been able to raise bail earlier, strolled easily down the aisle when he finished his testimony, past my parents and me, glancing warily towards us as he sauntered out of the courtroom that day, apparently a free man.

That was the prosecution's case: the unsure, wavering testimony of a reluctant eyewitness, the selective expertise of a Chinatown-based police sergeant, and a surprise jailhouse snitch. The Assistant District Attorney then wrapped the gang war theory around this tenuous evidence, appealing to public outrage at the unsolved Chinatown murders. He used the young eyewitness' reluctant testimony to play up the community's fear of the retributive power of the Joe Fong gang. He signaled the need for society, represented by the jurors, to put someone away and send a message to the gangs: their day of terror was over.

As it turned out, Richard's young lawyer, schooled in the fairness of the Constitution and the system, so fresh to practice, was not able to preclude or defend against this inflammatory innuendo. Richard's case was Coyle's first murder trial: he too lost his innocence as well that day.

As for Richard's unlikely banker's profile, the prosecutor characterized him as a Jekyll-Hyde personality, a polite, patient bank teller by day who switched to an evil alter ego at night, robotically killing upon the orders of his Svengali-like leader, Joe Fong. Objectionable speculation at best, but Judge Calcagno didn't seem bothered by this gratuitous, spontaneous psychiatric expertise.

They had pulled out all the stops, and, as horrified as I was, I was truly amazed at the extremely circumstantial nature of the state's case. This was a desperate case that should never have gone to trial. I thought that even this all-white, crusty, old-line San Francisco jury could see that. There would be a Perry Mason ending after all, but one provided by the jury, even this all-white one. The jury was the idealistic linchpin of our justice system, those common sense peers who would sweep away every prosecutorial smokescreen and penetrate every legal sleight-of-hand.

But the prosecutor gave an amazingly spellbinding closing statement. He had this jury in the palm of his hands, even had me going his way once or twice. Despite the contortions of his case, his style was crisp, sincere, and rational. None of the jurors seem to have any inclination to suspect that his reasoning could be faulty. No wonder he removed all the Chinese-American and African-American jurors, I thought to myself. These were his kind of jurors, I realized. I was now worried.

I thought the final nail had been pounded into Richard's coffin, but we were wrong. The worse was to come.

In a distressing "coincidence" on the eve of jury deliberations, California Attorney General Evelle Young called a major press conference where he denounced Chinese youth gangs as the leading organized crime threat in the state, a story that played on major local TV and radio news broadcast that evening and on the morning of Richard's jury deliberations.

The *SF Chronicle* reported:

> *The Chinese youth gangs named in the California Department of Justice report on organized crime are believed to be responsible for at least 13, and probably 15, murders in the Bay Area since 1969.... Because of their wide-spread involvement in gangland killings... Chinese gangs are fast becoming threats in the state and other parts of the country in cities and towns having Chinese communities.*

The Attorney General's Report replicated in all respects the contours of the police intelligence expert's Chinese youth-gang war theory. Was there some kind of secret script making the law enforcement rounds, I wondered? This report neglected to mention the Mafia and the Teamsters' Mafia-linked illegal pension dealings in California, then under active federal investigation. The report said nothing about tongs, gambling parlors, or police pay-offs. Chinese youth gangs, it appeared, were the primary bane of California's law enforcement problems.

Richard wasn't the only one imagining a well-orchestrated conspiracy. We were knee-deep in Bizarro world, and the insidious atmosphere of that courtroom now blanketed the Bay Area, all of California, like a torrid, noxious smog which couldn't be blown away. Yet, I kept hoping to trigger the magic phrase that would drop us back into the good old days. My parents believed in the justice of the system, my mom in the humanity of the jurors. We'll never know for sure how the previous evening's broadcasts and the morning paper may have influenced the unsequestered jurors, because the Judge didn't probe the jurors. I do know that after only a few hours of deliberation, the jury found my brother, Richard Wayne Lee, guilty of the charge of the first-degree murder of Poole Leong.

In that moment, we became green card holding permanent residents of Bizarro world.

I was stunned. So was my father. Mother was silent at first. What I remember most was my mother's reaction the moment she realized what happened. She hadn't understood enough English to comprehend the announcement of the verdict, and we were too stunned to tell her in the courtroom. It wasn't until the bailiffs unceremoniously shooed us outside that I told her in Chinese, "Richard lost."

Mother then let loose a wail that rose, dipped, and rose again. She placed her hands against the marble walls outside Department 22, and, as if beseeching a God that had broken a promise to her that day, started to wail louder, and louder again, and then again louder in an ever-rising aria of anguish. Between her wails, she wretched out Richard's childhood name "Dickie, Dickie, Dickieeeeeee!!!!" Between shrieking out Richard's childhood name, she banged her forehead against the marble. The corridor, had become her private wailing wall.

Mother had no soup to make that could balance the conflicting passions of justice and law, retribution and punishment, at play in the situation. There was no social ritual to invite a healing discussion between contentious parties. She had had no role in the fate of her most precious treasure, her child. She could not speak to the dead victim and ask him tell to her the name of the real murderer. All she could do was wail.

I think that all courtrooms should have a wailing wall, a psychological *pissoir*, an emotional vomitorium, conveniently located just outside the courtrooms of justice, a place to get it out of your system when you've had more than your fill of the system. Legal justice seems so cut-and-dried. Yet it is not. Never for the defendant. Never for the victims. Or for their "others," the families, friends, and community. Not even for judges, prosecutors, defense lawyers, and the police.

But there is no such wailing wall. In the halls of justice, no one has permission to wail unchecked. We tried to comfort Mother, but to no avail. She could not stop and we could not stop her. The male bailiffs in the courtroom, who had moved us out, stood there, uncomprehending at first. They were men. Tough guys. Then they looked ready to forcibly move her out to the streets. After all, other courts were in session and the process of justice could not be disturbed.

Finally, two women bailiffs gently touched her, and then comforted Mother. One was black and the other was white. They spoke to her in English, which she could not understand, of course. But Mother heard them, heard them when she couldn't hear Father or me. She heard them because they sang the secret melodies of those who know hurt in the heart. They were women and they were mothers. It was another kind of Clan Sisterhood, and it wasn't necessary to speak the same language.

They said they would take her up to see Richard. One of the male bailiffs indicated that was against procedure, but in a tone suggesting he wouldn't be a stickler this time. The women bailiffs called up to the county jail's turnkey and arranged for a visit. Because Mom didn't speak American, I could accompany her.

We rode the elevator up to the County Jail, escorted by these two women bailiffs.

We were shown into the cell, where Mom immediately grabbed Richard, hugged him, and started weeping. After a few minutes, she calmed down. She said we would visit him as often as we could and bring him Chinese food. She urged him to be good, do his sentence, and when he came out, we would be there for him.

I said to Richard that what happened wasn't right, and I was going to do something about it, find the real killer, seek to overturn the conviction in some way. Richard said he wasn't asking me to do anything, that I was under no brotherly obligation.

"You don't owe me a thing."

He stressed that I had my own life to live. This was his fate and he would live as best he could with it. Anything I decided to do was strictly up to me.

"Do what you got to do, but I'm not asking you to do anything," he underscored.

After about fifteen minutes, the two women bailiffs escorted us out of the jail, then back down the elevator. They asked Mother if she felt better. "Yes," she said. "That's good," one of them said. They walked Mother, Father, and me outside the Hall. Mother thanked them, smiling through her tears. They looked at each other, part of the same circle, members of the same secret society. And they were—the society of mothers with sons and daughters. Of mothers who hurt for their children.

Just another Clan Sisterhood.

Chapter 29 Rub the Hard-boiled Egg on the Bruise

Just like when you two were kids in the summertime. Scrambling on your hands and knees to climb up Telegraph Hill to Coit Tower. Slipping and sliding on the rock bar at Aquatic Park, where the baby crabs lived. Falling out of trees in Portsmouth Square. Racing here, dashing there. Wrestling on the sidewalk. Always playground fights. So of course you two came home with twisted ankles, skinned knees, and black eyes.

I'd clean the injury with warm water and soap. Then I'd boil up an egg. While the egg was still warm, I removed the shell. Then I slowly and gently rolled this egg against the injury. Back and forth. Round and round. The white of the egg turned blue as it absorbed the bruise.

When the egg was cold and purplish-blue, I'd toss it away. The egg had absorbed the hurt, the bruise faded away, and your own healing began.

As your mother, whenever my children get hurt in the course of life, I am like this kind of egg. I remain close to you, hover all around you, caring for you, feeding you and whispering affirmations to you. I absorb your hurts. I remove your bruises.

Richard's conviction was the only time I couldn't even lift a finger when my child got hurt. Yes, I was angry, sad, hurt. I cry even now thirty years later as we talk about this. After the trial, I woke up dizzy. Some days, I could not even get up and start my day. Other days, I wouldn't eat. I missed my boy, to see him behind bars, sentenced to life imprisonment. For his life! So young, a good boy. A mistake, the wrong boy.

Both Father and Bob took care of me, did their best to comfort me. Father stopped complaining, treated me nice all the time. Said it was Richard's fate, his life, not mine. Don't be so wrapped up that it sickens you. Then, instead of just giving me enough household money, he gave me his entire check to cash, to use it all as I pleased. I remember going to the bank to cash the check, so happy to have all the money for the first time in our marriage. I was in the line, and then I couldn't stand in line a second longer. I rushed home, closed the bedroom door, pulled down the shades.

Father understands some psychology – you know he's always reading this and that - and helped me to see that I needed counseling. He found a Chinese-speaking women's services center in Chinatown. They help battered women, even had a home for them. They also helped with mental issues, referrals, translations, just about any kind of problem a woman could have. For one week, they talked to me every day, from 9 AM to noon. Finally, they said there's nothing physically wrong with me, but that of course the trial had affected me deeply. I needed to take it easy, stay home, and sleep a lot. They recommended certain kinds of foods, happy films to see, and lots of visiting with friends. But mainly, I was to stay at home. One of their doctors prescribed medicine of 1/2 a pill a day. It made me sleepy, but helped me to me to stop thinking about Richard so much, to feel better during the day. I was to keep coming to the center every morning.

But that four block walk to their center became very difficult. You know how I am, I love the street chatter, calling my friends, touching the shiny vegetables, smelling the sweet fruits, checking the boxes of dried mushrooms, shrimp, and cuttlefish from China on the sidewalks. But I just couldn't walk it anymore. With every step, I just wanted to turn around and go home. So one of the counselors came to Ping Yuen every morning. She was so nice, too. We'd talk for several hours over tea and fruits. I always felt better when she left.

You know your father's wonderful that way. Even though we argue a lot about money, he doesn't like to see me unhappy. That's why he gave me his entire check. That's why he found the women's center. He even tried to tip the counselors, money for coffee and pastries. I never saw him do that before or again. They refused so nicely, though.

And that's why he never complained about Bob being my boyfriend, because Bob made me happy. That's a good side of your father, the side that didn't care what anyone thought of how he lived.

It was Bob who watched the children. Bob reminded them to stay quiet while I slept. Bob took them out to play, too, and then cooked for all of us, including enough for Father when he returned late at night. He bought me whatever treats I wanted, too. Later, when I got better, he drove me anywhere I wanted to go. Dim sum, fresh-baked buns and coffee, movies, and Sizzler's. Yes, he took me to Sizzler's a lot. I'd be eating my salad, all you can eat, too, and look up and there'd be all these happy people eating alongside me. Their smiles raised my spirits, made me happy for just a little while longer.

Clan Sisters came by, including the one who baby-sat Richard when you were kids. I forget her name now. They're telling me "Mo yeah, mo shloo," that there's nothing wrong. I'll be well soon, go out again to see movies, beat everyone at poker, and so on. They bought white, red, and orange candied fruits, big, sweet oranges, and Sun Wah Kue pies.

So, I got better and better. Soon, I could go with Bob and the kids to Golden Gate Park. I'd sit on the bench with a sun parasol — you know too much sun bothers me — as they played. We'd shard a simple picnic of sandwiches, chips, and sodas. I started to feel how wonderful life is, how happy I was to hear the children playing, the songs on the portable radio we took everywhere. We'd pet the goats and sheep at Children's Playground, and ride the old-fashioned merry-go-round there. We'd climb the old cable-car left like a toy in a sandbox and clang its bell like we were climbing up Powell Street hill. Sometimes we rowed boats in Stow Lake. Life was good. The days were good.

Then I wanted to play cards. Hadn't lost my wits as I could still read a gambler's moves like some people read the newspapers. Then, Bob and I went to Reno and had a good time. We went again, and again, and always went up on Wednesdays because that's when they served complimentary corned beef, red, steaming hot, with white potatoes and cabbage. Blackjack! 21! Became my favorite game. All you had to bet was a dime at blackjack in those days. Live bands playing for free. Free coupons for the breakfast buffet and free drinks while you played the tables.

After a couple of years, Richard seemed to be okay-okay in jail. That made me very happy, and before long, I told the doctor that I didn't need the pills anymore.

Sometimes it rains the right amount and the crops grows large and green. Other times the sun shines too strong for too long and the fields dry up. What can you do? That's the way life is. Just go from there, keep raising the crops as best you can. When I knew I was well again, that's what I did with Richard, make sure he stayed okay-okay. Even if in prison for life. Like the hard-boiled eggs from childhood, I rubbed Richard all over with Toisan ways, Toisan foods, and centuries old Toisan hopes of better years, marriage, and children. That's what I do with all my boys. Even if inside prison...for life.

Just like when you two were kids, getting hurt because of playing outside every day

I'd clean the injury with warm water and soap. Then I'd boil up an egg. While the egg was still warm, I removed the shell. Then I slowly and gently rolled this egg against the injury. Back and forth. Round and round. The white of the egg turned blue as it absorbed the bruise.

When the egg was cold and purplish-blue, I'd toss it away. The egg had absorbed the hurt, the bruise faded away and your own healing began.

Whenever my children get hurt in the course of life, I am like this kind of egg. I remain close to you, hover all around you, caring for you, feeding you and whispering affirmations to you.

I absorb your hurts. I remove your bruises.

Chapter 30 Healing Rites

A freight train named Unfinished Business had broad sided my American plan-what-am. But I clung to higher education's Promised Land, admiring the rare afternoon light as it sliced through my student apartment's living room window, warming my beloved books casually strewn about the coffee table, like lovers' garments from the night before. Outside the window, red, purple, orange, violet garden flowers hung off stalks in a profusion of Gramophone horns as humming birds with embarrassingly iridescent green and rouge chests whizzed their needle-beaks into stamen and pistils. So far from the concrete warrens of Chinatown. Just as life was getting good...this happens. I groaned at the advent of each too real day, of sixteen hours stuck in quagmire, not knowing what move to make, which direction to take.

Guilt, failure, shame, anger, hurt, resentment, and betrayal rebuked me. Guilt that I had enjoyed Asia that summer while Richard sweltered in the sweatbox of jail where a jailhouse snitch could set him up. Or more likely, the prosecution set up to lie about a confession.

Failure that I had not worked more closely with his lawyer, had not investigated the situation myself, had not found leads to the real killer.

Shame at Richard's conviction: how do I talk about this with Dale Benveniste from West Los Angeles, Richie Barton from Texas, Arthur Cotugno from Connecticut, or even Sherry Wong from Oakland?

"Oh, this Wednesday. I'm going to visit my brother in Tracy. What's he doing there? He's attending a vocational training institute. Just started."

Or could I honestly say, "Visiting my brother the convict. In for Murder One. One of those Chinatown slayings." And the implausible tagline, "He was framed, though."

Resentment at Richard that the tranquility of my life, our family's life, had been destroyed by whatever he had done, or had not done but was close enough to be sucked into, and that now, we found ourselves clawing the sides of a whirlpool.

Betrayal at a criminal justice system that I trusted. No - more than trusted, that I had faith in, believed in like a religion. Beyond betrayal, I felt the crazy-making need retribution against the cops, the prosecutor, the judge - all the bastards involved.

"Wake up!" I wanted to scream at my teachers and fellow students in class, in the drafting studio, or as we sat outside in the sun eating lunch. "A terrible thing has happened. Why are you all acting so godforsaken normal?"

They couldn't detect my distress, of course, and I didn't know how to tell them what had happened. Berkeley seemed a dream. Did I even belong here?

But Mother, my busy, energetic mommy, didn't seem to waste much time in regret or in rage. She was so vulnerable, so tentative those first few months. But she didn't throw out a lot of words railing against the justice system. She had a life to live. There was six-year-old John to raise, and her own aging mother to take care of in the housing project across from ours. Her Clan Sisters, too, called her out every day for coffee, gossip, and poker.

More than that, Mother unexpectedly had to raise another set of children—her brother's grammar-school-aged kids, Ada, David, and Victor. Married at a young age, their birth mother was ill-prepared for three children, and so, another man's promise of adventure took her away. But in the village way, there are no orphans. So it was that Mother found herself at midlife rearing four children as her own.

Mother didn't adjust right away, of course not. Those first few weeks especially, she suffered from bouts of melancholy. Downright depression. As such times, as during the ten days of Chinese New Year, she endlessly lip-synced the words of positive affirmations for freedom, success, and family for Richard, and forgiveness towards those who had wronged her. Those festive admonitions during my youth had all seemed liked silly old-country rituals, but they lifted her during this painful time. There was nothing celebratory about her mutterings now. She was praying desperately, like a Catholic nun white-knuckling her rosary, reciting umpteen thousands of Hail Mary's. Perhaps more accurately, she was like a Buddhist nun clicking off her beads, reciting endless *metta* prayers of loving-kindness towards all beings, and forgiveness in an ever-widening circle: from self to family to community, then ultimately including even those who had jailed her son.

To linger on hurt, anger, and regret would have led to a self-defeating bitterness, an outward rage toward an incomprehensible system and inward rage against her own powerlessness. Slowly, she wrestled her bitterness down to the mat, the deadly bitterness that paralyzes the chi force in each of us that she had nurtured all her life with her herbal soups. Life without active chi is akin to living death, to be a zombie, and I could see that Mother would never settle for that.

After a few months, she settled, accepted reality as it was, rather than as it should have been. She remained gentle, where I was seething. She simply took care of what was in front of her day-by-day, while I wanted to do something, anything, big enough to fix the mistake. She yearned to visit Richard at every opportunity, but I didn't look forward to prison visits, to be searched by guards, to be locked up ourselves for the day. To be violated by them again.

Her hellish wail in the Hall of Justice the day of Richard's conviction had sounded like the dying of a soul. But her Phoenix-like positive attitude, her renewed activity surprised me, and then inspired me to take events with some semblance of stride, to sustain the direction of my own life, and to be the big brother to my cousins as I loved John.

Just as when I was in Ward 75, Mother pressed us to visit Richard right away, assigning me the task the rules of how frequently we could visit. She kept on top of me to make sure we drove up as often as possible, three visits a month for each approved visitor. Then, we realized friends could even drive her up on different days than me so that, overall, we doubled family visitor days. It seemed that Mother's basic approach--or practice--was to surround Richard with the familiarity of family, a Toisan family, as often as possible. To rub us off on him. And invariably we were the first to arrive and the last to leave.

Still, I initially resented those prison visits, to be searched by guards, to be locked up ourselves for the day, to feel the violation again and again. Mother's hellish wail the last day of the trial was the dying of a soul. But her Phoenix-like activity surprised me, and then inspired me to take events with some semblance of stride, to sustain the direction of my own life, and to become the big brother to Richard again.

Invariably, we were the first to arrive and the last to leave. She sent Richard money orders for incidentals. Twice a year, she prepared and mailed a rather large birthday package and then a Christmas box that contained two cartons of cigarettes, Hershey's chocolate bars, packs of dried Ramen noodle packets, cans of Spam, bottles of Chinese oyster sauce and soy sauce, essentially every treat on the list of permissible items that could be stuffed into their prescribed carton size.

Then, three to four times a year, we moved in behind prison walls for a three-night family visit, staying in cottages built for this purpose. Bob couldn't join us, of course, for he wasn't legally family. But for days, he'd help Mother shop for the makings of three-days of Chinese feasting. Her sisters gave money. Her brother delivered a couple of pounds of the most delicious shrimp from his chef's job at Fishermen's Wharf.

After our first visit, Mom brought in her own complete set of Delaware cookware, her Chinese plates, and bowls, and chopsticks. The rudimentary visitation-cottages were well…rudimentary, providing only an incomplete set of white laminate plates, two or three well-charred pots and pans barely suitable for warming up canned foods or mixing in hamburger helper. The sagging and cracked furnishings seemed to have been rummaged from a fire sale of a bankrupt, low-rent rendezvous motet: Formica tables, collapsed couches, and sinking mattresses.

But Mother transformed each family reunion inside these dark, barren cottages into a Toisan hearth, subtly transporting us into our ancestral dining room in Suey Wan, where she herself had been loved in the simplest of settings and nurtured as a child during the horrors of the Japanese occupation. She strengthened Richard's body and as I could see, his spirit with his favorite foods.

By the time of our second family visit, I became more eager to participate in the routine, happily running whatever chores she assigned me despite the my now doubled-to-tripled demands on my schedule. Our first meal of each visit was an array of dim sum treats from Asia Gardens, then the best dim sum house in Chinatown. Car engine running, illegally illegally doubled-parked and fending off meter maids like a bandit team's getaway driver, I helped Mother make this final purchase before we hit the freeway, so Richard could eat the freshest dim sum.

She whipped up endless courses of the fresh, crunchy vegetables, thin-sliced meats, and steamed fish that had given both of us, and now John, our healthy, strong bodies. These patient, lavish preparations, far beyond satisfying hunger pangs and daily nourishment, created as normal a sense of family as was possible behind twenty-foot-tall electrified fences, a mere thirty feet from an armed guard tower whose klieg light and gun sights swept our family cottage all night long.

In the evenings, Richard sipped the herbal soups Mother had been brewing since early afternoon, the chi soups that had girded his chi-body and body fires during childhood, and as the changing seasons changed.

Within Mother's cocoon, Richard relaxed, found peace in the communal rituals of food preparation, family-style dining, and clean-up as he and mother engaged in a kind of practiced dance of gentle gestures, softened Toisan words, and unhurried shared tasks.

These were the simple family practices that perfected and passed on from generation to generation over a millennium, which even I knew so well from childhood. Despite famine, drought, bandits, twentieth-century warfare with its butterflies of death, and now imprisonment, our family just kept on living this way, grounding ourselves against the harsh externalities, healing each other, squeezing vitality out of the good fruits of the earth, our alchemical culinary knowledge transmuting that harvest, however abundant or sparse, however sweet or bitter, into renewed spirit and hope for a better tomorrow. Ten thousand sorrows followed by ten thousand joys, and sometimes all mixed up in no discernible sequence: this is life after all.

Over the years, it became clearer to me that our visits truly renewed Richard. As trapped as he was in this lower level of Dante's Inferno, by the end of each family visit the glare in Richard's prison-hardened eyes fell away by the second day of each family visit. His taut, cagey body, arms intentionally swinging freely at his side, ready to defend and strike, became relaxed. As he curled into an easy chair after each meal, those same powerful arms and rock-hard fists folded into his lap like a baby. As Richard recharged, the years left his face, like his body knew he was really part of something greater, something longer in time than a life-sentence, something bigger than his infamy as a murderous California convict, and his role as the victim of a cynical prosecution. He seemed to remember that he was from a lineage much nobler than his present circumstances. In those simple visitor cottages, I came to see that a prison experience could not only be endured, but also transcended. This too would pass and he might return to us intact.

When the departure hour inevitably arrived, Richard finished up his tasks of cleaning up for the next family while we packed our last bags. The further we walked from the cottage and toward the visitor's center, the less he acknowledged us. By averting his eyes, I knew he was disconnecting himself from us. As we looked back to wave our final good-byes, Richard's final smile would drop into a stoic line. He turned his back on us a second before the iron door to the outside thundered shut behind us. During the next couple of hours of his clean-up ritual, Richard undoubtedly put back on his mainline body armor in preparation. But underneath that armor, I felt certain that his inner being had been recharged, reharmonized, and reconnected to us.

Mother, too, put her armor back on, but it was the lighter, flowing armor of energetic, uncomplaining activity, and insightful chatting. She'd comment on Richard's face, his health, his attitude, and his job inside working the guards' canteen. Or that he seemed better this time, or more quiet, or his cold lingered a bit longer this winter. Like an agronomist, she assessed what she would bring up in the way of nutrients next time, to specifically fix this and that physical or attitudinal deficiency. Like a therapist, she considered what she would say to him, which apt words of wisdom to impart, during our next day visit.

From her example, I came to realize that all I should do was what I could do. I was not a Toisan mother, but I was certainly a third-year student at UC Berkeley with knowledge of, and growing access into the institutions of power.

Finally I was able to confided my plight to my two faculty advisors, professors Ken Simmons and Lars Lerup. I told them I didn't know what to do, but I thought to take a leave of absence to organize Richard's legal appeals. I might have to work two jobs to pay the lawyers and needed time to organize fundraisers. A leave often slides too readily into dropping out, and so Professor Simmons, an African-American who specialized in urban design solutions for the inner city, instead, reminded me that what the College of Environmental Design really taught was analysis and solution. Like many older African-American men who survived the terror of Jim Crow, Professor Simmons dressed low key, in dark and somber colors, so as to not attract undue attention. His words, however, were anything but low key. He stressed that the College's underlying philosophy, and the core power of its curriculum, was to teach us the ability to define the parameters of a problem with, in all its possibilities and limitations.

"Treat what happened to your family as a design problem and go from there," he told me. He clicked off the CED action litany: design practical solutions, but within society's reality—social, cultural, financial, and political. Research, hypothesize, and recheck your findings. Then and only then start formulate your working conclusions. Finally, engage the community in the implementation of the solution. Stay flexible, just as we have taught you here, in this school. And most of all, stay in school. Any distinction between your life and your schooling is artificial.

Professor Lerup, a tall lanky Scandinavian with wispy blonde hair to his shoulders, completely agreed with Professor Simmons. Also, he seconded this and then reminded me that I had successfully finished the rigorous two-year core curriculum, including a mind-boggling year of engineering, and that my last year of study would be a comparative breeze. Like Professor Simmons, Professor Lerup, too, specialized in designing exciting urban centers full of life, and creativity, and commerce. Lars was right, I would have a lot more time and energy in my remaining year at Cal. He too was adamant that I should not take a leave.

My faculty advisors help me feel like I still belonged at Berkeley.

I realized that if I had a hard-boiled egg I could roll to absorb the injustice of Richard's case, it would be these very tools I had sweated over in our student studios until 2 A.M. over so many nights for the past two years. But what did designing such a solution really mean? It's one thing to design a building, but how does one design justice and freedom? What they said made "sense," but although mentally convinced, I didn't know if I had it in me to carry on.

One Sunday morning, I awoke to all my doubts in a small attic room on the fourth floor of an old grand-dame Victorian mansion in the upper Haight-Ashbury. I pushed myself up from the firm mattress, and leaned my back casually against the wall. Sipping my coffee, I glanced through the small window overlooking Golden Gate Park, watching. In the distance, the towers of the Golden Gate Bridge snagging strands of fog as the sun lit the skies blue and the water green.

It was my turn to wrestle now. Would I do as well as Mother? My entire body was sore, as if I had been beaten from head to toe by a professional thug wrecking crew of thugs. It was more than the lumpy mattress: the soreness was within, filled with abject helplessness vying with an incendiary rage.

I needed clarity. Clarity, clarity, oh I pray, please descend upon me. What should I do? What can I do?

I knew that I could fake it by pretending this travesty hadn't happened and carry on the life I had created for myself at Berkeley. I'd run for student office, complete my master's degree in urban design, and transition onto the professional success track of America. It wouldn't be difficult to separate myself from my brother's conviction. After all, everyone would understand that it wasn't meI who was in jail. His actions weren't reflective of me. Besides, Richard had personally released me from any brotherly duty to help him.

Yeah, I could easily pretend Richard's life wasn't part of mine. If someone were to mention the "Chinatown gang-wars," I could feign ignorance. If someone more knowing were to ask, "Isn't Richard Lee your brother?" I could deflect it with something vague about fate, the different paths in life, and quickly move onto another subject. If Richard's story were to become an issue in my academic or professional my career, I could turn it around into a plus, i.e., I came from the same background and got out. Recite an enigmatic don't-judge-me-mantra like, "Some of us make it, some of us don't." Yeah, frigging converting his stain into my medal of honor, a testament to my character, focus, and ability to overcome obstacles that defeated others.

As for Richard, well, I would urge him to use his time in prison to better himself through correspondence courses, and what's more, I'd tutor him, too. Upon his release, I'd provide him a place to live with me for as long as he needed to get back on his feet. I'd set aside money for his education, or to start his own business, maybe a smoke shop like Benny's. Sure, I would help him transition back into society. That's what a good older brother would do, right? No one could ask for more, right?

Clarity, clarity… please…please clarity.

All well and good, except for one thing: I was witness to a frame-up. Of course, I felt an unacceptable shame on our family name. And like my mother, I felt guilty, that I hadn't protected my younger brother, hadn't stayed closer to him.

Yet, this sense of injustice was a separate kind of violation. The wonderful side of assimilation is that it actually instills in you the values of democracy. I believed in America. I believed in our Declaration of Independence and our Constitution: the right to life, liberty and the pursuit of happiness; and of equality before the law, due process, and fair trials. I believed that our America, our system, would correct this. In America's values of equality and fair treatment, and the justice system, I believe that America would set this straight.

Then, I mulled over the evidence as family shame alone doesn't justify reversing a truly deserved verdict of guilty. What if Richard had murdered Poole Leong? Just because he said he hadn't didn't mean he was innocent. Why weren't his alibi witnesses called? Did Coyle think they were they too easily discreditable as fellow youth gang members, like in other trials I had witnessed subsequently? Or were they liars and did Richard really have an alibi? Or was Richard protecting the real killer?

I looped everything through my head, time and time again. I believed my brother's assertions of innocence, and yet at times, he seemed such a stranger. Or did I need to believe in his innocence? The truth was, I hadn't been in Chinatown, and certainly not at the scene of the slaying that night, so perhaps I'd never know for the sure.

But I was at the trial. I witnessed it from opening to closing with my own eyes and, heard it all with my own ears. In America, there was a fundamental Constitutional right, that the verdict must come from a fair trial. I knew for a fact Richard was railroaded. Framed. You don't go after a man like that unless you didn't have a case, and but someone wanted him got, and you put him away regardless of guild or innocence or evidence. I had no qualms attempting to rectify that, to get him a second and fair trial, free of racial bias, dirty tricks, and media sensationalism.

That's everyone's right as an American.

Moreover, at another trial, of Richard's closest friends, Joe Fong and David Wong, I had witnessed the same thing happen to them. They had been framed in the same courtroom, by the same prosecutor, with the same police intelligence expert, and by the testimony of similar witnesses. Then, there were even other cases, involving other Chinese-American youth, and their lawyers and families protesting the same tactics, making the same claims of innocence.

That morning, I knew that I could not blithely ride the success train, continue with my life as it was. No matter how successful outwardly, I would be living a lie if I did not right this wrong that happened before my very eyes. I could not be and would never be a man unless I spoke up and dedicated myself to reversing this verdict, getting a new and fair trial.

A voice whispered that I was the only one in the family who could possibly begin to do something about it. Your parents can't because they have no understanding of the system. Richard can't from jail. John is just a kid. Richard's lawyer won't, because as bad as he may feel, and he feels terrible, it's just another case for the firm — win some, lose some.

Yet, I too felt trapped, stretched out on my own torture rack of competing directions: of doing right for myself and who could judge me? Or of doing the right by family and political values. In that moment, I broke down and wept, helplessly and long, keening a sad, miserable lament of the spirit.

But I really had no choice.

Unexpectedly and mysteriously, a steeling energy filled my body. My breath evened out. My mind became cleared. Where this clarity and resolve came from, this flood of energy, I couldn't say that day, didn't care that day. I was just in the experience Rather, I was the experience. That crystal moment of no choice but this one way, when I knew you can do this, only this. Do it. No choice. You must do it. No choice. You will do it. Clarity, clarity.

Blessed clarity.
Cursed clarity.
No choice, so start. "Just start," said a voice.
And so I started.

In truth, it had started with Mother, broken as I watched her so carefully, out of concern, in the days and weeks after the conviction. As I studied her emotional and mental resurrection, and then welcomed her back into my life. Her Toisan feet that just kept walking forward despite this season of disaster, these ten thousand daily sorrows. Her Toisan hands that just keep helping everyone in need, even as the bombs of emotional carnage fell all around her, just as the bomb had struck her war-torn childhood. Her Toisan energy sizzled, emanating off her like the sparks off an electrical powerhouse coil.

Like Mother, I threw myself back into real life. Now there was no longer a rift between campus and Chinatown. My family, three adults and four kids, spent peaceful days visiting with me in Berkeley, walking the campus, picnicking in the nearby hills, and barbecuing on my apartment balcony. I visited home more often, and Mother cooked my favorite foods.

Unexpectedly, I assumed the "parent role" for a while, not only planning family outings, but by boosting everyone's spirits and hopes, but also leading the way to clear Richard's reputation and our family name. In coming together, we somehow ducked under the emotional storms bearing down on each of our lives. Oh, the storms raged on, never so far away, but the hours were a bit more quieter, the days a little less difficult to get through. At times, I even forgot what had happened to Richard. Oh, the deliciousness of normality!

Like Mother, I dedicated myself my new life as I took on the work of raising money for Richard's appeal, investigating a changed Chinatown, beating the tom-toms to alert the Asian-American activist network of what was happening to many innocent Chinese youth down at the courthouse, and somehow finishing my degree. Eventually, I applied to law school as well, hoping that studying the law might help in Richard's appeals.

Like a monk taking vows of a simpler, yet more demanding path, I had carefully pared down to the essentials of life. No social life, no intoxicants, no money for theater, concerts, or movies. I wore the simplest of daily attire: white, crewneck JC Penney's t-shirts, loose-fit jeans, desert boots, and a dark blue Sgt. Pepper's jacket with four pockets. This jacket was not as an insouciant 60s Carnaby Street fashion statement: those four pockets held my calendar book, a notepad, pens, the day's catch of business cards, and a sandwich.

I determined to rise at 6 AM every weekday morning and with the dedication of a Saturday morning Jehovah's Witness, knock on the doors of lawyers, politicians, activists, and reporters alike - anyone who would give me a few minutes – to persuade them to look into Richard's case and that of other Chinatown youth.

"Please read the transcripts and you see. We're only asking for fair trials, not scapegoat legal lynchings, and to help get the real truth out about Chinatown criminality. So it could be cleaned up."

I would spend my weekends typing up the week's notes, planing next week's schedule. I clacked away at analysis, letters to the editor, any editor, and plan fundraising dances for Richard's appeals.

Because that's what it takes.

Chapter 31
Talking about Bad Times Brings Them Back

I don't like to talk about those times. The fighting. The killings. The tongs and the police. Richard in jail. All the lawyers and the newspaper stories. It's bad luck to do so.

In Toisan, it was tough enough to get through one year – plenty of bad things in any year. Who had time, or the strength, to remember bad things from the past? You talk about it and you feel bad. Then you get mad again and argue with everybody again. Then they get mad at you and, the next thing you know, everybody ends up suffering about something from a long time ago that isn't even happening today. What's the point of that?

In Toisan, we know it's smarter to focus on today, this season, each other, and what we have to do before dinner. That's why during Chinese New Year, we visit each other with fruits and candies, to leave a sweet taste. We apologize, forgive each other, and renew our friendship. No anger. No sadness. No resentment. No debts of any kind. Start the year clean, fresh, and positive

Did I hate the judge? No. Of course I was shocked at the mean sentence the judge gave Richard. Couldn't he see there was no case? So many years in jail for someone so young, a good boy. You know how I cried in the court. But I didn't hate him, or the prosecutor, or the police. What would hating accomplish? Would it make them better people, more honest, and fair? Would it make the witnesses tell the truth? Would it get Richard free?

In written Chinese, the character symbol for a common person's mouth is a single square, like a wide open mouth trying to say something. But the character symbol for an official has two squares, one on top of the other, connected by a column, and all topped by a large minister's cap with a tassel. This is their superior power, two mouths speaking at you. In Toisan we say, how can one mouth speak back to two mouths?

So, it is, there's no point to hating officials. Hate eats you up, drives you crazy, which defeats you, not them. They already forgot about you. That's Toisan philosophy.

As for Father, he said it was Richard's problem, not ours, saying "Nothing happened, nothing happened." Bob was reflective, that it was's just bad luck, that Richard was in the wrong place with the wrong people at the wrong time. But they didn't hate either.

Did I ever feel like revenge? No, it's crazy to talk that way and, besides, everyone knows better than to talk about getting even with someone. When a friend starts complaining about someone and talking about how they're going to do this and that back to them, I tell them to calm down. I tell them that really, it's not such a big deal when you think about it, is it? Then I point out that if they scolded you, there's probably some truth in what they said. She's your friend, so think about it a bit. Then I say, let's just wash all this off, as I'm doing now, and forget it. Life is good.

Did I even feel anger and hate towards the Japanese soldiers during wartime? We were so terrified all the time, who had time for anger and hate!?

But Richard's trial reminded me of China in this way, that people with money can get away with bad things and poor people can get put away for nothing. Officials respect you only if you're rich.

I remember how upset you were, how angry - you couldn't stand it because what happened was so wrong. But if f I were you, I wouldn't talk about those things in your book. Not the judge, the prosecutor, the police, the jail, the witnesses, the news reporters - none of it. You'll give renewed energy to the past. You'll bring those bad things back. Just don't talk about it. No one needs to relive that again.

Chapter 32
The Season of Ten Thousand Sorrows

In this I differ from Mother, and so I disobey her warning. Run the risk of her being right, that these memories, from our season of ten thousand sorrows, may very well arise from the dead past to accuse us once again.

Perhaps this telling comes from the American part of me, especially the denial-is-bad Californian school of humanistic psychology. I tell this tale, however, not as a kind of personal therapy. Thankfully, I am past that. Nor do I have any desire to refight old cases in the arena of public opinion or to get revenge on criminal justice officials.

But American upbringing, leads me differently. Mother grew up as a farmer's daughter in a disintegrating, chaotic, wartime China, when officials indeed possessed "two mouths," and routinely silenced the "one mouth" of country folk. I'm American-born and 100% homegrown and the "mouths" which speak for me, are the Bill of Rights and the fundamental right to life, liberty, and the pursuit of happiness.

But our lives are not Mother's Toisan ways, rites, and wisdom nor are Toisan ways a misty harkening-back to a romanticized past. For although Toisan ways were not the keys to unlock the American legal system, yet those ways, served a more important purpose: they held my family unbroken and in those places which broke, mended us.

Richard's trial wasn't our family's first legal encounter, just unexpectedly the worst. We had enjoyed dignified, benign, and fair engagements with the law. My father smoothly passed his immigration interrogation. A law firm helped Mother attain her citizenship. A kind judge, proud of her achievement, swore her in as a citizen that day so very long ago. A lawyer helped, with his knowledge of the fairness of the law, the rights of individuals, removed that unfair suspension from my high school record.

It was as American to fight to regain your rights as to have them, and liberty's cadence beat forth in my head as a drum roll.

So, I plunged into Richard's case like a workaholic steam engine, powered by triple-espressos, and my hard-earned Environmental Design skills. Just as my mother had visited me day-after-day when I was isolated in Ward 75, so, too, I dedicated my days to Richard. The first task was to establish the facts of the Chinatown environment, so changed from when I left three years ago. The slaying of Barry Fong-Torres had silenced Chinatown's outspoken, articulate, liberal activists. Fearful, very few of my old friends would speak freely with me.

One of my best sources turned out to be Richard himself, now serving his sentence at a state prison named Deuel Vocational Institute (DVI), an hour-and-a-half drive east of San Francisco.

In my three away, Chinatown had descended into the nightmare described in Bertold Brecht's play, *"Jungle of Cities,"* a grand, random drama of thundering, stark violence between rivals symbolizing contrary views of life: one was of the morally craven who desired wealth and power and the other was a paragon of astringent, idealism, sacrificing everything to protect freedom and personal choice. The drama unfolds against lies, corruption, debasement of the innocent and weak, intentional disinformation, and media manipulation.

With Richard's help, I was able to piece together the unfolding rounds of our own jungle of cities. He and his friends, including a charismatic youth named Joe Fong, somehow rambled into a pivotal role despite their teenage years. Bilingual, bicultural, outspoken, politically savvy, Civil Rights advocates, Joe Fong, David Wong, Richard Lee, and Raymond Leung exuded a natural leadership, forging deep friendships among both American Born Chinese (ABCs) and Fresh-Off-the Boat immigrants (FOBs). In their time, they had bridged the gap between between the Wah Ching and Leways youth, a task we Il Piccolo activists had attempted, but failed to achieve.

Too, Richard's group too challenged the old Chinatown leadership. Far from becoming the scapegoat for my high school stridency, Richard and his band spring-boarded off it. While we had conceptualize a student strike, they organized one and then marched from Galileo High School down to the Board of Education to lobby for more Chinese-American administrators. While we had talked about promoting our overly qualified Chinese-American teachers, their actions promoted Mr. Stanley Tong, my high school geometry teacher and a popular coach, into the position of Galileo's first Chinese-American principal.

Within Chinatown, they organized dances, street fairs, picnics, and cultural outings for at-risk youths for youth. In time, they and their followers became loosely known as Yau Li, initially meaning, "to have abundance." That was when the tongs began wooing members of Yau Li, just as they had recruited Wah Ching factions. They lavished Richard and his friends with banquets; they gave them well-paying jobs as doormen for gambling parlors, and made them errand runners for tong leaders.

By the fall of 1971, Yau Li had one foot in the heady idealism of the Chinatown liberal coalition and one foot in the lucrative rackets of the underworld.

Then, fights between youths spilled out into the streets. Some Yau Li wandered freely in and out of restaurants and theaters without paying, sometimes disrupting them with their fist fights. Others extorted money from merchants. This was a new definition of Yau Li became "to have profit," and the elders were not amused.

In May 1971, when Bing Kong Tong issued its infamous bulletin in May 1971. Matters had gotten completely out of hand. Written in Chinese, it warned all remaining lawless youth elements to obey, or they would "use any means necessary" to go after them.

In Chinese dialectics, rooted in the nature-based, yin-yang fluidity of Taoism, every position contains the seed of its opposing view; thus every viewpoint can readily change into that which it had previously opposed. Too, every conflict eventually narrows down to a two-line difference, and in that process, either the better position prevails, or the organization crumbles under the weight of its own contradictions.

And so Yau Li collapsed one night in September 1971, during a meeting at their clubhouse, a second-floor walk-up located in a dead-end alley in Chinatown's the heart of Chinatown. Richard and his friends argued that elders must not exploit the youth of the community, nor draw them deeper into crime, and that their future of Yau Li was in the larger Civil Rights struggle for all Asian-Americans.

The tong-affiliated members vehemently disagreed scornfully. Enjoying serious money for the first time, they saw their future with the old-timers. Chinese-Americans would never be accepted into the larger white society, they argued. Racketeers provided opportunities and money now, not after years of political activism. Anyone staying in Chinatown must obey the old-timers.

Then the tong-affiliated faction stormed out, dramatically scratching out their names and those of their friends off the Yau Li roster and stormed out. Later that night, at the popular late-night Sai Yon restaurant on Jackson Street just below Grant Avenue, the two factions ran into each other and a vicious fistfight broke out. Those who had led the walkout were severely beaten by Richard's faction.

Reaction was swift and deadly.

On October 2, 1971, on a busy Saturday afternoon, on Jackson Street and just a few store fronts up from Sai Yon restaurant, three young men shot Raymond Leung in the back and chest. A final shot, the *coup de grace*, was fired into his head.

Weeks later, three young men were kidnapped at gunpoint. Their tortured bodies resurfaced in three spots throughout the Bay Area during the first week of November: rice bags covered their blindfolded eyes, gagged mouths, and heads; their hands were hog-tied to their necks; and signs of torture marked their bodies. Two were youths I had once encouraged to stay in high school, but who had apparently joined a defiantly independent burglary crew beholden to no Tong.

Startlingly, these abduction-murders were clearly the work of professional assassins. The murders' message was clear: the crackdown announced by the Bing Kong Tong bulletin had kicked off in earnest.

No doubt, my brother, Joe Fong, and David Wong were also on that hit list. Richard said they avoided death only by avoiding Chinatown. He and his friends armed themselves, motivated more by self-defense than intent to war. In fact, this outcast group rededicated themselves to a nobler path, renaming their reconvened group, the Chung Ching Yee Association, a name that thundered out from the mythic Chinese tale, "The Heroes of the Water Margin."

As integral to Chinese consciousness as "The Odyssey" is to Western consciousness, these legendary martial arts heroes, unjustly driven exiled to the "watery margin" of a swamp, organized thousands of other exiles of farmers, shop owners and merchants fleeing the same tyranny into a huge rebel force. Their insurrection swept away the corrupt government to restore the mandate of heaven, that fluid, harmonious, mystical balance between emperor, subjects, and the cosmos -- so precious to Chinese social conscience.

The heroes' great meeting hall was named Chung Ching Yee, after the three virtues so lacking in the corrupt government they fought and so lacking in the old Chinatown order.   Loyalty to each other; Harmony among the brotherhood; and Righteousness in all conduct. Richard and his friends had defiantly declared themselves the rebel force.

These ideals struck me as not so different from the values of Mother's Clan Sisterhood. In their Chung Ching Yee council chamber legendary hall, these mythic heroes made decisions in an open, equal way, akin to "speaking round-and-rounds." They similarly advocated for the common good over personal avarice, and for the future of the nation over family aggrandizement values familiar to Toisan clans.

But in Richard's world, the savvy Chinatown elders and the underworld wing did not construe this cultural invocation as a call back to fiduciary governance, but as a challenge to the death: Chung Ching Yee must be crushed.

So that was the untold story. The complacent media parroted what the police fed them. Richard was a leader within this audacious, modern-day Chung Ching Yee when he was arrested, not the autonomic, right-hand hit man of Joe Fong portrayed in the trial.

Within months of Raymond Leung's murder, Joe Fong himself was wrongfully charged with three felonies stemming from three separate incidents. Despite several prosecution witnesses placing him at the scene of the murder on the first spurious charge, Joe Fong was acquitted because a white woman ticket seller remembered selling him and his date tickets for a movie, way over on the other side of town, a movie that began within minutes of the exact time of the shooting.

But Joe Fong, along with David Wong, were handily convicted at his second trial by the same triumvirate who had convicted Richard: Judge Calcagno, Assistant District Attorney Pierre Merle, and police intelligence officer, Sgt. Diarmuid Philpott. His alibi witnesses in this trial, were unfortunately only other Chinese-American youth.

Swiftly, these would-be leaders of a brave new youth movement were struck down, one-by-one, either by the gun or by the sword of the criminal justice. As with the protagonists in "Jungle of

Cities," it was unclear who was bad and, who was good; what was moral and, what was evil; who, if anyone, was winning, or what ideals had been trammeled in the combat.

What is certain is that the convictions of Richard and his friends changed little in Chinatown: its underworld rampaged on as Crazy Six, a former Wah Ching faction leader, and now head of the Suey Sing Tong enforcers, warred against the stronger Chinatown tongs from his base in Oakland's Chinatown. Other reorganized factions, old and new racketeering interests, old new alliances rose and fell against each other. The arc of death soared over the next four years, reaching a mortality toll of over thirty slain at its zenith and then climaxing in the horrendous Golden Dragon Restaurant massacre of Labor Day weekend, 1977.

A Hop Sing Tong member owned the popular restaurant and youthful thugs affiliated with Hop Sing Tong gathered nightly at the same table near the entrance, a table that served as a kind of office for them. That night, three masked men stormed in to assassinate the Hop Sing youth enforcers, but these wary thugs reflexively overturned their table, dove to the floor, and survived unscathed. Other diners, having no reason to anticipate a shootout nor the street instincts to do so, did not react so reflexively: five innocent diners killed and eleven others seriously wounded, several handicapped for life.

The unfolding of these events confirmed that Richard's case was larger than Richard. By focusing on Richard, the prosecutor and police had left untouched the tongs whose violence would later prove so deadly. Sensing the larger story, I focused on prodding the media into action. A few investigative reporters began investigating the Chinatown prosecutions. A May 1973 *SF Chronicle* front-page story supported Joe Fong's claims of innocence. The investigative journalist, Paul Avery, uncovered evidence of prosecutorial misconduct, the suppression of a confession of the actual gunman, Clifton Wong. He stated that Joe Fong was not even present in the car at the drive-by shooting. An alibi witness, a Chinese-American female, passed a rigorous lie-detector test paid for by the paper. Marilyn Baker, a TV reporter with the local PBS station, broadcasted several in-depth interviews with Joe Fong from prison. She too, became convinced of his innocence and the likelihood that others had been wrongfully convicted.

But the District Attorney's office refused to reopen the Fong case, and then Judge Calcagno denied Joe Fong's motion for a new trial.

A growing number of concerned community activists persisted. We did all the things a network of well-meaning poor people with limited influence supported by a few professionals can do in a situation like this. Pubic forums, private meetings, press conferences, legal fundraisers, fiery letters to officials and news media, demonstrations, contacting the Civil Rights Division of the Justice Department. Our strategy was, or perhaps desperate thrashing about is a more accurate description, we tried everything, pitching every one we met, optimistic that something would stick with some honest folks.

But we also conscientiously solicited the involvement of family members of the wrongly imprisoned into the campaign, at least those who could set aside their fears. Unconsciously, in this process of building a community-level consensus, we replicated the safety, confidentiality, and solution-seeking of a "speaking-round-and-round."

Well, something somewhere must have worked. Or perhaps some folks with greater influence quietly echoed our concerns to the right people. Or perhaps Barry Fong-Torres himself had long ago set it into motion, the reason why he may have been silenced. The FBI announced a major investigation into police corruption and gambling in Chinatown, as reported in the September 30, 1973, *SF Examiner* headline:

"Police Scandal Brews Over Chinatown Graft"

> *"A major bribery scandal starting with alleged gambling protection 'payoffs' by a dozen or more "Chinatown establishments" is about to rock the San Francisco Police Department, the Examiner has learned....... A joint police-FBI strike force investigation conducted over the past few several months has zeroed in on four patrolmen and a sergeant presently or formerly assigned to Central Station. Central Station includes all of Chinatown... where gambling and prostitution are believed to be widespread.... Police officers, at least one in uniform, have appeared under subpoena in a virtual parade before a Federal grand jury...... At least one of the officers who appeared before the jury during the past week, including a sergeant, are expected to be indicted on bribery charges...The. The number of police personnel who may be ultimately indicted could climb as the protracted investigation continues... "*

Confirming that a number of his men were under grand jury subpoena, Chief Scott informed the *SF Examiner* that

> *"[T]he multi-million dollar gambling industry in Chinatown has been the direct cause of a great deal of crime there and in adjacent areas, including burglaries, extortion and even murder. It has led to a climate wherein youth gangs have flourished.... There is reason to believe the most recent gang-type assassination in Chinatown... was directly linked to extortion within the gambling fraternity."*

Finally, a fuller truth was breaking through: Chinatown violence was more than just a couple of youth gangs shooting at each other. It was the outgrowth of a gambling industry, millions of dollars in scope. And corrupt police were involved. Richard and his friends, including Raymond Leung, the first slain, had not been silenced.

Still, the Chinatown elders who had cunningly survived a century in our American jungle of cities could not be so easily crushed. They outfoxed even the FBI, and lived to fight another round.

The FBI's key witness was Wai H. Ow, the infamous bagman who routinely paid off the cops, who was under a subpoena to testify before the Grand Jury. He could name policemen, dates, and pay-off amounts. Several days before, before the Grand Jury, this bag man was found dead, hanging by the neck in his own closet. Official cause of death was suicide, according to police investigators. Along with Mr. Wai H. Ow's death, the Strike Force probe also died and faded away.

So much for cleaning up Chinatown. Meanwhile, our family had our own problems. In early 1974, our appellate counsel Charles Garry, a renowned Civil Rights attorney and, as it turned out, the leading expert on minimizing racism through careful juror screening, gave us some bad news: the State Court of Appeals had rejected Richard's appeal.

Garry agreed with us that the legacy of racial prejudice against Chinese was very much alive and well in the San Francisco of the 1970s. He of course knew that one hundred years before, Chinese-Americans had successfully invoked the Fourteenth Amendment's equal protection clause in *Yick Wo vs. Hopkins, Sheriff*, securing the right to ensure equal enforcement under by local authorities; and that this Chinese-American case was later successfully cited by NAACP lawyers as legal basis for the landmark 1954 school desegregation case, *Brown vs. Board of Education*.

Ironically, the US Supreme Court had recently ruled that black defendants in state criminal cases were entitled to have prospective jurors carefully screened for racial prejudice. Perhaps they might had extend its applicability to Chinese-American defendants? After all, they had seen the connection between *Yick Wo vs. Hopkins*, a Chinese-American case, and *Brown vs. Board of Education*, an African-American case. Garry thus advised appealing directly to the US Supreme Court.

He strongly recommended that the community send an *amicus curiae brief*, or a friend of the court synopsis, outlining the largely unknown history against Asian-Americans in California, including the interment of Japanese-American communities in World War II. It's been a while since *Yick Wo* and memories fade, he said, and a brief coming from the Asian-American community is more credible than the assertions of his white law firm. So once again we started organizing and soon Richard's supporters – political activists, clergy from the local Council of Churches, university students, concerned private individuals, and outraged attorneys - raised the funds to print this brief and then obtained a sterling list of organizations and individuals concurring in the brief. The Asian Law Caucus, a recently organized group of law school graduates running a store-front community legal services clinic, mostly sons of Japanese-Americans interred during World War II, wrote the submitted the brief to the high court.

The American appellate process takes a long time and a lot of money. Through it all, our family patiently raised whatever funds we could. We kept hope alive in one another's company. Mother, Father, Bob and the four little continued to visit me in Berkeley for a backyard barbecue, a stroll through campus, and frolicking through the many sylvan delights of our regional park system. Yet, because of my growing public engagement with Richard's campaign and the issues around it, I knew they could be threatened, hurt, perhaps killed.

There is a bit of outlaw derring-do in my family's American sojourn, a willingness to bend the rules when we'd unfairly end up victims otherwise. At the height of the anti-Chinese exclusionary hysteria, my paternal Great Grandfather simply walked across the shallow riverbed of the Rio Grande into America one summer. His Mexican cotton farm had collapsed in some worldwide downturn in prices one year. My paternal Grandfather, born in America, was by birth a citizen, and his father somehow made sure that was properly recorded, regardless of his own dubious status.

When Father emigrated over to join his father, he faced the choice of being stranded in Angel Island for months, perhaps years, for failure to answer the draconian trivia exam about his village, even one whose pathways he knew by heart. Or he could buy a contraband copy of the exam questions that had somehow made it out of Angel Island to Chinatown San Francisco and then back to Toisan. Father wisely paid, surreptitiously studied in a hidden corner of the ship's deck each day, and then dumped the exam into the ocean a few days before reaching San Francisco. He was in and out of Angel Island in record time, and working within days of that.

In her turn, Mother, who did not read or speak American, memorized phonetics to pass her oral citizenship oral. She passed, was naturalized, and sponsored her mother and brother's immigration to America.

Motivated by a desire to protect and reunify family or to avoid unjust results, all my forebears had bent the rules of unfair laws, or as Mother did, creatively out-strategizing their testing methodology.

And so, my time came, too to initiated a subterfuge to protect my family . I circulated a rumor that my parents had disowned me. They disagreed with my criticism of the police, the judiciary and the tongs. That they thought my work on behalf of Richard's appeals was a waste of money. This rumor was of course designed to protect them: they lived within the shooting gallery of Chinatown, not me.

So, we met clandestinely, as we waited for the US Supreme Court decision. We also knew that new information not available at trial might also justify a new trial, evidence that investigative reporters could uncover, as media investigations uncovered in Joe Fong's. But no one was looking into Richard's case. Then good news! After reviewing the trial transcripts, Lowell Bergman, an independent investigative reporter, was so shocked at the flimsy evidence that he became interested. Our first break came when Bergman met with Porter, the jailhouse snitch. Porter told Bergman he had been forced to lie about Richard's confession.

I took the story to the *SF Examiner* and, after the meeting, William Randolph Hearst III and his editorial team assigned the story to Raul Ramirez, a highly regarded reporter recently recruited from the *Washington Post*. He would work with Bergman.

My parents were pleased. This good news helped us get through the bad news to follow, that the US Supreme Court declined to hear Richard's appeal, leaving the *SF Examiner* investigation as our last real hope. In mid-May of 1976, the *SF Examiner* ran its three-part investigative story. The first day's headline read,

Perjured testimony in Chinatown Trial: Curious conviction in gangland murder

The series filled in the blanks on the lingering mysteries of Richard's strange trial: Thomas Porter, Jr. stated in a signed affidavit that the prosecutor fabricated his testimony; that police induced him to testify under threats of violence and promises of leniency for himself and his pregnant girlfriend and co-defendant, Sybil Kenney.

May Tom, the sole eyewitness, stated that she was never sure of the killer's identity; that police told her she couldn't go home that night until she picked out someone from a police photo gallery of alleged Chinatown gang members. At the line-up, when she couldn't identify Richard, she was told instead to pick out the man matching the photo. Despite expressing her ongoing uncertainty, she testified only after being falsely told that her testimony wasn't that critical, as eleven others witnesses had positively identified Richard Lee as the shooter.

Weyman Tso, who was standing next to the gunman and fled the city after the shooting, stated that he saw the killer, and the killer was not Richard Lee.

The prosecutor and the police investigators declined to be interviewed.

Just after the *Examiner* articles, in a highly unusual move, two officers from the State Attorney General's office flew out to the federal penitentiary in Terre Haute, Indiana, to meet with Porter. They returned with another sworn affidavit. In this one, Porter recanted the affidavit relied on by the *SF Examiner* and reaffirmed his earlier testimony against Richard Lee.

What could explain this, yet another u-turn? Apparently, Porters was reminded that after his time in federal penitentiary, the San Francisco police had a hold on him for unserved time, a hold they could exercise or they could relinquish. That decision would, of course, be made at a later date. Porter didn't need a lawyer to understand the threat to his future liberty and safety.

I didn't know what to make of Porter. Yes, I felt anger, but more strongly, I felt a surprising sympathy for him. A sad and wizened sympathy, but sympathy nonetheless. Porter seemed both victim and villain. Perhaps he reminded me of Woody, my best friend in Ward 75, that kept my anger in check. Perhaps it was Mother's insistence on positive affirmations. The one true thing about him was that he was a practiced liar who traded fabricated testimony for a spell of freedom.

Someone so bright, and yet so trapped by the streets, whether of his own free will or under duress, Porter was intelligent enough to pick-up cues and package testimony convincingly for a prosecution who knowingly or cynically - and yes, criminally - used him. I could not summon that same sympathy for the prosecutors, the police, and the judge. They knew what a kind of person they had chosen were willing to testify falsely put on the stand under oath.

In the wake of the *Examiner* series, the state Supreme Court unexpectedly ordered the recalcitrant local judiciary to hear Richard's motion for a new trial. Relatives and supporters raised enough money to fly out witnesses from Oregon and Indiana and to pay some attorney's fees. Willing still to trust the justice system, we believed that if a new trial were ordered, a jury truly made up of Richard's peers, and free of bias, could arrive at a just verdict. We could live with that verdict, then, even if, as unlikely as it seemed, it might concurred with the first verdict.

However, through a highly suspect technical maneuver, the case ended up back before Judge Calcagno, who would not recuse himself. Pessimistically, our lawyers presented the new evidence uncovered by the *SF Examiner*.

In my mind, I thought it would not have been so hard for Judge Calcagno to at least admit, "You know, I let that guy Porter testify in my court and now I can see that was a mistake. The guy's a compulsive liar."

Or "Yeah, there was a lot of pressure to get someone back then. So, let me try this case again, fair and square, now that passions have subsided." Predictably, after several full days of testimony, Judge Calcagno ruled against Richard. There would be no new and fair trial and this ruling was, effectively, the death knell of Richard's legal campaign.

Shortly after that ruling, Pierre Merle and homicide inspectors Eddie Erdelatz and Frank McCoy filed a lawsuit and later won a $4.5 million-dollar libel verdict against the *SF Examiner* and the reporters before another old-line San Francisco Judge. The judge in that libel case was perceived as so anti-reporter that one participant was moved to an act of guerrilla theater: the placement of a paper toilet seat cover on the judge's chair.

In 1986, the California Supreme Court unanimously upheld the legality of the *SF Examiner* story and quashed the $ 4.6 million award. In the court's opinion, the reporters raised well-founded questions about the trial, and conducted a careful, detailed investigation over eighteen-months. They concluded that no libel had been committed.

But for Richard, Calcagno's denial shut his case down for good. There would be no further appeal. I was devastated, but Richard had a somewhat different attitude. At the end of the *SF Examiner* series, Ramirez quoted Richard as saying:

> *The way I see it, they put me here according to their law of the land. I can't fight it because they've got me in a situation where if you fight it, they'll just get you more, lock you up,*

charge you.... I have resigned myself right now to being here.... They've got my body in here. Physically, they've got me but my mind is still free. As long as my mind can still function freely and think what I want to think and feel what I want to feel, it's OK. I'll make it.

In all the years of working on Richard's case, I had cut off parts of myself to just make it through another day. I did it to help Richard, of course. Now I was completely devastated. Yet, here he was, not focused on the ups and downs of his own case, but solely on his internal journey. He was inside, I was outside, yet he possessed a clearer grasp of reality, was stronger in spirit, and freer than I was.

Could I have handled his suffering as well as he? I believed so strongly in the system that I gave up architecture and entered law school to help Richard and to be able to prevent these very travesties of justice. I was utterly downcast when the courts failed me. Richard rested no hope in the system, and thus it could no longer hurt him. He was neither cynical nor embittered. Not only did he have the strength to live through this day-by-day, but also he sounded like a blessed saint to boot.

How did he do it? It was Mother's Toisan ways, I knew. She had wrapped Richard with those ways, and, so protected, he lived immanently, above the fray of frustrating legal outcomes, the daily hell of prison, and interrupted, personal ambitions. I was hurting because I was attached to another reality, of the outer victory of legal and public vindication, a view one that I had bet my life, my energy, and money, and career on.

Mother had warned that officialdom's "two mouths" would out-shout the "one mouth" of little people like us. Turned out she was right... this time.

What had I failed to understand?

It would be Richard's example, his words in that last article of the series, that would help me to understand, to reconnect to all things Toisan, and to fully understand that Mother was a transmitter of its tried and true wisdom, as versed and trained as any spiritual teacher of any tradition, of any order.

Chapter 33 Mothering All the Children

You see, you must understand one thing about children. A child is basically good and will stay good. You must watch over the child, watch every little thing.

Now, some people would say Gawn was a bad boy, a thief, that I should have scolded him and never let him into my house again. But to me, he was just a boy being a boy. Yes, he turned out okay.

Gawn was the first son of the Vietnamese boat-people, a family who moved in next door…1977, something like that. A single mother with two young boys. Gawn was about eleven and the younger boy one, I don't remember his name, was about eight. They were Chinese-Vietnamese, Cantonese speakers. I don't know what happened to the husband, just that he was dead. Their mother worked during the day and so I watched her boys for her after school. The younger one was mentally damaged. Sometimes he got lost in his own world. He would be sitting there playing like a normal boy and suddenly his eyes would float off to the ceiling. He would start waving his fingers around like a dancer and then sing-song in a strange language that made no sense. But I would call his name, offer some candy, and after a while he came back. Someone must have hurt the younger one, maybe a pirate when they left Vietnam. They wouldn't talk about it.

They fled the Communists after their war, just like my own family. Many Chinese-Vietnamese boat people were forced onto boats into the South China Sea. Pirates attacked them. Aiiyahh, lots of suffering. I think they lived in a camp on Samoa, or some place like that, waiting until they got their visas to the United States.

I helped them to settle down. You know, enrolled the children in school, took them to the playgrounds, applied for medical coverage, and rode the buses with them until they knew the routes. I introduced them to the best places in Chinatown to shop. Vegetables, meat, and fish. I walked them downtown to Macy's, Emporium, and all the other stores.

They lived next door, the three of them in a small studio and so Gawn came over all the time. He liked my apartment, always clean and so much more room. Just made himself at home right after school and on weekends. Laid down on the sofa floor and rested. Watched TV. Did his homework. Played with John and your cousins Ada, David and Victor. I cooked extra food for him all the time because their his mother worked late. We were all like one family.

Gawn shopped for me, just like you and Richard when you were little. He always wanted to do some chore for me. Well-mannered and really smart. Gawn studied hard, earned good grades, just like you. Sometimes I helped him with Chinese School homework when his older sister was too busy.

Do you remember Richard's coin collection? Indian head nickels, Lady Liberty head dimes, old quarters, and so on? And silver dollars—real silver through and through, souvenirs from my winnings in Reno. Well, Gawn stole from Richard's coin collection. Sometimes Gawn played alone in your old bedroom and then left quickly, like he had done something he shouldn't have. I started checking, and always a few more coins were missing. But I never accused him. They had suffered so much, and were so poor. He just wanted to be a boy. Eat potato chips. Drink Coca-colas. Buy comic books. So how could I call him a thief? I just pretended it never happened.

After a while they moved away. The mother's sister was doing well, and they moved near San Jose, into a Little Saigon. New immigrants don't seem to stay long in Chinatown anymore. They move out the first chance they get. Well, later Gawn went on to college and got a good job. For years, he visited me every Chinese New Year's and with gifts. Bags of tangerines. Dried coconut candy, plums, red watermelon seeds. Whole roasted duck. Crackling skin barbecue pork. So many Chinese New Year goodies. And red envelopes with lots of money, so much more than he ever took from Richard's coin collection.

Now, if I had treated him like a bad boy, scolded him, told all the neighbors, banished him from our home, and made him feel like he was really bad, you think that would have helped him? Of course not. Gawn was too good in far too many other ways. Just like any other kid, his mouth watered for treats. He took only a little bit of money, after all. You must understand children. A child is basically good and will stay good. But you must watch over the child every day, every little thing. That's the way to raise a child.

That's why I tell you so many times that in the village Toisanese mothers stay close to their children all day long. Even if my mother was working in the fields during spring planting or fall harvest, she made sure to eat lunch with us, and check in on us several times before dinner. That's the only way to make sure children turn out well.

Chapter 34 A Chinatown Grows in Prison

There is a 1974 Associated Press Wire newspaper photo from those years of the first sixteen year-old boy, Chi-ko Wong, a Chinese-American from Los Angeles as the first teenager to be tried and convicted as an adult in the state of California. He's starkly framed against the side of what must be a very tall door, as if pausing between two worlds. Behind him is a guard, which we know only because we see a corner of one side of his head.

But perhaps the oddest, most starkly troubling element is Chi-ko's own choirboy face or "baby-faced" is the Associated Press reporter's description.

In the photo, Chi-ko himself, a Chinese-American from Los Angeles, is barely five feet tall, sleight of built, skinny, and rendered optically thinner by his child-size Sunday school jacket and is adult-size prison shirt and jeans. He looks too much like a child to be contemplating the steely prison door studded with rivets framing him, and several times heavier, in front of him, or to require the vigilance of the tall, burly California Corrections Officer blandly monitoring him.

Chi-ko's wrists are manacled to a metal belt around his waist. From the slant of the back of his head, he wrists are so tightly manacled to a metal chain around his waist that his elbows involuntarily bend backward. He's facing his mother, whose own face is hidden by the knuckles of her right fist, which perhaps hides her tears, too. Then it sinks in that this is a child, and he's going into an adult prison...for life. Perhaps he's staring at the floor to obscure his tears, unable to face this one-way door to years, if not decades, within the corridors of the California State Penal System.

Although he's not facing the camera, Chi-ko was the poster child for the new policy of trying teenagers as young as fifteen as adults for certain violent acts (in his case, a conviction of murder in the first degree), a graphic announcement that California had officially given up on the idea that all youth rehabilitation Chi-ko's facelessness seems to reinforce the universality of the message, "Mothers watch your babies, this could be you."

A river of teenagers have since been tried and convicted as adults, and more heinously, incarcerated with hard cons who victimize them, turning them into more vicious and cunning criminals, before their return into society. Many states now actively contemplate the execution of convicts for felonies committed before the age of eighteen.

This turn in American jurisprudence officially started with Chi-ko Wong, a Chinese-American teenager. It unofficially started with the decision to try Richard, Joe Fong, and David Wong as adults. They were, youths barely out of high school and eligible for youth authority incarceration when arrested. These trials reversed the compassionate policy that even eighteen and nineteen year olds were unformed enough, despite the gravity of their charges, to be able to turn their lives around in the more benign, and nurturing, environment of the California Youth Authority.

But Richard and I never got to discuss such weighty policy issues during our earlier visits. In fact, it took months of visits before Richard would even describe to me his first days in the state prison known as Deuel Vocational Institute (DVI). From his perspective, why should he? After all, I too was the stranger, familiar only because of our childhood closeness, but unknown after years of mutual independence. I had left for Berkeley, but perhaps in his eyes, I had left Chinatown too. I helped to start an internecine battle within Chinatown, but perhaps in his eyes, andI left him to finish a fight I started it, and to suffer the consequences. Finally, I left for what he called my "vacation," and despite his apparent consent and his lawyer's concurrence, had left him in jail to be set up. I hadn't exactly watched his back these past few years. So how trustworthy was I? How worthy was I, of him?

All I could do now was to show up, visiting Richard as often as I was allowed to under the guidelines. First to arrive, and last to leave. Always with enough money, despite my stringent student finances, to stuff coins into the machines for overpriced, stale sandwiches, chips, candy bars, and soft-drinks. I drove Mother and sometimes father to and fro, too to this prison an hour-and-a-half east of San Francisco. I booked the dates, then processed all the paperwork for family visits, and then got everyone there and everything in through the tight security check.

At first, our topics tended to be legal: the progress of the Garry law firm appeal, the new evidence in Joe Fong's case, Bergman's remarkable interview with Porter, the *SF Examiner* investigation, and the slow emergence of his case as a cause celebre. The family was the other safe topic: our family outings, to Marine World/, Africa USA, a picnic on Mt. Tamalpais with its bird's eye views of the entire Bay Area, or that rare, warm day at Santa Cruz beach.

I don't know when that turning point clicked-in, when we went 'round the bend of our estrangement, but Richard started to share his narrative of life within DVI prison. He actually never really narrated, but dropped hints, telling clues that I deciphered over my long drives home and arranged into a sketch of life inside.

One day he said inmates called DVI the Gladiator School, because of the violent race gangs who ran the prison. Richard was the first and thus only Chinese-American in DVI for months. Within a society organized by racial gangs, Richard was a one-of-a-kind outlier among outlaws. He may as well had come from Jupiter.

Those first few days, slowly making his ways among the hardened convicts, always glancing from side-to-side or, occasionally looking over his shoulder, his arms and clenched fists swinging free, ready to block a prison-made blade, to lash out in return out. But, to his growing surprise, he discovered that his "beef" or "jacket," the very conviction of first-degree murder, however wrongful, and his "rep," as the assassin-on-command of a mythologized, cold-blooded crime boss protected him from the prison predators who reflexively preyed on young first-timers.

Soon enough, Joe Fong and his co-defendant David Wong joined him, and their equally impressive conspiracy-to-commit murder convictions stemming from one of the first drive-by shootings in California confirmed their media-inflamed crime family legend. So, the prison gangs kept a respectful distance.

Richard said at DVI, inmates ranged in age from eighteen to thirty years olds old. He described the race-based inmate gangs that ran the prison. DVI was Nuestra Familia turf, a Chicano gang and the largest single group of the fifteen hundred inmates. Their the Mexican Mafia were their bitter rivals, and any Mexican Mafia member negligently or intentionally assigned to DVI would be dead or certainly critically maimed within a week. Two other race gangs included the white supremacist Aryan Brotherhood who wielded power over white inmates, and the small Black Guerrilla Family(BGF), inheritors of George Jackson's revolutionary prison legacy . Yet, despite their large numbers, BGS commanded limited sway over African-American prisoners, generally unorganized , and hence not a dominant force despite their superior numbers. Each gang ran a share of commonplace rackets—drugs, prison-brewed alcohol, cigarettes, grocery items, male prostitution, smuggled in knives and, prison-made weapons called shanks, and of course, violence for hire. Cartons of cigarettes were as good as currency.

I couldn't believe that such a place existed on earth. I couldn't comprehend how anyone could survive here with their dignity intact, their body unmarred by violence, or their sanity unscarred. Frightened, for Richard, I became doubly motivated to secure his release. Yet, somehow he and the increasing number of Chinese-American inmates sent to DVI managed to survive intact.

One summer, Richard groused his frustration at the inmates annual summer "Gladiator games." California's Central Valley blazes with long days of unclouded sun in July and August, heating up these young, overheated, testosterone-laden inmates to a boiling point. The gangs actually looked forward to ritualistic Gladiator battles in the arena of the prison courtyard. They prepared their weapons, strategies, and priority target lists with an anticipation more typically associated with high-schoolers planning for their first prom. On the appointed date, at he very hour agreed to, a time mysteriously known to every inmate but not the guards, weapons magically appeared out of thin air. Jagged shanks, sharpened metal torn from metal bed frames, clubs embedded with nails and razors, forks wrapped around fists with their tines turned out like claws, and smuggled-in butcher knives all slashed the air into skin, tendons, bone, and vital organs as wave after wave of shrieking inmates fell upon each others.

Within minutes, old scores were settled as territory and rackets changed hands. The guards belatedly fired tear-gas, rubber bullets, and real bullets to disperse the fighters. DVI would locked-down the for days, sometimes weeks. Each cell was shaken down for weapons and drugs.

Richard's ire was that even a safe non-combatant, he too was locked-down, his cells now a sweatbox in the unrelenting summer heat.

"Couldn't they pick a cooler season to fight?" he grumbled.

At once frightened for Richard and then fascinated at this insider's anthropological report, I slowly felt some relief. Somehow RichardIt was clear that he and his friends were removed from the fray, a sideline group secure its own small, but safe corner. During that visit, in the background was the unabated din of hundreds of inmates yelling their insanity and rage, like the Devil's version of speaking in tongues. Richard was oblivious, relieved to in the air-conditioned visiting room. On those days, I stretched out our visits as long as possible, lingering despite the guard's signal that we needed to give the table up for other visitors.

But significantly, Richard was talking now, reciprocating my stories with his stories, sharing even if in tough-guy, clipped, neutral terms about the daily fears, dangers, and triumphs of his life. We were connecting again as brothers. I was getting to know him as I had not known him since our drifting apart.

Richard was my brother again.

During another visit, Richard casually mentioned that he personally had forged an alliance of mutual protection with the Native-American inmates, a group fewer in numbers than even Chinese-Americans. Together, numbering approximately thirty inmates among DVI's population of fifteen hundred, the Asian/Native alliance did not challenge Nuestra Familia, the Aryan Brotherhood, or the Black Guerrilla Family. In a series of meetings, they respectfully announced their intention to stay out of prison rackets and prison warfare, desiring simply "to do the time" in peace. They shrewdly pointed out that despite their limited numbers, they were large enough to relentlessly and brutally retaliate against anyone, or any group, who might harm any one of them.

"We may go down, but so will the fools who mess with us."

That was the only break that came young Chi-ko Wong's way, after that iron door clanged shut behind him in 1974. He ended up at the Gladiator School, if that can be described as good luck. But there, Richard placed him under his personal protection and of their new Asian/-Native alliance. Anywhere else, with his child-like look and size, Chi-ko would have been victimized in the most horrid ways.

I was blown away, that in this lower circle of Dante's inferno, in this dark hole of human misery and rage, Richard reached out to others. Not Joe or David, but Richard himself worked out a flexible solution, one worthy of Toisan pragmatism. Not a gang, but a mutual-protection society. Remarkable, this alliance between Native Americans and Chinese-Americans, until I then realized that cross-cultural alliance building was nothing new to Richard. He had and his friends had breached the divide between ABCs and FOBs. When that alliance broke down with the assassination of Raymond Leung, they simply created a new one, Chung Ching Yee.

Of the prison gangs tested the tensile strength of this new alliance, but the alliance held and from that point forward, Native Americans and Chinese-Americans were, for all intents and purposes, left alone.

But the most interesting topic was Richard's take on time. For the typical busy American, or for a workaholic as I was then, there is never enough time. In my Quixotic campaign on behalf of Richard, I careened through my days faster than a greyhound chasing the rabbit at the races and mightier than a storm-driven westerly wind exploding through the Golden Gate. Yet, time seemed to be so scarce that I drove faster while crossing the Bay Bridge two, three and even four times in a single days to meet with and talk quicker with growing numbers of more supporters, lawyers, and reporters. Not enough time and so I got up, got up earlier, drove even faster, and stayed up even later so that I could create more minutes here, a quarter-hour there, maybe up to a half-an-hour there. If I stopped too long at a stop light, was stalled by a receptionist or by a counterman waiting for my sandwich-to-go, the immediate atmosphere felt lighter, sucked empty of oxygen, because my time was always slipping away, dropping off the table, floating off into space, melting into Insufficient Funds status.

But Richard, when Richard talked about time, he talked about it like it was dense, massive, and immovable. For him, there was too much of it to begin with. He talked about *doooo*ing time, as if it were a pool of mud he pushed through all day long. As if wearing away a giant boulder by rubbing it down with palms of his hands.

If an inmate at the next visitor's table complained he wasn't doing so well, Richard intoned, "You just got to know how to *dooo* the time. You just got to *dooo* the time."

Then I imagined him waking up to a hundred 50-lb sacks of sand, strapped to his shoulder, hoisting each bag from his cell to breakfast in the dining hall, to the showers, through work, lunch and dinner, the visitors room, and finally to evening activities, until the bags of time completely eased off his back by day's end.

Richard was doooing the time.

And, the next day, he would wake up to another hundred bags of heavy time.

If only I could have swapped my vanishing minutes for his superfluous hours, and moved up his release date.

Later, when it became clear that appeals would take years, that Richard would be in for a long, long time, even if we did ultimately prevail, I started to imagined his body calcifying within the walls, then freezing like a prehistoric bee perfectly preserved in amber. In a Polaroid photo of us at the time, I'm smiling easily, lithe in a tight disco shirt seamlessly tucked into form-fitting white, flare-bottom jeans, long hair blowing off to the side as I lean gently against his shoulder. But Richard stands solid like a Stonehenge column, nondescript in basic prison blues; his arms extended stiffly like pistons by his sides.

Yes, he was losing fluidity, the careless, dancing, hand-flinging, walk-skipping, okay-to-change-your-mind pirouette of the free.

My response was to live the life of two people, to make up for what he was missing. So I moved at the speed of life of two people, nonsensically believing I could gather up a store of life-equity that I'd transfer to him in our visits and our conversations. So I began to filled him up with stories of the interesting people I was meeting, like Harvey Milk, the Gay organizer, of Margo St. James, the former hooker turned union organizer, and others representing people victimized by the criminal justice system.

I pestered him with my personal insights into the lives of Charles Garry, Mayor George Moscone; and a meeting we had with the Governor's Chief-of-Staff. I kept him on the newest dance spots, the I-Beam, the Mind Shaft, the City with its ceiling-high jukebox DJ booth, and described the latest disco dance crazes. I detailed the décor of this and that new inexpensive restaurant, or how Sai-Yon Restaurant's Duck Broth Yee Foo Won-ton soup was slipping in quality.

I regaled him with stories of, my new girlfriends, what hot tubs felt like, and that strange mystical-cowboy movie, *"El Topo,"* by the Chilean *avant garde*, surrealist director, Alejandro Jodorowsky, an erratic narrative of violence, resurrection, strange allies, all wrapped in Catholic symbolism, signifying a profundity that eludes the audience. I drew him into the fun of our recent annual Lake Tahoe family vacation, which cousin learned to swim this year, how it differed this year, hoping it would make him feel like he had been with us.

On and on, I would blather, like a desperate rescuer.

Richard was restrained in so many ways. He couldn't grow his hair below the nape of his neck. He couldn't grow a beard. He couldn't wear colorful shirts, flare bottom pants, psychedelic tank tops, Superfly knit sweaters, and leathers. All he could wear was blue.

I even grew my hair even more outrageously long, because Richard couldn't. A full yard, falling to below my waist, way past the chic urban hippie's mid-back trim. Like the biblical Samson, I felt power in the fierce defiance of my unclipped locks. Later I discovered that ancient Chinese martial arts heroes grew their hair long, way below the waist.

I'd read more newspapers and books, party harder, expand my cultural and social circles even wider, master more subjects, make three times as many friends, all to somehow save up for him, transfer to him half-of-my-equity of life's vitality and experience.

Richard always listened respectfully to my One Thousand and One Tales of San Franciscan Nights. He just kept reminding me, that all he could do was "to dooo the time..." But, from time to time, an ephemeral smile disclosed his pleasure at a good story, or that his spirits rose at the growing number of supporters. I learned to spot, then listen for, these songs from his soul. Yes, I grew my hair long for Richard too. At least in my mind, I was doing so. Soon, he would get back out to where he really belonged. Thanks to my stories, he could be normal, not having missed a beat.

Eventually, he started to comment, he was glad at some progress in his case, that I was doing okay in school, and having some fun. But, basically he remained the strong, silent type. So, I learned to lie in wait, waiting for a twitch of interest in my always new and fresh menu of vignettes. When I detected a slight upward turn of a grin or a nod of his head as one eye stared at me, enlarging quizzically, I would expand the story line, embellish the facts, animate my hands, facial expressions, let loose, hold, and then squeeze my metaphors and adjectives like a long accordion solo. If he laughed, I scored. If he wryly commented, I double scored and if he exchanged a story, that was a rare, triple-score moment. Whenever I scored, I'd launch into more stories, hoping the fervor of the bonhomie would carry him through until the next visit.

But, basically, Richard stuck to doooing the time, push-strolling gracefully through the time's mud that was up to his neck, rubbing down time's boulder with his palms.

Was I trying to make up for my entertaining chatter to make up for the lapse of not being there for him the summer before his trial? Probably there's truth in that too, but there must been a moment when the scales evened up, when that debt, never articulated and perhaps only a weight on me, was completely repaid, with interest and late fees. Then, I realized that silence was a convict trait, and learned not to overreact to it as a psychosis, of his losing connection with the outside.

I started to relaxed more into Richard's silences, less anxious to tell my stories. Silent sitting together were just as fine a visit as lively ones. I was there, he was there. He was safe. I was safe. That's what mattered now.

After the *SF Examiner* investigative series ran, Richard quietly dropped another piece of information. He had been assigned to an escalating series of favorable day jobs. This latest one, managing the Guard's canteen, actually took him outside of the prison, away from the daily prison madness. This was unusual, if not against policy the unwritten rules that lifer so early into his life sentence could not be trusted outside the fence. Who wouldn't bolt for freedom if a choice between decades behind bars or the blue sky?

Richard speculated that the guards wanted to "...do right by me."

One vertebra at a time, I uncurled slowly upright against the hard back of the visitor's chair, blinking rapidly, taking slow breaths, as I sought to reconcile this with my attitude. Like the members of many other prisoner families, I had lumped the prison guards into the corrupt system that had put Richard away. They were the ones enforcing his odious imprisonment. Most of the

—

guards seemed dour to me, none particularly alert, and fitted the stereotype of bureaucratic lifers, whose physical fitness waned and waistlines broadened, the closer they got to retirement.

But over time, I discerned that this nonchalant watchfulness was the heart of their work. Watch and watch some more, day after day, whether we visitors noticed or not.

I did not doubt the stories of prison guards who routinely manipulated prison gangs, favored one faction over another, or who meanly beat inmates, arbitrarily threw them to isolation, and spitefully added time for fighting back. Richard himself complained of several particularly mean-spirited guards.

But at DVI, what I observed was that mostly, they watched, interpreted, and meted out punishments and benefits based on what they saw. I came to conclude that most guards had heard it all, seen it all, and dealt with it all. In ways I initially loathed granting, I came to realize that many of the prison guards possessed a levelheaded wisdom about inmates. They knew who could or couldn't dooo the time well… and made sound judgments about their families.

Something about our family must have touched their hardened hearts. Something about Richard must have affected their view of him. Perhaps it was the way he protected Chi-ko Wong, or the way he forged the alliance with Native Americans. Perhaps it was our clockwork regular visits and our penchant for being the first in line to sign up for our lavish, family stay-overs. Perhaps all this and followed by the *SF Examiner* series led them to conclude that Richard had been framed. After all, they knew that innocent inmates were not that unusual, had made the acquaintance of many in their careers. They couldn't grant Richard a new trial, but they could "do right " by him in other ways. In any case, the guards started to "protect" Richard.

It was as if a jury of prison guards found Richard innocent as charged, and amended his conditions of imprisonment to render him as free a man as possible within their part of the criminal justice system. That first outside assignment placed Richard in a safer and saner place, as we later came to realize, and was but the first of many outside assignments, each of increasing freedom and ever-widening mobility. As hard as we worked on the outside to win his freedom, Richard had diligently and quietly worked from the inside to push through the walls of his imprisonment. He was taking care of himself in this strange reality for which nothing had prepared him.

Just like Father when he came to America; and like Mother, too.

Richard wasn't just *dooo*ing the time now, he was transmuting it, creating freedom.

Chapter 34 A Time to Stop

I watched you sitting on the floor, on a pillow, one of many pink and blue ones, with seagulls and waves. Hunched forward, your law books all over the low table as you studied. You always loved books, became so concentrated when you read. Even as a kid it was like no one else was in the room, not even hearing me when I asked you come to dinner. You were drinking water out of a Chinese earthenware jug you kept beside your books. Plain tap water. Said you liked water, and no, I shouldn't bring you juice or sodas next time. Your friends called in, probably about the case, raising money, for you'd scribble something in your calendar book.

I know water tastes sweeter out of a jug, but to me you looked miserably impoverished. Not even a chair to sit on, I thought, drinking only water. I felt so bad that we didn't have money to help you with school, to live an easier life.

We visited you more after you moved back to San Francisco. For law school. You gave up architecture to help Richard, you said. We needed to understand the law, you said . But not just for Richard, so you could help other people, too. I was proud of you, a poor boy smart enough to become a lawyer. I'm sure many rich kids couldn't do that.

After the Golden Dragon, everything was really tense in Chinatown. Everyone was angry, looking for someone to blame, to get back at. The police, the Six Companies, the family associations, the tongs. Grant Avenue emptied out as soon as night fell. Not just tourists, but the local white customers and people from Marin, Oakland, and San Mateo. They all stayed away now. Even Friday and Saturday nights, when Chinatown restaurants stayed busy until 3 a.m. an4 a.m. Kum Hon, Woey Loey Guey, Jackson Café, and the Golden Dragon – all the waiters just standing around now. So, the night-time restaurant business died, hundreds of thousands of dollars in lost business every month, said the Chinese newspapers. The Golden Dragon Massacre really hurt Chinatown.

So, I was even more concerned for you, speaking out against the Six Companies, police corruption, and how the tongs s used young Chinese like tissue paper. Then your name appeared in the newspaper. The police were trying to link you to Joe Fong.

I was worried they would blame you too, just like they blamed Richard for the troubles. Someone might even kill you, I feared. You were back in the city, living closer to Chinatown, now, and it would be easier than Berkeley! Then, I heard rumors, and one day, one of my Clan Sisters who ran a gambling parlor, the only woman in Chinatown to run a gambling parlor, came to see me. She was close to the tong bosses. She talked in a general way, nothing specific. She said that times were dangerous, a good time for critics of Chinatown to stop.

That's why I came by that day to visit you. It was in the afternoon, after school, when your father worked. Bob drove all of us. John, Ada, David, and Victor, still kids then under my care, came with me. We surprised you since we didn't call first. We joined you on the floor, on those seagull print pillows, some pink and some blue, placed around the low Japanese table. You asked if we wanted to stay for dinner.

"No need, I came by to talk to you about something very important. We will leave after that." I said.

You sat down and waited for me to speak. I asked you to stop. Stop everything you're doing involving Chinatown. Just stop.

At first you refused.

I said to stop working on Richard's case. You have done everything you could. No one could have done more for his brother. The court system doesn't care. We have lost at every turn. It was time to accept that. You have sacrificed enough. Time to finish law school and find a job. Then pay off your school loans. Make a living. Get married, have children.

It is time to live your own life, I said. When Richard is released, we will help him then as we have helped him in prison. He's doing okay-okay now. Good boy. Nobody is harming him. Maybe it's better he's where he can't be killed.

I said you should stop working with the street kids in the youth agency, that you've done enough for them, too. Time for new people to do their part.

I said stop criticizing the police, the gamblers, and the tongs. Chinatown is not going to change because of one person. It may never change.

I said I have already lost one son to prison. I didn't want to lose you, too. Then you were quiet for a long time.

You said that my reasons made sense. Then you said that you would stop. You would call everyone today and tell them the family had asked you to stop. That you could not refuse us.

Chapter 35 Defeat

Acquiescing to Mother's request didn't come easy. The afternoon visit took me by surprise. The kids looked at me with so much love in their eyes. Emotionally, Ada, David, and Victor were as much my kid brothers and sister as our own little John. I had long ago accepted Bob as a member of our family. They would really be devastated if...anyway, their love stopped me in my place. I could listen now as I turned off the cruise control of my manic drive.

Mother spoke from a place of courage, clear headedness, and respect for me as an individual. She spoke, as always, with love. Richard had the right to appeal Judge Calcagno's decision *ad nauseum*, but a favorable outcome was unlikely. Similarly, the compelling legal campaigns for other Chinatown youth had petered out. To expect redress from the courts was a quixotic fantasy.

Mother's intervention was uncannily timely. I was feeling the futility, the fatigue, and the insanity of turning around the San Francisco's judiciary. Our family's scarce financial resources were depleted, and squaring off against the dwindled legal options, we could not in good faith solicit more from our steadfast supporters. After completing my final year of law school, I would be devoting months preparing for the California bar examination, the toughest law-license exam in the nation. After that, I had to start repaying my student loans, a great portion of which had gone to cover Richard's appeals. Slowly admitting defeat to myself, I had been coming terms the congenital perversity of Chinatown machinations, that this was a dragon too savage to reason with, impossible to subjugate.

That was why I replied "yes" so readily that afternoon. In my heart, I knew it was over, and in my spirit, I knew that little would change. On my own, I couldn't bring myself to quit. But having given my word to her, in the presence of the kids and Bob, my word to Mother was like a sacred vow. I kept it.

Any relief I felt from this decision rapidly spiraled down into a new misery. I felt like a complete failure. We had lost. So much energy expended, day after day, year after year. So many people involved—priests, ministers, union leaders, undergraduates, politicians, community-service directors, lawyers, and my classmates. So much money raised, gobbled up by the legal system—all a waste. They had gotten away with it. Richard, Joe Fong, and others were still in jail—and there wasn't anything we could do about it.

As for Chinatown? The FBI Strike Force had caught only a few small fish and the big fish swam away to play another day. Chinatown was aflame in the wake of the Golden Dragon Massacre. Vengeance was in the air. Was I still a target, even as I called it quits?

I focused on finishing my final year of Hastings law school and I was nowhere near my 3.9 GPA at Berkeley. I spent most of my free time with Francine, the modern dance performer with whom I had been living for two years, helping to raise her daughter, Sherry.

With my free-and-easy disco seventies lifestyle, how had I ended up in my own family? Very simply, Francine and I had fallen in love. Still, so many men drew the line at becoming Daddy, and shockingly, many single mothers with children agreed, shunting their child aside whenever the man magically appeared. My friends skeptically wondered at my willingness to play the daddy young Sherry never had, especially with law school, Richard's appeals, my work, and co-organizing a controversial youth center. I was surprised too, but the decision had come easily. I saw a young, vivacious girl who never had a daddy, who craved a family. In true Toisan fashion, I didn't hesitate for a moment to step up to this role. After all, there were no orphans in my mother's village, so how could there be in my life?

Like most dancers, Francine worked a paying job, photographing tourists at San Francisco's finest hotel rooftop lounges. Many evenings, I ended up den father to Sherry and a surprising number of single girls (all white) of single mothers, lending an ear to their teen-age dramas of boyfriends, misunderstandings with other girls, homework, school difficulties and especially, peer pressure around sex and, drugs. For me, this cobbled together family was a tonic, the one place where I could drop the mental and emotional load of the rest of my life.

But even this oasis was no longer off-limits. In the media maelstrom following the Golden Dragon Massacre, my name surfaced more than once in the mainstream media. This was the way media logic worked: Richard was at DVI with Joe Fong. The Executive Director of the youth agency I helped to co-organized was a regular visitor of Joe Fong. Therefore media concluded I was a member of the Joe Fong Gang. In the TV news rating wars, Chinatown slayings were a long running hit, a precursors of today's reality TV drama series. New plot twists-and-turns week after week, and an ever-dwindling cast of characters, as old players were killed, and each fresh murder spiked ratings for days. Breaking the story first prevailed over accuracy and damage to individual reputations and their lives.

The local ABC television affiliate was particularly unrestrained, and openly connected me to the Golden Dragon Massacre, an event I had no involvement in, no connection with, nor any knowledge of, before or after, outside of what was generally reported in the news. Words hurt, but bullets killed, and their inflammatory newscasts virtually painted a bull's eye around me with the subtitle "Shoot this Man." It wasn't hard to conceive what would come next. The *SF Chronicle* would parrot the lead. Then Chinatown papers would reprint their articles as gospel truth. That last step was tantamount to my death warrant. Yeah, I was running scared for the first time in my life.

It took the intercession of a senior partner of a large downtown law firm, James Brosnahan, then the president of the San Francisco Bar Association, for this popular newscast to agree to establish some facts in support of their assertions of my involvement before flinging my name into the public consciousness. Overnight, my name disappeared from the airwaves.

Was my life truly in danger? Yes, and that became clear one weeknight when I picked Francine up from her workplace and drove us back home. During the half-block walk from my parked car to our 17th Street flat in the Castro district, I noticed a late-model car full of young Chinese men parked across the street, and facing our doorway. Their engine was running although the car was legally parked against the curb. Several of them had longish hair, the kind of stylish *Superfly* hairstyles favored by many of the youthful tong enforcers. Tong enforcers always had souped-up muscle cars – TransAms, '442s, and Mustangs.

In 1978, the Castro district was a pluralistic neighborhood of white Russians, Swedes, Italians, bohemians, hippies, and the first wave of gays from all over America. Chinese-Americans did not frequent the neighborhood. Moreover, our street was infrequently traveled, since it appeared to be little more than a driveway, splitting off from the confusing intersection of Market , Castro, and 17th streets. The presence of young Chinese men was out of character, and glaringly so especially at this late weeknight hour.

I warned Francine to move quickly away from me and into the house. I dragged my pace so that if they leapt out of the car firing at me, she would at least be out of the line of fire. The young men stared directly at me. Their car's interior light came on as they opened their doors, possibly readying themselves to spring out.

"This is it. It's over," I thought.

But, weary from work, Francine did not quicken her pace, and, in the shadowy light of 17th Street, it may have been hard to tell who I was. Or perhaps it was seeing me with a tall, attractive, elegant, blonde Caucasian woman that psychologically threw them off their game. For them, it was easy enough to kill Chinese-Americans; their instincts were honed to do that. But to kill a white person, even accidentally, was taboo. It was easy enough to kill in Chinatown, with those warrens of busy streets they knew intimately and into which they could confidently vanish. But the Castro was alien landscape. In any event, they hesitated, giving us just enough time to get into the house safety.

Barely.

I triple-locked the doors, and rushed Francine and her daughter Sherry to the back of the long apartment, advising them that if they heard any shooting, they should dash down the back stairs to safety. At the insistence of friends, I had purchased a shotgun when I returned to the greater risk of San Francisco. While I abhorred violence, a shotgun was a home defense weapon. Still, I had never fired it as I believed the sight of one was sufficient to dissuade would-be attackers. I took it down from the closet shelf where I had secreted it from Sherry, loaded birdshot shell in the right barrel for a warning shot, and a Double-O shell in the left to take care of business.

"I may go down, I thought, but I'm was going to take some fools with me," I mumbled, echoing the mantra of Richard's Asian/Native Alliance. I returned to the front living room, shotgun in one hand

and a box of Double-O shells in the other. Shutting off the lights, I crouched by a bay window, raised it up slightly, cocked both barrels, and placed my finger on the two triggers.

Their car was still directly across the street, engine running. The young men, eyes squinting, peered toward my windows. They seemed to be debating. I stuck the shotgun barrel out the window, aimed it at them, and moved it around so that it picked up the gleam of the light of the overhead street lamp. They evidently saw I was armed and ready to shoot. After a few long moments, car doors slammed, headlights flared up, and they rocketed up the steep 17th Street grade. I slept that night on the sofa in the front living room, the loaded shotgun next to me.

During the next few weeks, we received endless anonymous calls, all in perfect American. In the three years there, we had never received a single crank call. Some directed warnings to me. Others made crude sexual suggestions to Francine and Sherry if they answered the phone. A few asked questions as to who lived in the house and the nature of our relationship.

I noticed a new neighbor across the street, a professionally dressed Japanese-American, who unerringly left for work at exactly the same time I left for my morning classes. Well, I actually never saw him walk up and down a stairway, but there he was every morning, car warming up. I didn't make much of it as people moved in and out of the Castro daily. But one day, while at the Civic Center Wells Fargo Bank, the same one Richard had worked in, I saw him step out of his car, having pulled over a speeder, and place a whirling red light on the roof of his sedan. He froze as he recognized me, then nodded acknowledgement that he had blown his cover. I never saw him again.

The feeling of death stalking me did not end as even my dreams augured death's inevitable appearance. One night I had the most graphic dream of my life, a nightmare so real that upon awakening I was unable to distinguish it from reality. In the dream, I was corralled by a group of young Chinese gunmen who fired point-blank into my body. Their bullets kept tearing into me as I crumpled to the ground. My lungs gasped for air. I blacked out. My spirit left my body, watching as one young man bent over to discharge the *coup de grace*, the bullet into my brain.

Then, just as suddenly, I was in the midst of a mysterious, metaphysical struggle. I was refusing to die. I slowly willed myself to come back to life. This wasn't about making deals with God, promising to live a new and different way if He would cut me this last piece of slack. No, this was a stubborn refusal to die, to be ignobly killed. I chose to live the rest of my life and, suddenly the steps of the slaying reversed themselves, like a film rolling backward. When I stood up, my breath returned, the holes in my body mended, and soon I was breathing and healthy. The assassins had vanished too.

I awoke, bolted upright, chilled, and with a rock of fear and disbelief in my stomach, convinced that I had cheated death.

Had the encounter with the young Chinese men discombobulated me so much that their thwarted plans found their way into my dreams? Or was some deep place in me warning that the danger was still great, that death was on the rampage, and that only my deep love of life would keep me alive?

I didn't know during those dangerous days that this was the beginning of the end of an entire era for me, a macabre, dance-of-death-ending that went beyond Richard's case and Chinatown and my lust for life. Death, as it turned out, was indeed filling her dance card, collecting partners in a gruesome dance marathon.

On November 18, 1978, my Café Flores irregulars began hearing rumors about a mass suicide in Jonestown, Guyana, where over one thousand members of San Francisco's utopian community, the People's Temple, had emigrated en masse. The news initially reported a mind-numbing hundred deaths by mass suicide, then quickly leap-frogged to an incomprehensible nine hundred plus victims. There was confirmation that Jonestown security had had murdered Bay Area Congressman Leo Ryan and three aides.

I remembered my dream. Death was indeed dancing and harvesting. But we were far from last call.

On November 27, 1978, less than a week after Jonestown, former City Supervisor and ex-police officer Dan White assassinated Supervisor Harvey Milk and Mayor George Moscone. Supervisor Dianne Feinstein, later to become a California U.S. Senator, may have been on his hit list, but was out of her office that day.

Harvey, as we called him, had openly supported Richard's campaign for a new trial. Best known as an advocate for gay rights, Harvey was unlike many in the white gay community for he viewed the gay rights struggle as part of the overall fight against bigotry. That was how we met, as members of Citizens for Justice, a coalition of African-Americans, Chicanos, Asian-Americans, gays, and women seeking to transform the city's criminal justice system.

At twenty-eight, I was their peer, in my own San Francisco wide version of the Il Piccolo band of activists. In our modern way, we were all knitting a new "village" of sorts, united by our common experience of bias and our belief in change. As a sardonic nod to our mutual criminalization by San Francisco's finest, we coined an unofficial name, "Criminals for Justice." All were equal and no one dominated. We spoke in round-and-round fashion as we began to piece it together the patterns of police brutality, including the policy of transferring rather than firing known "mad dogs," sadistic police who beat people senseless. They were transferred from district to district instead of firing one thus abused their power for years. Our task was to monitor them and then curb them, and, ultimately, to change the police culture. Harvey was more than a celebrity, he was our friend, an indispensable voice in our circle.

In my already fragile state, Jonestown and the assassinations were signs that it was time to move in another direction. The decade came to a personal close for me when the singer Joan Baez summoned us to a "healing concert," a novel idea for the times, at dusk on Christmas Eve, 1978. Thousands flocked to Civic Center Plaza across from City Hall, the site of the assassinations. Joanie sang song after soothing song and together we sang "Amazing Grace," our candles held high, signifying that our inner fires had not been extinguished by tragedy, but burned strong still.

And then we drifted off into the night.

My own inner fire, though, didn't hold up. From that Christmas Eve until well into the Chinese New Year of 1979, my burnout spread throughout my mind and body like an illness. From Chinatown's Civil Rights summer of 1968 to now, the decade had fed me, but ultimately took more out of me than it provided. I could not imagine myself physically waking up to another day as an activist.

To be sure, we had accomplished a lot . Chinatown and San Francisco changed for the better forever. In time, historians may well view the Chinatown civil rights movement and its internecine warfare as part of the larger citywide political transformation of the 1970s. We had set a boundary of fairness toward all Asian-Americans within the legal system, a line that became difficult for the criminal justice system to cross. Asian-American community leaders had brought Attorney General Evelle Younger to heel for his stereotypical portrayals of Asian-American communities in that press conference naming Chinese youth as the most dangerous threat of organized crime, broadcasted by the media on the morning of Richard's jury deliberations.

The media now questioned police sources, investigating Chinatown stories with confidence and objectivity. Asian-Americans integrated the police department and one of the new recruits, Fred Lau, Chinatown resident, Chinatown youth worker, and co-activist, rose steadily through the ranks to become San Francisco's first Chinese-American police chief. Even the FBI Strike Force investigation of gambling and police corruption may have had its genesis in the my efforts, Joe Fong, and various defense committees, to expose Chinatown organized crime. Richard, Joe, David, and especially Raymond Leung had not been silenced after all.

But Richard continued to sit wrongfully still in jail. All those larger changes, and my role in them, had the satisfaction of a Pyrrhic victor. It was great for society, but where my work was most personal, we had lost.

Or so I thought.

Section V
Renewal & Continuation (1979–1983)

Chapter 36
Rage under a Mother's Gaze

In those first few years in prison, Richard was angry and so distracted and confused that he barely followed our conversations. I was deeply hurt, and angry too. My son in prison for something he didn't do. Police using liars to put him away. He was a good boy. Ran errands for Benny's Smoke Shop as a child. Held summer jobs all his life. Worked at the bank and was going to college. The courts made a mistake, why couldn't they see that? I suffered, oh how I suffered.

We couldn't really talk except during family stay-overs. Richard really enjoyed those and he was more himself then. He enjoyed chopping vegetables with me, slicing meat, and watching me cook. He always washed the dishes, more than he ever did at home. It was like he was making up to me in some way.

Those were the times when we talked, chopping, cooking, and cleaning up. I told him that what was done, was done. Whatever his mistakes were that put him into prison, they were the past. He had to look to the future when he got out. "You are young, your future is waiting for you when you come out," I said over and over.

Richard told me how violent the prison was. Every day some kind of fight. Every day someone hospitalized or killed. And so I drilled into him at every family visit. Stay out of the fighting! Don't let anyone make you angry! Don't do anything bad, so they can't keep you in prison a day longer! You know how I am, how I say the same things over and over to my children. Stay out of trouble! Just get through your day, day by day! Just stay out of the trouble!

Richard always said, "That's exactly what I'm doing, mom. That's exactly what I'm doing."

Richard enjoyed playing with little John, still a baby then. John didn't even know he was inside a prison. Richard was gentle and patient, teaching John this and that, like a big brother should. He was never strict with John. Richard even brought books into the stay-overs, to teach John reading. I think he got those books from his friends inside, like from David Wong.

After a while, Richard was more at ease. He wasn't angry all the time. Not so confused. Just kind of relaxed, like he was used to everything now. Accepted what had happened. He was cooking for the guards, then. After work, he spent time with David and Chi-ko, pan-frying night-time snacks of Ramen noodles, with Spam instead of Chinese barbecue pork, American vegetables from his job instead of bok choy, and lots of oyster sauce from his Christmas package.

About that time, we went back one last time to that same stupid old judge and he turned Richard down. Even after the newspaper stories, the new evidence!

Of course, I wish we could have won. Richard was still young. He could easily start his life all over again. He had stayed out of trouble in prison. Still a good boy, everybody could see that. But anyway, the main thing was Richard was okay-okay now. That was the most important thing to me.

I had taken some pills during the first two years of Richard's jail time. Just a half a pill a day. Made me sleepy, dreamy, so I didn't think about Richard in jail. Still, after each family visit though, I was depressed for a week, thinking this, and thinking that. After a day visit, I would suffer for a few days.

Then I noticed Richard was doing better in prison. First, he seemed strong, healthy, with an inner peace. Then the guards started treating him like they knew he was innocent, giving him special jobs outside the prison fence, cooking for them, many different tasks. But anyway, the main thing was Richard was okay-okay now. That was the most important thing to me.

That's when I told the doctor I was getting better. I stopped the pills.

Years later, they transferred Richard to a redwood forest camp. There was no fence, only tall trees, and the air was so fresh, you felt better breathing it. Nothing like a prison at all. After a few months, Richard's face turned so much softer, like he had become younger. He whistled when he walked. He greeted us with great, big smiles. He hugged me for long times. Richard was like a free man there. He would even drive off to a town for a couple of hours during our stay-overs. To pick up supplies for the camp, he said. He took long walks with Father, William, and John, deep into the woods. As long as he got back by dinner, no one seemed to mind. I was never concerned that Richard would escape. He promised me he would be a good boy and he was.

As for me, I enjoyed cooking Richard's favorite dishes ,pan-fried Hong Kong-style sam see chow mein, with the triple meats of pork, chicken, and beef combined with crunchy sprouts, sliced celery, and black mushrooms; home-made won ton soup with baby bok choy and thin-sliced oyster sauce beef; and whatever other dishes he wanted for dinner. Guards dropped in to eat, especially Sgt. Carpenter who was so nice to us.

It was there that Richard and I made plans about his life back outside. I told him to look forward to marriage and kids. Getting a job and making money. What could be more wonderful than raising his own children?. Richard agreed, said that was what he was going to do. He promised that when he got out, he was no longer going to get involved with foolishness. He was going to stay away from Chinatown.

I was happy again. There was going to be a happy ending to all this. My boy Richard was unharmed, in good. His mind was fine, and he was young enough to start all over.

You know me, I kept saying these words over and over, every time I saw him. You used to call it "bugging." But I tell you, that's what a mother must do. Oh, children hear you with their ears, but not all the way through their bodies, and into their stomachs. That's how I get through to all my boys. I said to Richard, over and over: Family, marriage, children. Work and friends. All waiting for you when you come out. That's how I got through to Richard.

Chapter 37 Healing

I did not attend my law school graduation. My absence was an unobserved act of personal protest. I had given up my personal dreams of architecture, of designing nourishing urban landscapes on the one hand and crafting small personalized homes on the other hand. I had loved the discipline's creativity, fondly remembering late nights in the studios drawing plans and renderings and building models. Richard's appeals would take years .A law degree could help in Richard's legal campaign; a master's degree in architecture could not. Moreover, the idealistic part of me wanted to protect other innocents families. But three or four years later, here I was, at the end of the day, law degree in hand, and Richard was no closer to freedom.

Burnt-out, I was burnt out, and, casting about for an entirely new direction, for as it turned out, the adverse media coverage had curtailed once accessible job options. Friends in government didn't savor that later revelations about me, even speculative ones, could harm them politically. As for hanging out my own shingle, who would hire a lawyer who had pissed off the entire judiciary and police?

I was down to two choices: I could move to another city or move into a new field free of local influences. I decided upon the latter, and with Hastings's core of international law and practice courses on my resume, plus my Chinese language skills, I searched for a job in international law and transactions. Bank of America took me on.

Standing inside the lurching, overcrowded No. 8 Market Street bus on my first day to work, I almost didn't make it. The downtown bound bus crawled by a prophet-like man waving a large cardboard sign that read "Wage Slaves, Free Yourselves." Was the universe signaling this was a wrong turn? I had cut my long hair into a corporate style held in place by gel. I wore a fresh blue blazer with pressed gray slacks, a starched white shirt, and a Windsor knotted red-white-and-blue striped tie. Part of me suddenly wanted to exit. Dump this costume.

But no, I had made my choice, and I would stick to it stoically. I worked enthusiastically that first year, even serving in the coveted position of chief assistant to an international bank-wide task force of senior officers from every major division, including my hoped-for assignment, World Banking. I also bit my tongue so often at my colleagues' racist and sexist jokes that a groove formed on it. A new hire, I had to pick my battles, and changing their mentality was a fight I could not even start. The burn-out, thankfully, subsided, but during the second year, a funk slowly replaced it, and then grew into a depression.

Unlike my mother, I was not skilled in deflecting negative states of mind. I didn't know to whisper mantras of positive affirmations. Instead, like a workaholic, I had buried my feelings in a frenetic overdrive of activity. The demands of Richard's case, college and law school, grassroots electoral politics, a youth agency, and my life with Francine and her daughter had left me no time to feel. Now, in my late twenties, free of even family demands after Francine and I parted ways, with a comparatively undemanding nine-to-five job with, lots of personal time, long-suppressed feelings unlashed themselves into the unbattened-down spaces of my life. I discovered that I was drowning in my own underground river of ten thousand sorrows.

I contemplated suicide.

In 1980, I was perilously unaware of post-traumatic stress syndrome or the corrosiveness to mental health from the accumulated carnage of so many young men. Something called "healing" needed to take place. To everyone, I looked great in my three-piece suits and my job sounded wonderful. Look, there was my spanking new law license hanging on my office wall. But inside, I was sinking into a malaise where I often stopped caring about anything. Not romance, work, friends, causes, and at times, not even my family. Live or die, at least death delivers finality's repose.

The only way I had to admit this descent to myself was when riding my Triumph motorcycle. It was an impulse buy: I needed some kind of triumph, even if only a brand name. The bike's clean lines, dusky red gas tank, blinding chrome, and its double-pipes with web-like heat deflectors offset my misanthropic self-loathing. The roar of its 650 cc engines and, its sudden bursts and responsiveness, re-endowed me with a sense of mastery over life. It sounds bullshit trite, but the bike and I truly became one that year. My legs existed only to carry and clamp my upper-body onto that Triumph, so I could begin living.

Riding became a daily choice between life and death. Easy enough to mask suicide as an "accident," I ripped around the hostile San Francisco streets, racing against the vanishing point between packed lanes, popping my clutch into ephemeral openings like a drowning man chasing his own oxygen bubbles. I instinctively downshifted back from oblivious drivers a nanosecond before they merged into where I had just been. I shot red lights during the rush hour, roaring past wall-sized delivery trucks and startled pedestrians alike, jackrabbiting on and off the sidewalk as if it was another traffic lane. The crazier the moves, the deadlier the risks, the more alive I felt, and the less I wanted to die. It finally dawned on me that I was consistently choosing to live.

The Triumph may have brought me back to life, but my healing really began, however, when I joined the Angels of Light Theater Company. Perhaps I was unconsciously searching for a new community, a Clan of some kind. For me, I discovered that the Angels of Light captured the essential compassionate essence of Mother's Toisan village.

On the surface, the Angels were like the bohemians in the musical *Moulin Rouge*, living for the flames of romance and the magic of theater. They were "gender-benders," with personas switching daily between personas of male, female, and androgyne; dressing to the nines either way or in some clever cross-sexual farrago, their genders betrayed only by their voices. Mainly gays, lesbians, and bisexuals, a few, like me, were strictly heterosexual. But with the Angels, sexual orientation didn't matter in the slightest, for at heart an Angel of Light was polymorphously sexual, alive in a constant state of revel and lust for every person, detail, taste, and moment. Their company became as fresh air reviving my dying embers.

Their stage productions came into being through a series of unpaid sessions not unlike a speaking-round-and-round. Each member freely contributed their own plot ideas, characters, songs, dances, and special effects as other members took those suggestions and refined them, until, at the end, they had a script, the music, the choreography, and the sets.

Their resourcefulness inspired me, since I too was depleted of resources, patching together my new life. Every Angel's costume was created on a shoestring—items from second-hand clothing stores and other people's cast-offs, all sewn together by one simple Singer machine. The majestic, mesmerizing, 12-14 feet high prosceniums and ever-changing scenery were constructed of discarded cardboard boxes, held together by duct tape, and propped up by scavenged two-by-fours. In my backstage role, I came to know the cardboard backside of these lovingly painted and glittery panoramas of illusion— Scott Tissues, Post Grape Nuts Cereal, Tide, Colgate, and other household names – that I lovingly reset performance after performance.

They split each weekend's profit regardless of star status. Just like Mother's village, shared and share alike. At a mere five dollars, the ticket price was intentionally and outrageously low for the early 1970s. No one was ever turned away for lack of funds, and single mothers with children were admitted free, oftentimes returning weekend after weekend.

Mother was pleased that I had found such fine new friends. So, one Chinese New Year, the core Angels trooped over to Chinatown for a special vegetarian Chinese New Year's dinner at Mother's. They marveled at the celebratory colors of shiny tangerines glistening with green leaves, the garish red and gold wall posters of millennia old affirmations, and the red buds of spreading quince blossoms next to the family altar, as if they had stumbled upon a secret civilization. They bowed to our ancestors, smoking incense sticks in hand. But most of all, these offspring of middle and upper class America loved the simple, utilitarian homeliness of Mother's housing project apartment, decoding what many could not, an interior design language of ancient authenticity.

They gasped at each new dish: black mushrooms over mustard greens, Buddhist Lo Han *jai,* deep-fried mushroom puffs with crunchy celery in light soy sauce, tofu squares with lotus roots, bamboo shoots and cashew nuts, and many more Toisanese treats. Crunching away and gushing gratitude to Mother throughout the dinner, Mother and the Angels took to each other like long-lost kin in an unexpected reunion.

In gratitude, they invited Mother and the kids as special guests to their greatest, most popular production, *Holy Cow!* a spiritual immersion disguised as a musical. Many Angels had journeyed to India, steeping themselves in tales of the mythological pantheon of Hindu deities. Returning as adepts of Indian music, they composed an original score of traditional Hindi music fused with jazz, new wave, and Western classical music. Others, now masters of intricate Indian dances, wove their graceful, enchanting dancing into the drama.

Seated front and center, and despite their lack of comprehension of most of the dialogue, Mother, Bob, and the kids were thunderstruck. In the play, the maharajah's evil advisor opened by announcing his presence with gunpowder explosions, mere feet away from my Mother, Bob and the kids, who screamed with delight as stage lighting transformed the plumes of smoke into red, green, and gold columns that ascended to the top of the fifty-foot ceiling of the converted canning factory. A glittering Chinese-style dragon swirled out and then broke apart into a chorus line of tap-dancing demons. The enchantress, the sinuous Robin, undulated in her yellow, skintight, full-body leotard, a cobra closing in on her prey, hissing and softly singing a mesmerizing melody to a solo instrumentalist.

After that night's final standing ovation, still dressed in their costumes, the core Angels filed out to greet Mother, paying homage to her own very special presence.

Viewing *Holy Cow!* night after night from my vantage point as a backstage hand, I felt the play's magic wash away the sludge in my spirit, rejuvenate my innocence, and, and remind me of life's ten thousand joys. The story's ultimate triumph of good over evil, always and forever, resurrected my hope for Richard's freedom and well-being.

But it was as fellow travelers into the shadow side that was the Angels greatest gift. I slowly realized that each one of them not only openly lived their shadow side, but also imbued their *Holy Cow!* characters with it, their shadow sides expressing themselves fully on stage. They treated life's ugliness as normal, with full faith that always, always, the light side and good would prevail. Feeling safe to do so, I soon unleashed my shadow to run into the night with the this parallel troupe, self-dubbed the Demons of Darkness - like a wild pack of wolves. I let loose my stored-up rage and unreleased frustration, transforming into a seething, don't-give-a-fuck, motorcycle-riding punk rock night-clubber, a full-on expression of my own duct-taped, pine board–propped, cardboard-patched, dark side persona.

To exorcise the cancer of negativity eating my spirit, I slam danced, weekend after weekend . To slam was therapy. Feel it. Live it. Express it. Get rid of it. I leaned against ceiling-high speakers, craving the booming rapid-fire bass and jarring harsh guitar runs that blasted through my body. Then I jumped onto the floor to slam again and again, way past last call and ending up at all-night parties until dawn. Like a wild pack of wolves, we ran until dawn. That year, the twenty-eighth year of my life, I bled out the deepest-seated, evilest portion of my depression. When my nihilism disappeared, I sold my motorcycle and bought a sensible Honda Civic hatchback. I stopped slamming and joined a gym.

And my career at the Bank of America took off. I was happy again. My parents and Bob were proud, dropping in to visit me in my high-rise, bay view office. In the evenings, I tutored John, and on some weekends, he and the kid cousins slept over.

As Chief Legal Officer and a vice president for one of Bank of America's international subsidiaries, I discovered that my multicultural personality helped me succeed in countries where my American colleagues had hit an impasse. My counterparts—whether Saudi Arabian, Yemeni, French, German, English, Venezuelan, Chilean, Argentinean, Singaporean, Japanese, or Chinese – detected my openness to them and my sincere interest in their culture.

I usually went against the faultfinding grain of my legal training, and yes, the superiority complex of so many international corporate officers then, respectfully probing into the human reasons why a good customer would default. In doing so, I inadvertently created speaking round-and-rounds. Once the other party recognized that I wasn't out to get him, but seeking to work things out, he and his lawyer started to parcel out the important facts, express their most urgent concerns. We could then take turns suggesting solutions, and together fashion one.

As it turned out, most defaults were necessitated by unanticipated business exigencies. Our financially troubled clients had treated our travelers' cheques as a temporary loan until they got back on their feet. Just as my mother did not see little Gawn, the coin-taker, as a thief, but understood his basic human goodness and his little boy's need, so too I searched for the human necessity implicit in each situation. Just as Mother's village sought to work things out because we are all in this together, like-it-or-not, I saw these hardworking businessmen as invaluable members of our global business community. In their gratitude, they always paid back and ended up delivering ongoing profit to the Bank just like Gawn had returned to Mother all the value of all coins he had filched and much more, year after year.

The power of my improvised speaking round-and-round was not hampered by differences in language. It seemed that if one could create the right atmosphere, a kind of vibration or spell of resolution, the process worked its own way. In one meeting in Paraguay, held entirely in Spanish, I was somehow able to follow the discussions, interjecting timely comments in American, and advancing the speaking to its resolution stage. Afterwards, the other side remarked, incredulously, that I had followed the conversation like a native speaker.

In Saudi Arabia, before a specially impaneled sub-ministry of the Saudi Arabian Monetary Authority, I replicated the same process and reached an equally fair resolution, despite differences in language and the application of the mysterious Islamic Shar'ia legal systems. I had uncovered the Shar'ia concept of the *Amana,* a concept not dissimilar to the Toisanese concept of a community trust, which depends upon trusting one another's word, honesty, and cooperation in order for communal survival. I reminded the ministers of the spirit of their *Amana*, its roots in an earlier, communally dependent time, an honor honed by the barren, baking, waterless desert of Saudi Arabia. I proved that that the Bank had honored its side of the *Amana* in all our dealings, that we expected no less in return. They deliberated briefly and recognized our debt as a priority claim. My own Toisanese *Amana* was rooted in the uncertain dictates of a different climate, but they could feel that I understood it deeply.

But in cases of unapologetic downright fraud, I came down hard. A former governor of Zulia, the biggest state in Venezuela and its oil state, in his role as CEO of a major savings and loan, defrauded us of hundreds of thousands of dollars worth of Bank of America Travelers Cheques. His family indulged themselves on a wild spending spree, with our travelers' cheques, throughout the Caribbean and Western —Europe as common Venezuelans suffered from downward spiraling cycles of currency devaluation. After a friendly, unproductive visit at his Maracaibo City headquarters, the defrauder informed my attorney that he personally would see to it that I would be shot if ever I set foot on Venezuelan soil again. After all, he mentioned casually, the price of a hit was a mere thousand dollars in US funds.

Presumably, he would pay the gunman with travelers' cheques stolen from us.

How could this gentleman have known that his arrogant corruption steeled me, and that his death threats wouldn't frighten me in the slightest? If anything, his threat summoned forth the ruthlessness forged in of Chinatown battles.

I sardonically mentioned to our attorney that why doesn't he send me a bill for $1,000 for special services and take care of the thief. "That's a good idea. That's a good idea." I then made it clear that I was kidding, that Bank of America didn't whack people who didn't pay up.

Instead, I did not hesitate to bring down the law, as hard as the law can be, against an arrogant, corrupt, wealthy, elitist croon. He was who one who robbed by the pen, and then shielded himself behind his privilege and power. Early one morning, coordinating a number of retained private attorneys in several countries, we simultaneously attached and froze all his bank accounts outside of Venezuela. Within a week, the "gentleman" paid up in full.

University and law school had qualified me for a career in international banking, so my family's belief in the value of a college education was vindicated. But, fundamentally, my way of doing business was a reflection of my Mother and the Toisanese way of living with others. In approaching any problem, I instinctively sought a common solution, engaging in a *tai-chi* dance of harmonious balance in my relationships with all people, a skill my mother, by her example, had instilled in me. I applied the speaking-round-and-round of her Clan Sisterhood, assuming that people were honest, even if human enough to succumb to desperation.

One of the perks of my success was that I could peruse the morning papers over my first cup of office coffee as the sun rose slowly over the Bay waters and warmed my quarters. One morning, a small article about a motorcycle fatality the previous afternoon caught my eye. A young man had raced his Ninja motorcycle at speeds of up to 50 mph down the lurching obstacle course of Mission

Street. Weaving in and out of traffic, he roared down the narrow space next to parked cars. Running his final red light, he was struck broadside by a truck. The biker was DOA.

Once upon a time, that could have been me.

Chapter 38 About Place and Home

Your father and I have lived in the projects for over forty years now, you know. I never wanted to leave Chinatown. Once your father, though, saw a chance to buy some flats in North Beach in the 1950s or 1960s. Only $15,000 way back then in the 1950s. Worth millions now, I am sure, with lots of rental income. But I only felt good in Chinatown and refused to move. So, he didn't buy it.

The newer immigrants think of Chinatown as a place for poor people. They think you should leave as soon as you make some money, especially if you live in the Ping Yuen housing projects. My brother Wah and my sister Tien bought a house together in the Sunset district. My sister Yoong has her apartment building on California Street. "First sister in America and still living in Chinatown, in a housing project, yet!" they say to me.

I say, "Where would you be if my husband and I hadn't sacrificed so much to get you here?"

I know a lot of Clan sisters who didn't care about their relatives stuck in China. They were having such a good time they forgot about their family! Didn't even write letters! I didn't have to work so hard to send money home and then suffer when your Father argued about every penny. I didn't have to make up stories to confuse him and sometimes take a beating. I didn't have to be so nice to Mr. Wong and Mr. Lee so they would like my sisters, thinking they must be like me, you know. Sometimes I get a little angry at their ingratitude. And they disrespect your father, too. Your father and I had it the toughest and but for us, they would all still be stuck in Hong Kong, in that overcrowded, crime-infested slum name, So Uk Choon, with the squat toilet room that is also the shower, kitchen sink, and laundry room.

But thankfully, there're a lot of us who don't feel we got stuck in Chinatown, especially those who came in the 1950s. Chinatown is our community and everything we want is here. It's also pretty safe now, after the muggings and robberies of the 1980s. Especially with the new gates and guards that we won in our rent strike in 1980. My husband was one of the tenant leaders. You remember that, don't you? You had just become a lawyer, working for Bank of America. You advised the president of the Tenant's Union.

The Cheong kids from Kearny Street, Jerry and Sonny, live in nice parts of Sacramento. Big Shots now, I hear. Their sister, Maxine, has her own house in San Francisco. Yet, Mrs. Cheong refused to move in with any one of them, even though she lives alone since her husband passed. She likes bumping into her friends, talking with the shop owners. And the old Wongs who lived across from us at Kearny Street, they never moved out either.

The best place is not always what looks good on the outside, or where the most successful want to be, but a place where you feel good walking, where your friends are, where you can easily get everything you need to be happy. A place where life is.

Maybe Americans move so much because they want the new feeling. Yeah, I know the new feeling is necessary. That's why I change the furniture every few years. New sofa, new stove, new table. I go to Levitz store. They always have good prices for solid furniture, and they deliver for free, too. William just took me to Ikea. Ooh yahh! Lots of good sofas, chairs and kitchenware. Very cheap, too! And the housing authority repaints the entire apartment every few years. Yeah, that's how I get the new feeling, like I'm in a new home, but without moving.

Besides, moving all the time makes you feel lost. Staying in one good place for a long time makes you happier, your family stronger, and makes a better life for everyone. Maybe in China, our Clan stayed in one place for so long because, at first, we didn't have a choice. But it turned out for the better, to have a place you know you can always return to, be welcomed and remembered. To speak a language that is yours, and to recognize each other by that tongue wherever you go. And if we bump into each other somewhere else in the world, to recognize and help one another out, sometimes a little bit, sometimes a lot.

That's the way it was back there. Poor, but always happy. Always busy, dawn to dusk. Always using your head, figuring out the next best way of doing the same old thing. I remember the rice paddies, so shiny and quiet in the morning. And the green vegetables, so beautiful when they grew, their leaves and blossoms spreading full.

Makes me feel so good to remember those days. So much joy.

Richard in jail was my toughest time in America. William's friends helped out a lot, and I thought for a while, that maybe we could even out the power, that in America perhaps common people can right wrong decisions. Maybe we might have, maybe we almost won. But as it turned out for Richard, all those friends weren't enough.

That's why I spent all my time thinking about our visits with Richard, planning our food, and sending the gift packages. I don't know much about officials, but I know about people, how to nurture them when they're unhappy, or in trouble. That's the way it was in the village, attending to each other, keeping one another happy, no matter what. Richard's okay-okay now.

Maybe I stayed in Chinatown so long because of this same reason. To recreate a way of life that I had left behind in China. Maybe I stayed in Chinatown because I don't know any better. But I cannot imagine living anywhere else, any other way.

Chapter 39 A Quiet TriumphVictory

I had not been the only one wrestling with a shadow side. Richard too had been struggling.

During a 1983 visit, Richard nonchalantly dropped an amazing admission. I had driven up on a Sunday morning, after a water-skiing party weekend at a friend's lakeside cabin on Clear Lake. Given my slightly hung-over state of mind and the long drive, the visit stayed low-key. Richard seemed somber himself, even mildly distracted. We spoke little, but we no longer needed to articulate our connection with each other. We were not only brothers, but also fellow warriors who had fought well in an unexpected war. Although we had lost, and one of was us was still a prisoner, we had survived. We leaned our backs against the wall across from one another, our legs stretched out along the length of the picnic table benches. Richard lit up a cigarette from time to time.

Then, as if talking about nothing, quite casually, he recounted an incident at DVI of some years back. An inmate had violated Richard's honor. Under the rules of prison society, Richard had to retaliate, probably through combat, possibly to the death. If he failed to do so, he would be perceived as weak, open to further victimization from one prison gang or other. Richard went so far as to hone a shank, a homemade blade. He prepared to do "what a man has got to do."

Then, a countervailing impulse surfaced. Richard felt the presence of all his supporters. One by one, he recited their names, remembered the myriad faces of those who believed in his innocence, or at least that he deserved a new and fair trial, rose. He remembered those kind strangers who had actually visited him in prison. One by one, he thought of their words, and how the sunlight was that day they visited him.

And so then he paused in his preparation to do "what a man has got to do"

He reflected on our family who had stuck by him. He thought of Mother cooking him feasts during family visits, mailing him money orders regularly, and faithfully sending birthday and Christmas packages every year. Her unceasing and never-changing mantras of advice: "Stay out of trouble. Stay away from the violence. Don't do anything bad that will keep you in prison a day longer," reverberated in his mind. He remembered his promise to her, "This is what I'm doing, mom."

He remembered Father's dismay, suffering, and shame at his own helplessness. He thought of our little brother John and of how good it would be, when he was outside to be a big brother. He undoubtedly thought of me, who had set aside my own ambitions to champion his case.

A deep appreciation that he had not been forgotten welled from within; that although he lived in the sticky, toxic, and lethal web of the Gladiator School, he could refuse to abide by all their rules. He was the son of brave Toisan refugees, immigrants who persevered through all the unkindness, difficulties, and insults to provide him a decent community, a family home, food, clothing, and time to study.

Any retributive actions, however justified by the dictates of prison culture, would hurt the reputations of many kind strangers. Thus, Richard clutched at his membership in the community of San Francisco, especially of Chinatown, a home he would return to one day. In spite of everything, Toisan Chinese had forged a viable community and he still belonged to it. There, his parents still lived, people spoke his first language, restaurants still served his favorite foods cooked the old fashion way. Familiar streets awaited for him to walk them once again. So he could make peace with Chinatown too. He soul wrestled in this way many days and many nights.

Slowly, Richard released himself from the wicked spell of the fatalistic prison code. He put down the shank, once and forever. In peaceful ways, he worked things out. The grudge was settled and the gangs left him alone.

I listened to Richard, but whether because of my own torpor, or Richard's casual way of speaking, I did not register the significance of his words during the actual visit. It wasn't until I was about an hour into my four-hour drive home that the import of what Richard had said struck me fully.

Exactly like a lightning bolt.

Like the Cantonese martial arts heroes of our childhood Hong Kong movies and true to the ideals of the mythic Water Margin heroes, the vows of *Chung Ching Yee*, the fraternal values of Loyalty, Harmony, and Righteousness, Richard had made a moral choice under the most dire of circumstances.

I quickly realized that Richard too, had been empowered by the example of Mother. Richard had journeyed beyond prison's perdition and reclaimed his own best self. As my wheels squealed around the tight curves of a rushing river that ran alongside the highway, a metaphor came to me of how well Richard had pressed through the treacherous white waters of this internal moral passage, snatching the victory of staying human from its deepest whirlpools. I realized that the victory one seeks is not always the victory one needs. It would have felt so felt glorious to have won in the courts too. Certainly it was a victory I had yearned to taste. But at that moment, I overflowed with the joy of this private, unglamorous, internal victory. I knew that this was immensely truer and of longer more-lasting value.

We had lost the legal case, but we had not lost Richard. Richard had triumphed.

In contrast, I thought of another DVI inmate, another highly publicized Chinatown frame-up murder case from that era. Chol Sol Lee actually won his appellate battle against equally impossible odds by having two murder convictions reversed (the second one a prison slaying). But that inmate had been on his own too early, without the same nurturing from childhood. In fact, his exoneration was the basis for the movie, "True Believer," starring James Woods in the role of Chol Sol Lee's real life attorney, the well-regarded Tony Serra. Like Richard, Chol Sol Lee had been convicted by another flawed Chinatown-related line-up, a group of three unreliable witnesses. A Sacramento judge, on the basis of suppressed material evidence, reversed Chol Sol Lee's wrongful conviction. Chol Sol Lee was acquitted in a second trial.

Yet, unlike Richard, Joe Fong and David Wong, Chol Sol Lee, a Korean-American who served time at DVI with them, had not been able to hold his place against the predatory prison environment. He was invited to join the Asian/Native American alliance, but instead, Chol Sol Lee became a member of Nuestra Familia. On orders, he killed another inmate in a prison yard altercation. His attorneys, Tony Serra and Stuart Hanlon, after successfully reversing Chol Sol Lee's original wrongful conviction, proceeded to reverse the murder conviction for the inmate slaying. Their argument was that the State had wrongfully placed Chol Sol Lee in a situation where, in order to survive, he had no choice but to kill in self-defense. Therefore, he could not be legally held responsible for the second murder, which never could have happened but for his wrongful incarceration.

Chol Sol Lee was overborne by the unexpected circumstances caused by his wrongful conviction. And it wasn't just Chol Sol Lee. Many inmates succumb, whether in prison rightly or wrongly, to prison's bizarre society. Certainly there was no mother recreating a timeless family hearth in family visits, whispering affirmative mantras in his ear, reminding him to avoid trouble, and reassuring him that he was young enough still to make money, marry and raise children. When released, that other young man eventually returned to a life of crime, became addicted to drugs, and was eventually incarcerated again.

Yet, that Richard wasn't similarly overcome, not even by that clear, but mysterious provocation that led him to prepare to kill another, is an instructive distinction. That said a lot about how Mother had not only nourished him with Toisanese food, but also fortified his core Toisanese character through her repetitive mantras.

At the moment of that realization, I recalled a similar moral decision of my own. Sometime in 1974, I had collaborated with several others to organize a youth service agency that focused on hardcore street youth and younger youth-at-risk who were often turned away by other agencies. Part of my role included counseling young adults who were capable of deadly violence, including a young man named Gerald.

Gerald was different from most of the youth we served. In his early twenties, he dressed stylishly, often in an expensive white linen suit. His thick 22-carat gold chain was adorned with and expensive jade amulet that dangled over his open-neck pastel shirts and his taut, Bruce Lee built.

"Provides protection against death," he said.

Once, during a martial arts practice, Gerald dazzled us with a close-to-the-body, swirling, double-knife set, Markedly unembellished and emphatically deadly, the set with emphasized efficient, close-in stabbing into all major organs of the body. Equally striking, was that he refused use of the traditional twin knives, more ornamental than functional, but insisting instead on two common 12-inch kitchen knives.

Eventually, Gerald revealed his true identity to me, as a highly trained killer and member of a secret criminal society based in New York's Chinatown. He had graduated from their deadly training academy, named *Hung Men* (Red Door). *Hung Men's* campus was discreetly nestled among the large private estates of upstate New York.

In Chinese organized crime, "*Hung,* " the color red symbolized its dark side, the blood of violent death, not the invigorating lifeblood that marked Chinese New Year's red envelopes. *Hung Men* translated culturally into something like "The Gateway into the Arts of Blood Violence."

There, Gerald relayed to me, he had learned to clean, reassemble, and fire numerous handguns, submachine guns, and rifles, as well as the best time and place to assassinate the target. He was drilled until he could maximize the terror potential of each gun during a robbery to maximize terror and confusion or alternatively, swiftly assassinate his target victim. He learned the craft of torturing people for information, by striking at different parts of the body with his fists or with clubs, chains, metal pipes, blackjacks, and brass knuckles. *Hung Men* which taught him the efficient 12-inch kitchen-knives set he had demonstrated to us.

After his training, Gerald worked as an enforcer and then as a commando-style armed robber. In the early 1970s, Gerald was promoted to a heroin courier. One day, he described to me the six-hour Toronto-to-Manhattan pipeline. In the morning, he'd fly to Toronto's Chinatown to pick-up a well-wrapped packet of heroin. In the afternoon, he delivered this return it to his bosses in New York Chinatown. The next morning, another courier walked the packet across Canal Street to Mafia contacts in Little Italy. By the morning of the third day, the heroin was cut and coursing through the arms of addicts in Harlem, the Lower East Side, and Brooklyn.

Gerald fled Manhattan's Chinatown because he had botched a job, or as I speculated, robbed one of his own bosses. I knew Gerald hadn't originally come to us to turn his life around, although, as we discovered long after he left the agency, he did turn it around. But it was not our policy to turn away anyone who behaved within the four walls of the center and who didn't otherwise deliver trouble to our doors.

It was Gerald's perverse way of expressing gratitude for whatever respite we provided him that prompted him to offer to assassinate Judge Calcagno. Perhaps too, he was testing me to see if I was "for real," unlike so many others in his life. Would I really walk the talk of peace, of working through the system, and actually refuse the easy way out? In truth, if a Gerald had made that same offer a year sooner, I am not sure that that I could have refused. In the Bay Area of the 1970s, deadly violence against authority was not unthinkable. Nor did I lack malice towards Judge Calcagno. If a ten-ton truck had hit him, I wouldn't have been heartbroken about it.

I had only to say yes, and our family would taste revenge. But like Richard, I passed my test. I turned Gerald down.

By then, I knew that violence never resolves differences, but only causes more violence. The power of Mother's seasonal Chinese New Year practice of releasing the wrongs of the past year, forgiving those who have harmed you, and thereby making room to let in the New Year's offerings, finally penetrated my skeptical Western upbringing.

On that long afternoon drive home from my visit with Richard, it slowly dawned on me that, like Richard, I had not lost either, that I too had won. Our family we had truly won, for we had not lost our humanity.

In our localized version of an epic, archetypal struggle, the Lee family stayed human. And Mother led the way during this most intimate of battles, these most private of victories. For over a millennium, like so many Toisan-Chinese before us, we had sourced a sustenance that carried us through life's ten thousand sorrows. That power, as I discovered one special day in a small, humble village square, was the power of Toisan-Chinese culture. The source was our relationship with our land. But for me, my mother was simultaneously the embodiment and holder of this legacy. It was she who transmitted it to me, by living as completely as possible the Eighth Promise, the promise to live the compassionate path of her Toisanese lineage. By her example, Mother taught me that compassion includes the gift of forgiveness. She taught me that to hold onto hate and feelings of revenge damaged me and blocked the wonderful providence that patiently waits to enter our lives. Through our own ten thousand sorrows, our Mother helped us to find our way back to the ten thousand joys. In this way, Mother fulfilled her Eighth Promise, the silent promise she made to Grandmother Chun so many decades ago.

EPILOGUE: The Present

A Millennial Chinese New Year in Toisan

That first visit to Toisan in 1983, turned out to be the keystone of a reintegration of self, the first physical experience of the land of my ancestors. Until that day, I had always felt as if I had been dropped out of the sky, birthed one perplexing day in America, focused exclusively on an American future, unconnected to my parents's past.

As I sat with my relatives in the makeshift village square, that my toes, my feet, and then my entire skin began tingling with some extraordinary energy. I started to effervesce, as if I were showering in bubbling champagne. Then I felt the energy move deeply inside me, like an underground stream surging through my chest, up my neck, and finally shooting out the top of my head. I felt like I would explode with joy, the hearty joy of coming home, of knowing fully who I was and where I'd come from. This was the joy of belonging, the joy of a simple village, of these quiet farmers who knew who I was despite never having seen me before. Here my spirit could percolate up from the soulful artesian wells of my kin, from our land.

Some may call this a mystical or spiritual experience of some kind. Perhaps it was that too, but I don't remember it as especially religious at all, just "right."

My grand tour of China's ancient magnificence had affected me profoundly, but not like this, no, not so physically at all. Standing upon my ancestral land was like standing next to the tuning fork of my soul.

For those of us who raised in America's mobile lifestyle, I think that few of us appreciate the power of place, of how place molds a people's character. So many questions have since jumped out: What creates the resonance of a place and its people? What makes Toisan people so…well, so Toisanese? I knew that Hawai'ians speak of the *mana*, their individual soul force that is so inextricably connected to and dependent on their *aina*, or homeland, that when deprived of their own land, their *mana* suffers. I had read that for countless millennia, Australian aborigines trek the mysterious song lines of their own ancient land in rites of initiation. Had the demands and bounty of this land similarly forged something so unique, a *terroir* of personality and character?

That day was the first time that I realized that even before my birth, I had a complete past and came from a complete people. I remember sensing the living power underneath the soil of my ancestral village; a gargantuan mother-root bulb thriving, streaming Toisan *chi* essence into me wherever I called home, that I was just one of her many shoots. My state of mind was joyous, a hilarious joy as my body continued to bubble like fresh-popped champagne, and I chuckled and laughed at every little thing. I was, oh, so happy.

In 2000, as a gift to myself on my fiftieth birthday that coming January 16, I invited Mother to celebrate Chinese New Year with me in Toisan. It would be the first year of the new millennium, and in 2000, Suey Wan would be a thousand years old give or take a few years. My fiftieth birthday to its one-thousandth birthday. But in the Toisanese way, we don't celebrate individual birthdays, but a collective Clan birthday, once a year, during the Chinese New Year period. The thinking is that we survive together or perish together, it's not about you alone. So, if the village makes it through another year, every one adds on one more year during that collective birthday celebration. In 2000, I simultaneously turned fifty years old and in a way, one thousand years old.

This would be not only our first time traveling together to China, but my first Chinese New Year celebration in China and, for Mother, her first Chinese New Year season celebration there since she left in 1949. Traditionally, Chinese New Year is celebrated at home, and since America has been our home for half a century, Mother initially refused to fly off until we had our New Year's dinners. But upon reflection, she fashioned a flexible solution. We would hold an unprecedented, early preemptive but still heartfelt Chinese New Year's dinner, mere hours before our midnight flight to China.

We landed in Hong Kong at dawn on the morning of Chinese New Year's Eve. A comfortable boat ferried us in four hours through the green waters, banks, and hills of the Pearl River Delta to Toisan. The local bus from the pier dropped us off at our simple but clean hotel, located smack-dab in the middle of Hoisin's historic district.

In 1983, my first time here, the historic district was the whole of Hoisin. In under two decades, its population soared from 30,000 to more than 300,000 strong and growing. Concentric circles of new residences, high-rises, and factories spiraled out for miles from the historic district. Hoisin was now a manufacturing boomtown of athletic shoes, home entertainment systems, and brand-name clothes and household wares sold at Macy's, Target, and Walmart.

I was grateful that someone had had the foresight to preserve this charming neighborhood of seventeenth- and eighteenth-century Western and Chinese buildings, with its captivating winding streets intended not for automobiles, but for pedestrians and horse-drawn wagons. Perhaps the magistrate-husband of Mother's adopted sister Kow Woon had established the special zoning before leaving for Canada? My nightly promenades through its quiet streets were unexpectedly reminiscent of my magical, midnight saunters through other historic districts, like the town of Aix-en-Provence in the south of France and the city of Oaxaca in southern, Mexico.

That first night, Mother telephoned her Clan Sisters and before long our room was full of happy young women in their twenties and thirties. They lavished attention on Mother. And their infectious joy visibly transformed Mother into a younger woman herself, despite the jet lag and her years. Just another young girl yukking it up at a pajama party.

I could only share a hotel room with Mother for the first few nights. I soon discovered that I would need my own room if I wanted undisturbed sleep and privacy to write. Her Clan Sisters dropped in continuously, at all hours. At 11:00 p.m. each and every night, the assembled sisters descended to a restaurant conveniently located on the third floor of the hotel for its final sitting, the *sell yeah,* (traditional late-night cuisine).

This ornate, large and popular restaurant belonged to a Clan Sister from Mother's own village. I Hugely successful, it specialized in completely fresh ingredients, *dim sum* cuisine *a la* Toisan, and with three daily sittings daily. The morning *dim sum* opened at 7 a.m. and ran until noon. The dinner banquet-style dining sitting started at 5 p.m., winding down around nine. And the late night snack packed them in from 11 p.m. until the food ran out. We ate there a lot, in the mornings and then every evening, at 11 p.m. The sisterhood routinely gabbed for hours before returning to the room to continue their *ji-ji-jah-jah* chitchat.

There, Mother held court for several hours more until sleepy-eyed, the sisters began peeling away home. Unfailingly, one or two Clan Sisters always slept over, turning our room into a slumber party. They started casually ducking under my Mother's covers and lounging on chairs, their pajama-clad legs dangling over armchairs, and everyone drinking hot tea and nibbling on dried fruits, blissfully oblivious to my male presence. One night, one of the sisters even innocently tucked herself in next to me for her stay-over. Then and there, I decided it was high time to move into my own room if I were to get any sleep or privacy for my writing.

I had expected the Clan Sisters to be Mother's age. Oh sure, childhood friends visited, but most of the sisters were in their twenties and, thirties, and a few in their forties. These younger Clan Sisters treated Mother with the greatest reverence. Belying their youth, they sincerely delighted in her company. My Mother, like her mother before her, had the reputation of being a uniquely compassionate, kind, and helpful Clan Sister. One of a kind and first-class. She had inherited her mother's position as the respected grand elder of this Clan Sisterhood.

During the day, the younger sisters accompanied Mother everywhere. They affectionately held her hands as we strolled through the old town, slicing through the thick crowds of Chinese New Year. They protectively cradled her arms as we crossed busy streets against the chaotic traffic of bicycles, motorbikes, pedicabs, and autos that miraculously never hit anyone. The sisters made dental appointments and restaurant reservations for her. They tracked down stores with the best prices and then bargained on her behalf. They arranged for cars to take us through the countryside to our ancestral village, all at their own expense.

One morning, Vee Son drove us out to Suey Wan for the traditional offering of gratitude to our ancestors. The ritual recognized our connection to them, they who had worked hard and lived well so that we could be born into a loving family and a safe village. Kow Woon's fiery friend Hung, now retired from his job as a postman, opened up the doors. As the protector of the spirits of the house, he had the only set of keys.

Vee Son set off a four-foot-long double line of red firecrackers before the entrance front door. The ear-splitting bursts cleared the home of dead energy and unwanted spirits. Presumably, firecrackers also awakened the good spirits of the house who would welcome us.

The house was musty from being shuttered. Apparently Hung's duties of protecting the spirit of the house did not include cleaning, or, for that matter, protecting the material well being of the house from the elements. Water had leaked onto the upper floor. But as the sun light streamed in and the breezes swirled through the rooms, the house seem to refresh itself, to come alive once again as a home. With a few swipes of a wet cloth, we easily cleared the dust from the ancestral shrine and the dining table. Old plates, rice bowls, and chopsticks appeared from cupboards. We burned incense, and Mother and I bowed three times before our family hearth in acknowledgment of our connection to this village. We offered to our forbears chopped white boiled chicken; barbecued pork; libations of wine, water, and soda; and tangerines with stem and leaves still attached. Then, in that practical Toisan way, we took the food off the altar and made a Chinese New Year's meal of it.

Later, an endless procession of Chuns came by to welcome Mother. Like her younger Clan Sisters of the night before, the clan was genuinely happy to see her.

After cleaning up some the old rough-hewn shelves, I noticed something that I had somehow missed during my first visit in 1983. There, on the highest shelf of the family altar, discreetly tucked against the wall, was a simple, tiny quite small statuette of Kuan Yin, the feminine Buddha of Compassion. Mother confirmed that she had sat there for decades, had been there all along, even during my first visit in 1983. How had I missed her?

Like holy Mother Mary in Christianity, Kuan Yin aids the desperate and heals those in greatest pain and helps the desperate. In Buddhist lore, Kuan Yin broke with the male patriarchs of the early Buddhist religion over their doctrinal viewpoint that only a man could attain enlightenment. Kuan Yin, originally an androgyne, transmuted herself fully into a woman, vowing she would attain enlightenment in a woman's body or not at all.

She did attained her enlightenment, and then, like the historic Buddha, took the Bodhisattva vow that she would not leave this earthly plane until all beings were free of suffering, and until each one in turn, had attained their own enlightenment. She further vowed to help all who called upon her in their suffering. The discovery of this statuette verified my sense that the compassion of Kuan Yin had always been part of my family's ancestral spirit fires. I knew that now. There were remarkably, no other Buddhas or any other statues despite the hundreds of religious figurines in the colorful ecumenical Chinese pantheon of Buddhism, Taoism, Confucianism, and Sino-Christianity found in so many homes.

I reflected upon Grandmother Chun and her reputation for compassion. I had not known Grandmother Chun well. She lived only a few years in America before she passed. Low-key, loving, undemanding, and considerate, she always smiled, even as her grand children spilled goopy soups onto her lap. My strongest memory is of her sitting serenely in her armchair, wearing her traditional black cap with a jade amulet, as her grandchildren crawled all over her lap, shoulders, and armchair as if she were a climbing structure. She then resembled those porcelain statues found in so many Chinese homes, the cherubic, robed Buddha with children hanging all over him. In actuality, I still knew so little about her, and so I began to ask questions.

In the village, everyone knew all about her. More than that, the conversation always lit up at the mention of her name. Backs straightened, voices leaped up a couple of octaves, and hands began to gesticulate wildly as the speakers sang her praises. It was like witnessing the start of a Holy Spirit possession. "Oh, she was just the kindest woman. Never an unkind word. Never raised her voice. She was good to everybody. She helped everyone. You know, she took Kow Woon in and raised her as one of her own daughters."

"And your mother is just like her, a very good person."

To the villagers, this matrilineal compassion of the Eighth Promise had passed from generation to generation and finally to Mother. The transmission was subtle, a quiet, living force. Yet this force had proven to be reliable, nurturing, and powerful in my life and is my true inheritance.

I arranged to spend a night in my mother's childhood home. That afternoon, my next-door auntie invited me along to select my favorite vegetables from her garden patch. With the steaming plates of fresh organic vegetables, she served a hot soup, rice, and a young chicken she had butchered a few hours before. In the evening, provided me a thermos of hot water for instant coffee in the morning. I felt as precious as one of her own sons.

Later, awake in the dark for hours, I reflected upon my one thousand years worth of ancestors. I started feeling their presence and soon I sensed currents of energy that seemed strong, old, and yet very much alive. Presence after presence swirled and rolled in and out of that house. Eventually, I thought of Mother's father. He was a gambling man, before the Japanese invasion. But who left for Burma during those destitute Japanese war years to make money and send it home. But one day, a Japanese Zero dropped a bomb directly on his busy laundry, killing him and all his workers. I wondered at his courage and determination, to stifle his wasteful habit and at his courageous journey go so far from home to such a dangerous place to earn money for his family. An inexorable and mighty love of family miraculously transformed him. And although he died before I was born, I was grateful for his sacrifice. So too I recognize that this Grandfather was the source of Mother's canny gambling skill, which made the difference between whether we had new clothes, notebooks, and ballpoint pens for the school year or not.

I then thought of Mother's elder brother, a gentle scholar and gentle beloved teacher of children, who died while under investigation by the victorious Communists. I felt his sensitive terror, and ultimately his ultimate desperation. I then felt his presence, in the very house where he had jumped or been pushed to his death, as if seated on the chair next to me. I became frightened in the presence of that gloomy spirit.

Then, when I remembered this house was blessed with the loving, protective presence of Kuan Yin. I remembered that Grandmother Chun was Kuan Yin personified, and that I was in Grandmother's house. Joy and well being swept over me as I nestled in deeper under the dense cotton comforter, and fell into a deep, satisfying asleep.

In the mid-1990's, after leaving a highly lucrative partnership, a relationship, and a materially opulent lifestyle in the old-wealth town of Hillsborough just south of San Francisco, I started meditating and formally learning more about Buddhism. In lectures and readings, I realized that many of the ethical guidelines of Buddhism's fundamental eight-point path of living right had been modeled by Mother: always speaking kindly, refraining from hurtful speech, acting from good intentions, considering the impact of your actions, applying the right effort and focus in your actions, and of finding a way of making a living that did not hurt others. Cogently, she long ago forgave the ones who had hurt her the most: the Japanese Zero pilots and marauding soldiers, the Communist investigators, and those who put Richard away including Judge Calcagno, the assistant District .Attorney, the police expert, May Tom the manipulated eyewitness, and Thomas Porter the jailhouse snitch and liar.

In those retreats at Spirit Rock Meditation Center, I also learned that in Tibetan Buddhism, the most advanced students practice a metaphysical healing technique known as *tonglin*. *Tonglin* involves taking into one's body the physical disease, mental illness, or emotional suffering of another person. That person is then healed, but the healer now holds the negativity, and risks being sickened in turn. Advanced practitioners transform this negativity into positive energy, and put it back out into the world.

My mother, her mother before her, and the many matriarchs before them had all practiced *tonglin*. *Tonglin* was the same as the egg Mother rubbed to remove the pain of her sons. I came to understood now her steady, silent mantra was her *tonglin* practice of transmuting deep suffering into positive energy.

In Toisan, *tonglin* and other well-known Buddhist practices of loving kindness and forgiveness, especially at Chinese New Year, were implicit in daily village life. Yet, at the Buddhist retreats I attended, these teachings were presented as something newly discovered, and in a way that felt separate from our daily American lives. I realized that this was because my teachers were the first major generation of American Buddhists, that it would be some time before these teachings would become so indistinguishable from their own lifestyles that it not have to be "taught" in classes. In contrast, Mother and our village began living this way over twenty generations ago, and through centuries of life's ten thousand joys and ten thousand sorrows, they had become second nature. Our Clan was incapable of extrapolating them out as "teachings," separate from the rest of their lives.

Kuan Yin's presence on my family's altar now seemed inevitable, so natural as to be unremarkable to anyone else but me, an American.

That night, as I again tapped into the source of energy encountered on my first visit here in 1983, the mother-root underneath the surface-alive, wise, and mysterious, and constantly streaming her vitality to me through a hidden mesh of energy channels, I knew I was but one more shoot darting out from this ancient, fecund, gargantuan mother plant. The most beautiful flowering of our Toisan mother-root is the compassion of Kuan Yin. I remembered once again that I contained all that is Toisan, the collective wisdom, the strength, and above all the compassion of my ancestors. Like my mother and her mother before her, I too have the potential to blossom into this full flower of compassion.

Season after season.

In 1983, my first time in my mother's house, I was not yet ready for this teaching. In 2002, at the age of fifty, I was finally prepared to see Kuan Yin's quiet, beaming face, her power in the heart of my family's life. I was home. I was finally home.

A few days later, I flew back to the United States, to my other home in Berkeley, California. Here, in this land called America that was so strange to my Mother when she arrived in 1950, I am completely at ease. Curled up on an antique American mahogany bed, under a warm goose-down comforter, and covered by an American quilt, I slept as deeply as that recent night in our ancestral home. Months before that New Year's trip with Mother, I had placed a small statuette of Kuan Yin on my fireplace mantle, presciently replicating the one on my family's ancestral hearth.

Well, I am finally equally at home, in America and in Toisan.

And because the power of Kuan Yin had been a millennium-long matrilineal transmission through Grandmother Chun, directly to my mother, who then passed it on to me. So, I have come to recognize my mother as more than a good soul and an admirable woman.

In truth, Mother has been, and remains, my greatest wisdom teacher.

Closing Reflections

I promised my Mother and my clan many things before I left and I completed them, one by one. Even though my husband could be difficult, he really was my partner. Without him, I could not have fulfilled the promises.

I fulfilled my first promise, to raise my children to be Chinese so they could one day return to their ancestral village. All my sons speak Chinese and are comfortable with Chinese ways. John and Richard speak mostly Cantonese, but William speaks the best Toisanese, also some Cantonese and a little Mandarin. But my sons will not be returning to China: they are American and America is our home.

I fulfilled my second promise to my two sisters, to find suitable Chinese-American husbands for them so they could come over. I've matched other Clan Sisters with husbands, and many of them live in America now.

I fulfilled my third promise to become an American citizen so I could sponsor the immigration of my mother, my brother, and his family over to America here.

As to the dream of Sun Yat-sen and a Republican China, well, we celebrated every October 10 (the Nationalist Party Independence Day), welcomed President and Madame Chiang Kai-sek of Taiwan whenever they came through Chinatown, sang the Nationalist anthem, and saluted the Nationalist flag at banquets. But according to my Clan Sisters who stayed, and from what I have seen, the Communists did a pretty good job of making China safe and strong.

As to my fifth promise, to keep my children connected to the village, I faithfully wrote letters home and sent back baby and school pictures where they're mounted in my old house. Since the 1990s, I've gone back regularly, mostly with John and once with William. Richard hasn't been back yet. He's too busy raising his two daughters, but I hope one day soon, Richard will make the time, too.

The sixth promise was to keep the Clan Sisterhood traditions alive in America. When I first got here, I organized women from other villages and together we helped make the soups for mothers and babies during birth-time and organized the red-egg parties. Our Toisan sisterhood got larger, as more Toisanese women migrated over. We talked over family problems, just like in the old days. We lent each other money and babysat each other's children. We discussed items in the Chinese newspapers that affected our lives, and voiced our concerns to the family associations when we could. We helped new sisters get settled, attended family association events together, went to every restaurant's' grand opening, and found good sales downtown. Many have passed on now, but we still get together to gossip over coffee and rolls, $4.00 lunch specials at Uncle's Restaurant, and dim sum. If someone new comes over from China, we still make sure to introduce them to everyone, let them know we're here to help them.

I fulfilled my seventh promise, to cook the energy soups for my family. I still make them for my sons. That's why they're so healthy. Everyone says they look ten or fifteen years younger than their age. William wants to learn how to make them. Easy to make I say, be sure to simmer any soup for at least three hours. I've been giving him herbs to practice with.

But most of all, my biggest promise, the Eighth Promise, was to raise my children the way my mother raised me, and to teach them the Toisan ways. I've stuck with them through the worst times. Just raising them by myself was hard enough, and they don't know how much work being a mother is. But when they got into trouble, oh, that was really hard. William in the hospital by himself. Later fighting the high school principal. Richard in jail for so many years. John running here, running there like a sleepy, lost chicken in the night. I've sat up late into the night until they came home. I've been with them every step of the way. I've taught them to be nice to everyone, to help people you meet along the way, to not hold onto grudges or resentment at wrongdoing. That's the best way, cooperate and work together for the future.

This doesn't mean you should let yourself be taken advantage of, or that you shouldn't stand up for yourself. But you must try to work problems out in everyone's best interest whenever you can, if you can. My sons had to learn to let go of bad things. They know now that bad feelings can trap you by keeping you angry, desiring revenge, and finally doing something to someone that makes them do something back to you. They know that life is too wonderful to waste this way. That's what we Toisanese believe, that letting go of the bad prepares a place to allow in the many joys in life: new friends, new travels, new fortunes, the next delicious restaurant, healthy and happy grandchildren, a nice sunny drive over the mountains to Reno, and maybe win at 21 blackjack. The ten thousand joys of life are just around the corner.

If I died and a supreme being granted me a choice to come back to this world or to stay in heaven, what would I decide? Oh, I'd come back—no question about it.

And oh, yes, of course, I would ask to live in America!

An American Promise

One winter afternoon some years after our Toisan trip, my mother paid me the highest compliment.

"You cook just like a lady," she said in American.

I was puzzled. It was a cold day for a visit, and so I had only made her a simple cabbage soup. But, she said, this is a chi soup. True, I had taken the time to use local ingredients, organic and freshly plucked from the soil: a head of Santa Rosa cabbage, several garden-grown carrots and tomatoes, a fat red onion, and two cloves of garlic with a chunk of some home-baked, free-range turkey added to sweeten the soup. After I brought the soup to a boil, I had simmered it for three hours in the time-honored Toisan way of building the chi fire. In that critical gourmand way of Toisanese Clan Sisters, Mother remarked upon the comforting feeling of the soup's fire clearing her chest as it went down. She remarked on its sweetness, its nutritiousness, asking whether I had used pork to give it such a wonderful body or herbs to make the fire.

No, I had not.

The secret to the chi recipe was not exotic ingredients or ancient technique: the secret was one I had learned from my mother, the secret of the Eighth Promise. Its most precious ingredient was compassion, that singular appreciation for each person, that ability to see the "Nue-e," the child in each one them and thus, the desire to make them completely comfortable. I have no children. I am an American, not a Chinese. But with this soup I make a Promise to my own Mother, an American Promise, to keep alive the ways of the Toisan even as, like my Father, I continue to find my way on American soil.

For Toisan once was only a place, but now it is a state of being, an interior sensibility of home, no matter where I may reside in this world.

– The End –

Made in United States
Troutdale, OR
10/10/2023